Puritan Temper
and Transcendental Faith

PURITAN TEMPER AND TRANSCENDENTAL FAITH

Carlyle's Literary Vision

A. Abbott Ikeler

OHIO STATE UNIVERSITY PRESS

Library of Congress Cataloging in Publication Data
Ikeler, A Abbott, 1943-
Puritan temper and transcendental faith.
Bibliography: p.
1. Carlyle, Thomas, 1795-1881. I. Title.
PR4434.I4   824'.8   72-6296
ISBN 0-8142-0176-8

for MY FATHER AND MOTHER

CONTENTS

PREFACE

Before beginning, I ought to define what Carlyle meant by the word *Literature*. He usually thought of it as a term for creative expressions (poems, plays, novels, stories, and speculative essays), although in later years he often expanded the definition to include all printed matter. In such cases, literature was not only art, but reviews, periodicals, "Dryasdust" histories, and "Books in general." Occasionally he distinguished between "Poetry" and "Story-telling," but he seldom maintained genre distinctions for more than a sentence or two. Carlyle was more concerned with moral categories (the "true work of Art" versus the "daub of Artifice") than he was with technical ones. Nonetheless, we *can* say that whatever else he may have meant by the word "Literature," he almost always intended it to include the works of the imagination. It is in that sense, unless otherwise stated, that literature should be thought of in the following pages.

For their advice and aid in locating Carlyle materials, I should like to thank the keepers and staffs of the manuscript departments in the National Library of Scotland, Edinburgh, and the Victoria and Albert Museum, London. The assistant librarians at King's College General Library were also helpful in answering my almost daily questions. I owe a special word of thanks to Professor Jean Vigneault, who pointed out a large body of contemporary Carlyle criticism in the British Museum. Thanks are also due Professors Brooks and Slater of Birkbeck College, London, Patrick Yarker of Kings College, London, G. B. Tennyson of University of California, Los Angeles, and H. R. Coursen, Jr., of Bowdoin College.

I am particularly grateful to Bonnie Haselton for proofreading each chapter and for listening, with infinite patience, to the scholastic and critical problems that the preparation of this work involved.

LIST OF
ABBREVIATIONS

Works	*Works of Thomas Carlyle*
Cromwell	*Oliver Cromwell's Letters and Speeches*
Essays	*Critical and Miscellaneous Essays*
FR	*The French Revolution*
GR	*German Romance*
Heroes	*On Heroes, Hero-Worship, and the Heroic in History*
HFG	*The History of Frederick II of Prussia*
Last Words	*Last Words of Thomas Carlyle (Wotton Reinfred, Excursion to Paris, Letters)*
LDP	*Latter-Day Pamphlets*
Lectures	*Lectures on the History of Literature*
LS	*Life of Schiller*
PP	*Past and Present*
Sterling	*Life of Sterling*
SR	*Sartor Resartus*
WM	*Wilhelm Meister*
Note Books	*Two Note Books of Thomas Carlyle*
Letters	*Letters of Thomas Carlyle, 1826–1836*
New Letters	*New Letters of Thomas Carlyle*
Goethe Letters	*Correspondence between Goethe and Carlyle*
MSB Letters	*Letters of Thomas Carlyle to John Stuart Mill, John Sterling, and Robert Browning*

Puritan Temper
and Transcendental Faith

Chapter One

Carlyle on Literature: Conflicting Views

> We make out of the quarrel with
> others, rhetoric, but of the quarrel
> with ourselves, poetry.—W. B. Yeats

For the student of Victorian prose, drawn to Carlyle by the early essays and *Sartor Resartus*, there are few antidotes more effective than *Latter-Day Pamphlets*. In *Sartor*, the hero's struggles are subjects for poetic rhapsody and outrageous humor; in *Latter-Day Pamphlets*, Peel's problems inspire only tedious invective. In 1831, Carlyle's landscape is fabulous and obscure, his style "jeanpaulian,"[1] his irony playful; in 1850, he focuses only moral heat upon the prosaic, in a voice that is remarkable for its shrillness and redundancy.

This apparent contrast of early and late Carlyle disturbed his contemporaries as much as it does the modern reader. Despite an initially poor reception in England, *Sartor* had circulated widely among British artists and intellectuals by the 1840s. Mrs. Tillotson points out Arnold's liberal borrowings from the Teufelsdröckh saga, borrowings that enriched such poems as *Empedocles on Etna*.[2] Browning also valued the buoyant artistry of *Sartor*—an approval he manifested not only in his verse but in personal friendship.[3] Even minor romantic novelists of the period adapted the steps of Teufelsdröckh's mystical ascension—Everlasting No, Centre of Indifference, Everlasting Yea—to fit their narrative fictions.[4] The vogue was as intense as it was general: "An American man of letters, Mr. C. G. Leland, writes in his *Memoirs* that he bought Carlyle's *Sartor Resartus,* first edition, and read it through forty times, of which he kept count, before he left college."[5] Mill, Tyndall, even Huxley found the nonutilitarian Carlyle to be a "wholesome influence" who held them by the sheer "force of his genius."[6] It was from this quarter, understandably, that critical hostility first came. In 1846, Mill and Carlyle quarreled over the justice of Cromwell's Irish massacres and their friendship "was practically at an end."[7] With the serial publication of "The Nigger Question" and the other *Latter-Day Pamphlets,* Carlyle's popularity fell sharply with the young Radicals and poets. Arnold later said, "I never much liked Carlyle,"[8] and he made the reasons for his revulsion explicit in *Culture and Anarchy.* The ties with Browning grew increasingly casual—loosened in part by Carlyle's impolitic advice to him to rewrite *The Ring and the Book* in prose.[9] Browning criticized his friend's moral pragmatism in "Red Cotton Nightcap Country" and regretted that the older Carlyle saw "the poet in a social, rather than an aesthetic context."[10]

The sense of betrayal felt in the literary community was justified by their reading of the individual texts. In *Sartor,* Carlyle finds art sufficient unto itself:

> Another matter it is, however, when your Symbol has intrinsic meaning, and is of itself *fit* that men should unite round it. . . . Of this latter sort are all true Works of Art; in them. . . . wilt thou discern Eternity looking through Time; the Godlike rendered visible.[11]

But in *Latter-Day Pamphlets,* he has lost all trust in eloquence, spoken or written:

> With horror and amazement, one perceives that this much celebrated "art," so diligently practised in all corners of the

world just now, is the chief destroyer of whatever good is born in us. . . . Know this: there never was a talent even for real Literature, not to speak of talents lost, and damned in doing sham Literature, but was primarily a talent for something infinitely better of the silent kind. Of Literature, in all ways, be shy rather than otherwise, at present![12]

Carlyle's apostasy is a matter of tone as well as creed, and his followers found the didacticism of *Latter-Day Pamphlets* unreasonably strident. In these serial tracts, the comic strain of *Sartor* gives way to obsessive earnestness: imaginative coloring shrivels into flat, journalistic commonplace. Yet perhaps it is unfair to set Carlyle's only complete "novel"[13] against an anomalous piece of political propaganda in order to point up a shift from artist to "anti-poet." Whatever case there is for Carlyle's declining opinion of literature, poetry, and the poet grows more justly out of a general survey of his works. Let us look briefly at some of the arguments and evidence that support such a claim for simple, chronological disjunction in Carlyle's view of literature.

Before 1838, the titles alone are sufficient to indicate his preoccupation with artists and men of letters: *Wilhelm Meister* (1824), *Life of Schiller* (1825), *German Romance* (1827), "Jean Paul Friedrich Richter," "Goethe," "Burns," "Voltaire," "Novalis," "Boswell's *Life of Johnson*," "Diderot," (1827–33), *Lectures on the History of Literature,* "Sir Walter Scott" (1838). After 1838, Carlyle's attention appears to have turned abruptly toward moral practitioners of the political sort and toward issues that are primarily social: "Chartism," "Petition on the Copyright Bill" (1839), "Dr. Francia" (1843), *Oliver Cromwell's Letters and Speeches* (1845), "Shooting Niagara: and After?" (1867), "The Portraits of John Knox" (1875). Superficially at least, the writings reinforce such a dichotomy between aesthetic and moral, literary and practical, advocacy.

In the 1824 sketch of Goethe, prefatory to *Wilhelm Meister,* Carlyle is effusive in his praise of the poet and the poet's role:

> Poetry . . . exists not in time or place, but in the spirit of
> man; and Art, with Nature, is now to perform for the poet,
> what Nature alone performed of old . . . for the fiction of
> the poet is not falsehood, but the purest truth.[14]

The hero of the age, as of all ages, is neither king nor conqueror,
but the novelist and poet who can lift us toward sublimity and
truth:

> If he [the reader] know and believe that poetry is the essence
> of all science, and requires the purest of all studies . . . he
> will find that in this Goethe there is a . . . temple for the
> Spirit of our age, as the Shakespeares and Spensers have
> raised for the Spirit of theirs. . . . If it seem that I advo-
> cate this cause too warmly . . . I may be allowed to remind
> my readers, that the existence or non-existence of a new
> Poet for the World in our own time, of a new Instructor
> and Preacher of truth to all men, is really a question of more
> importance to us than many that are agitated with far
> greater noise.[15]

Yet *Past and Present,* written in a mere seven weeks, and published
in 1843 amidst Carlyle's research on Cromwell, indicates a new
and radically different allegiance. Earlier standards have been
juggled, and action has got the upper hand of eloquence: "The
spoken word, the written Poem, is said to be an epitome of the
man; how much more the done work."[16] And in a passage that
endorses both the indecorous and the anti-intellectual, he equates
practicality with divinity:

> How one loves to see the burly figure of . . . this thick-
> skinned, seemingly opaque, perhaps sulky, almost stupid
> Man of Practice, pitted against some light adroit Man of
> Theory. . . . The cloudy-browed, thick-soled, opaque Prac-
> ticality, with no logical utterance, in silence mainly, with
> here or there a low grunt or growl, has in him what tran-
> scends all logic-utterance: a Congruity with the Unuttered.

> The Speakable, which lies atop, as a superficial film, or outer
> skin, is his or is not his: but the Doable, which reaches down
> to the World's centre, you find him there![17]

Certainly Carlyle's antagonist here, the "adroit Man of Theory,"
is meant primarily as a caricature of Bentham, James Mill, and
other mathematical hedonists, but it is difficult to imagine the
poet or the aesthetician in league with a "sulky, almost stupid
Man of Practice."

The artist's sympathy with Carlyle is further strained in reading
The History of Frederick. In the first volume he makes little
attempt to disguise or condemn the insensitivity of Frederick's
father—a man notable only for his cruelty. In order to justify
Friedrich Wilhelm's preoccupation with "War Sciences," and his
mistrust of the arts, Carlyle is compelled to ridicule literature as
fictitious, idle nonsense:

> The wild man has discerned, with his rugged natural intel-
> ligence (not wasted away in the idle element of speaking and
> of being spoken to, but kept wholesomely silent for the most
> part), that human education is not, and cannot be, a thing
> of *vocables*.[18]

In judging the effects on Frederick of his father's severity, Carlyle
is contemptuous of literary enthusiasts:

> However it may go with Literature, and satisfaction to
> readers of romantic appetites, this young soul promises to
> become a successful Worker one day, and to *do* something
> under the Sun. For work is of an extremely un-fictitious
> nature; and no man can roof his house with clouds and
> moonshine, so as to turn the rain from him.[19]

But 1858 and the character of Frederick the Great are a far cry
indeed from the sentiments of Novalis and of his expositor in 1829.
In that earlier essay, Carlyle displays a reverence for poets that is

nearly excessive. Considering the passage just quoted, one is hard put to credit what follows to the same pen:

> Novalis' poems are breathings of a high, devout soul . . . his pure religious temper, and heartfelt love of Nature, bring him into true poetic relation both with the spiritual and the material World, and perhaps constitute his chief worth as a Poet. . . . He, alone among the moderns, resembles the lofty Dante; and sings us, like him, an unfathomable mystic song.[20]

Moreover, Carlyle sees Novalis's meditative intensity as "the highest and sole duty of man"—a view of things that would elicit growls of disgust from the semi-articulate Friedrich Wilhelm.[21] Two years after the "Novalis" essay, Carlyle still favors an education in the arts as the soundest approach to virtuous behavior. Schiller, his subject in 1831, is a familiar one, and the young Carlyle has few doubts of the efficacy of poetry:

> That high purpose after spiritual perfection, which with him was a love of Poetry, and an unwearied active love, is itself, when pure and supreme, the necessary parent of good conduct, as of noble feeling. With all men it should be pure and supreme, for in one or the other shape it is the true end of man's life.[22]

There can be little question that such sympathetic criticism of German aesthetics is in baffling contrast to Carlyle's later militarism: only fourteen years after "Schiller," he writes in defense of Cromwell's rough-hewn letters:

> The Intelligence that can, with full satisfaction to itself, come out in eloquent speaking, in musical singing, is, after all, a small Intelligence. He that works and *does* some Poem, not he that merely *says* one, is worthy of the name of *Poet*. Cromwell, emblem of the dumb English, is interesting to me by the very inadequacy of his speech. Heroic insight,

valour and belief, without words—how noble is it in comparison to the adroitest flow of words without insight![23]

One readily seconds Carlyle's last statement, but of all the appellations appropriate to Cromwell, certainly the least of these is "Poet." It is not, however, the first time Carlyle indicates a preference for active, silent heroes. Five years earlier, in the 1840 lecture on "Hero as King," he places Cromwell's genius ahead of the poetic kind. Once again, his praise of the soldier-monarch is heightened by a dismissive attitude toward the "vocables":

> The rugged outcast Cromwell, he is the man of them all in whom one still finds human stuff. The great savage *Baresark:* he could write no euphemistic *Monarchy of Men:* did not speak, did not work with glib regularity; had no straight story to tell for himself anywhere. But he stood bare, not cased in euphemistic coat-of-mail; he grappled like a giant, face to face, heart to heart, with the naked truth of things! That, after all, is the sort of man for one. I plead guilty to valuing such a man beyond all other sorts of men.[24]

The value of a man appears to be measured by his moral utility—his ability to "accomplish" truth, to perform practical, righteous deeds. For the most part, Carlyle has deserted verbal and literary heroes as morally ineffectual; the poet has no worth unless he ruthlessly subordinates the delineation of the beautiful to the preaching of virtue. Even then, he would be more usefully occupied in "doing" some poem. Speaking of the older Carlyle, Julian Symons agrees with Arnold in labeling him a "Philistine":

> His remarks about art were now those of a self-satisfied Philistine. His earlier doubts about the validity of literary art . . . had extended and changed. Now, at an intemperate moment, he said curtly to Espinasse that his attempts to popularize German Literature had only increased contemporary confusion; it was not literature at all, he often implied and sometimes said, that was wanted . . . at the best

his view of art was now ordered wholly by its usefulness—a word which he interpreted in the most limited sense.[25]

What makes his altered allegiance exceptionally ironic is the use Carlyle had earlier made of the very word "Philistine." In a footnote to the 1824 Goethe essay he attacks the critic Nicolai, who "wrote against Kant's philosophy, without comprehending it; and judged of poetry as he judged of Brunswick mum, by its *utility* . . . a man of such spiritual habitudes is now called by the Germans . . . Philistine."[26] The early Carlyle does not limit his aestheticism to the fine print at the bottom of pages; in "The State of German Literature" (1827), he openly condemns those who would apply the standard of moral pragmatism to the works of an artist:

> Art is to be loved, not because of its effects, but because of itself; not because it is useful for spiritual pleasure, or even for moral culture, but because it is Art, and the highest in man, and the soul of all Beauty. To inquire after its *utility*, would be like inquiring after the *utility* of a God, or . . . the *utility* of Virtue and Religion.[27]

The shift, then, from sympathy to antagonism looks explicit, thorough-going, and, it would appear, fairly rapid. Carlyle's affection for Goethe and the German Romantics is still very warm in 1832, but by 1840 many of his writings begin to reflect the crotchety tones of a hardened moralist. It is difficult to find the precise watershed in these years, but most critics agree that there is a gradual decline in Carlyle's opinion of poetry and prose fiction throughout the 1830s. Symons links the change to his distrust of story-telling: "As Carlyle grew older he became more and more inclined to place the making of verses with the writing of fiction as a trivial occupation in a serious age."[28] He finds this disaffection most marked in thoughts and writings after 1838, but Harrold believes the break from aesthetics and "things German" is not completed until the end of 1842, with the writing of *Past and*

Present.[29] Wellek speaks of his "desertion" of literary criticism after 1840, and G. B. Tennyson concludes his discussion of Carlyle's poetry at the same year.[30] Tennyson's chronology of the poems, which are few and generally insignificant, covers only the decades of the 1820s and 1830s: "As he aged, and as his opinions and strictures on art became more severe, his own output diminished."[31] Lehman, too, although his investigations are limited to Carlyle's heroes, sees the decay of a poetic standard and the substitution of a moral one.[32] This is not to say that Carlyle ever divorces the beautiful from the good, but merely that over the years his priorities change. It is significant in this regard that Carlyle repeatedly misquotes Goethe's exhortation to live in *die Schöne* as a call to live in "*[dem] Wahren.*"[33] But altering the thrust of a poet's message is the least of Carlyle's artistic heresies. More often the man who had campaigned for literature in his youth dismisses it altogether in old age: "The fact that he at one time or another advised practically every poet of his day to write prose and that in moments when he was given to wild exaggeration he even deplored the fact that the poets of the past had written poetry is so well known it has become a kind of joke."[34] That the high-minded enthusiast for German aesthetics should soon achieve a reputation as a bitter opponent of the arts may seem inconceivable, yet even his close friends began to call him "a gigantic anti-poet."[35]

Carlyle's letters, as well as his essays, testify to a waning faith in literature. He writes to von Ense in 1842: "There is now for me very little speculation and almost nothing of the so-called Poetry that I can bear to read at all."[36] A few years later, when he is understandably preoccupied with the Puritan Revolution, he tells his wife: "When I think of an Oliver Cromwell . . . and other such phenomena, I am very indifferent on the Book side. Greater, I often think, is he that can hold his peace; that can *do* his bit of Light instead of speaking it!"[37] Here Carlyle's private opinion is almost a paraphrase of his public one in the *Cromwell* preface, except that in writing to Jane he has chosen to corrupt the meaning of "light" rather than "Poet." In the period from 1852 to 1865, which his wife familiarly called "the Thirteen-Years'-War" with Frederick the Great, Carlyle's irascibility ripened. Art and literature seemed to him then worse than useless; in fact, he argued, they were insidious pursuits that sapped the mind of vital energies. Part of his discouragement was in the nature of his subject, for he saw that Frederick was an "unfortunate" choice, hardly "worth doing." Carlyle's disillusionment deepened as he neared the end of the project: "Writing books is a task without proper encouragement in these times."[38] When a young man sent him a manuscript play in 1862, hoping for preferment or at least constructive criticism, he received a sharp rebuke:

> It is my standing advice to all young persons who trace in themselves a superior capacity of mind, to select, beyond all other conditions, a silent course of activity; and to disbelieve totally the babble of reviews and newspapers, and loud clamor of Nonsense, everywhere prevalent, that "Literature" (even if one were qualified) is the truly noble human career. Far other, very far! since you ask my opinion, the greatest minds I have known, or have authentically heard of, have *not* been the speaking ones at all—much less in these loud times—raging with palaver, and with so little else from sea to sea.[39]

Such rhetoric notwithstanding, the minds Carlyle knew were almost exclusively literary, and excepting Mazzini, Buller, and perhaps Robert Peel, his acquaintance with political heroes was severely limited.[40] One feels some sympathy for the young man in question, who, knowing something of Carlyle's circle of friends and of his early essays on literature, expected a more genial response.

The early letters and notebooks do, in fact, underscore the young Carlyle's dominant trust in the arts and his eagerness for a literary career. In 1831, he admits to himself, "The only Sovereigns of the world in these days are the Literary men."[41] To worship one of his poet-heroes at close range, he had established, seven years before, a correspondence with Goethe. Although their exchanges often turned on mere trivia, the epistolary friendship was rooted in a mutual respect for art as a source of spiritual elevation.[42] Again and again Carlyle is comforted by the apparent awakening among his contemporaries of what Goethe calls a "new World-Literature":

> For your ideas on the tendency of modern poetry to promote a freer spiritual intercourse among nations, I must also thank you . . . they command my entire assent; nay, perhaps express for me much which I might otherwise have wanted words for . . . under you and Schiller, I should say, a Third grand Period had evolved itself, as yet fairly developed in no other Literature, but full of the richest prospects for all; namely a period of New Spirituality and Belief . . . a new revelation of Nature, and the Freedom and Infinitude of Man, wherein Reverence is again rendered compatible with Knowledge, and Art and Religion are one.[43]

For Carlyle, as late as 1831, there is still no higher vocation than poetry: "Literature is now nearly all in all to us; not our speech only but our Worship and Lawgiving; our best Priest must henceforth be our Poet."[44] Even during his precarious career as translator, reviewer, and would-be novelist, he seems content to spend the rest of his years in writing: "I look forward with cheerfulness to a life spent in Literature, with such fortune and such strength as may be granted me; hoping little and fearing nothing from the world."[45] Carlyle often conceived of the artist as the ultimate hero: as early as 1814 he wrote in the margin of a textbook his ambition that "unseduced by the world's smiles, and unbending to its frowns, I may attain to literary fame. And though starvation be my lot I will smile that I have not been born a king! ! !"[46] Despite the adolescent bravado in this—defiant romanticism glorying in its own vicissitudes—it is nonetheless a position that Carlyle holds in practice all his life and, in theory, for at least another twenty years.

By contrast, half a century later, in his "Inaugural Address" as rector of Edinburgh University, he sternly repudiates the attractions of literature. No longer is poetry the "purest truth" or art the theme of modern heroes. For the young men of Scotland in 1866, Carlyle sees no "use" in their exploiting whatever genius they may have for articulation, no practical purpose in books of any kind:

> Keep out of Literature, I should say also, as a general rule.
> . . . It would be much safer and better for many a reader,
> that he had no concern with books at all. There is a number,
> a frightfully increasing number, of books that are decidedly,
> to the readers of them, not useful . . . speech, in the case
> even of Demosthenes, does not seem on the whole, to have
> turned to almost any good account. He advised next to
> nothing that proved practicable; much of the reverse.[47]

Are these what they immediately appear to be—the rantings of a bitter old man? Are they, as many critics have suggested, the product of impatience nurtured on disappointment? There is no doubt that Carlyle grew restive in later years, and fame was no comfort to him after his wife's death. He complained to Froude that although men called him a "great man," no one did what he had told them.[48] Perhaps his strictures on literature rise out of a commonplace frustration: the inability to realize a personal creed in a social context. It is, in part, such an evangelical urge that led Ruskin from art into politics and finally into madness.[49] Similarly, the stridency of later Carlyle is, at least in some degree, born of the pessimism of an artist who finds his audience sincere in nothing but its complacency. Like Ruskin, he sees that for most men the only sentiment is self-pity; the only wealth is money. G. M. Trevelyan voices the view that many readers of Carlyle privately

entertain when he looks at the writings as a descent toward the
no-man's-land of irrationality:

> His early writings . . . seem to me eminently sane. Perhaps
> the fact that they were written for reviews kept his genius
> in bounds, like the form of a Sonnet. And both *Sartor* and
> the *French Revolution* though strange in style, seem to me
> wise and sane both in thought and feeling. With certain
> reservations I should say the same of *Past and Present* and
> *Cromwell*. It was after 1851 that his genius declined. Like
> Wordsworth, he wrote very little that was first rate in the
> last thirty years of his long life, except his *Reminiscences*.
> And with his powers of writing, his *powers of thought and
> feeling deteriorated.*[50]

Considered in this light, Carlyle's apparently declining opinion of
literature is directly attributable to blunted sensitivity; that is, to
his age and a kind of chilled humanity. The shift from artist to
humbug, from aesthete to Hebraic prophet is then no more than
the usual movement from a liberal youth to a conservative dotage.
Spontaneity and humor are, over the years, supplanted by emphatic self-righteousness. We have only to compare the outlandish,
Swiftian comedy of *Sartor Resartus* to the rigorous epigraph that
opens *Past and Present*—"*Ernst ist das Leben*"—to feel the limits
that experience and earnestness have raised around the aging Carlyle.[51] Look to the pomposity of Wordsworth's later poetry, or to
the shrillness of Emerson's last essays if you would understand the
diminution of Carlyle's talent, and the unpalatable nature of his
final words on art.

Such, at least, is the commonly accepted answer to the conflicting
opinions that Carlyle at one time or another holds on literature.
There is certainly, as we have seen, a great weight of evidence from
his works and from his correspondence to support the view
Trevelyan, Harrold, and others have put forward. Their solution,
however, depends upon some degree of internal consistency at

each stage of Carlyle's development. That is to say, the "progress" toward rejection of artistic values should be gradual, and there ought not to be included within a given period or work those violent contradictions which are manifest in a comprehensive survey of his writings. If, on the contrary, Carlyle displays a consistent ambivalence toward art, at every age, then the theory of deteriorating sensibilities will not answer at all.

A reappraisal of his opinions, both public and private, does indeed indicate a divided allegiance, but it is not one that will submit to a chronological solution. At closer range, those writings of Carlyle after 1838, which we have loosely classed as unsympathetic to literature and often anti-intellectual, reveal a peculiar loyalty to the arts. The Edinburgh Address of 1866, in which Carlyle warns students to stay clear not only of a literary career and books in general but even of academic rhetoric, nonetheless acknowledges a debt to poetry. There is surely an obvious inconsistency in closing a speech that has dismissed literature as uninstructive with a long poem of Goethe's; but Carlyle's paradoxical approach surfaces explicitly a few pages earlier. He decries the modern age as wholly irreverent, and believes it to need, beyond all other reforms, a new education in devoutness. In a paraphrase of *Wilhelm Meister*, Carlyle stands with Goethe in his commitment to an aesthetic ultimate:

> The highest outcome, and most precious of all the fruits that are to spring from this ideal mode of educating, is what Goethe calls Art . . . music, painting, poetry . . . . He considers this as the highest pitch to which human culture can go; infinitely valuable and enobling.[52]

Another curious, and perhaps subtler, example of Carlyle's complicated attitude toward the artist appears in a letter to his wife in July, 1865. The circumstances that evoke his unusual response need some explanation: Trollope had just written an unfavorable review of Ruskin's *Sesame and Lilies,* condemning its prose as effeminately "graceful" and unsuited to questions of high moral import.[53] Balanced sentences of finely wrought delicacy have, so Trollope argued, no place in a discussion of social evils.[54] In his attempt to follow Carlyle as a prophet and moralist, Ruskin fails, and would be wise to reapply his talents to womanish subjects like the criticism of painting. Trollope concludes by praising Carlyle's unpolished haranguing as the best manner in which to attack the immorality of the present age. In short, unconcern for felicitous phrasing is held up as the touchstone of sincerity and practicality. Trollope's verdict closely corresponds to Carlyle's judgment of the Cromwell letters twenty years earlier, and one would expect no censure of such a review from an "opaque Practicality." Yet he writes to Jane, in the mood of a provoked aesthete:

> Ruskin's *Sesame and Lilies* must be a pretty little thing. Trollope, in reviewing it with considerable insolence, stupidity and vulgarity, produces little specimens far beyond any Trollope sphere of speculation. A distylish little pug, that Trollope. . . . Don't *you* return his love; nasty, gritty creature, with no eye for "the Beautiful."[55]

Moreover, since Carlyle had apparently not yet read *Sesame and Lilies,* his attack on Trollope's philistinism must have been purely instinctual.[56]

Even in the *History of Frederick,* literature is not always scorned as mere "clouds and moonshine." Carlyle does approve the emphasis placed on practical military education by Frederick's father, but there is also a curious sympathy for the "effeminate" elements in the prince's nature. Frederick's mother and his tutor encourage the boy's interest in Latin and the fine arts—a practice which Carlyle considers a humanizing influence on the young Prussian.[57] It is such training, in fact, that later equips Frederick to entertain poets and *philosophes* at court, for scattered among the battle plans and troop movements that dominate Carlyle's life of the king are accounts of regular and extended visits from Voltaire. Carlyle gives them full play, quoting copiously from the letters and conversations of the Frenchman whom he has, in another work, derided as the chief of *"Persifleurs."*[58] In a moment of what can only be called romantic indulgence, Carlyle transcribes three rather dainty little madrigals of Voltaire, calling them "really incomparable in their kind; not equalled in graceful felicity even by Goethe, and by him alone of Poets approached in that respect."[59] It is startling, perhaps, to find phrases like "graceful felicity" in the mouth of a "thick-skinned" "self-satisfied Philistine," yet the aging Carlyle often rises to defend the poetic temperament. His "Sketch of Edward Irving," finished in January 1867, includes the caustic parody of a practical Scotsman, in a tone that recalls the comment on Nicolai forty years before: "a hardheaded fellow, Utilitarian to the bone, who had defined poetry to Irving once as 'the *prodooction* of a rude *aage*.' "[60] Thus, amidst the clatter of Prussian cannon and roundhead musketry that fills the pages of Carlyle's later work, there is a quiet, insistent countermelody.

Nowhere is this other voice given finer or fuller expression than in *The Life of John Sterling.* Less than a year after the publication of *Latter-Day Pamphlets,* at a time when Carlyle was frustrated and belligerent over the condition-of-England question, he composed an evenly paced, well-turned biography of a literary friend. The impetus for the *Life* was not a rush of uncontrolled grief, for Sterling had been dead seven years—years during which Carlyle had apparently grown antagonistic toward writers and contemplative men in general. Six years earlier, in *Cromwell,* he had classed poets as a people of "small Intelligence," and only months before had called eloquence "the chief destroyer of whatever good is born in us."[61] His choice of Sterling is made stranger still by his subject's ineptitude as an artist, for the man was little more than a dabbler in romantic prose, and a poetaster in verse. Carlyle certainly numbered many more consequential persons among his literary heroes; a biography of Goethe or Byron or Burns (for all of whom he had an almost irrational affection) might be easier to explain at this stage of his life. Most critics are unable to reconcile

Carlyle's sympathetic picture of Sterling with his usually vigorous condemnation of the dilettante class. H. D. Traill despairs of a schematic answer to Carlyle's sentiments and looks at the book as a genuine anomaly:

> After all, we are thrown back upon the assumption of a "personal magnetism" exercised by Sterling over a few distinguished minds, and associated probably in this particular case with some subtle appeal to that curious vein of tenderness which lay among the deeper stratifications of Carlyle's rugged nature.[62]

The "vein of tenderness" is here, as always, alloyed with criticism: Carlyle maintains throughout an ambivalent attitude toward art and literature, alternately approving and censuring Sterling's activities. At one stage the two men debated the problem of whether to write in prose or in verse; Carlyle argued hotly against the "fiddling talent," dismissing it in favor of "plain speech":

> My own advice was, as it had always been, steady against Poetry. . . . Why *sing* your bits of thought, if you *can* contrive to speak them? By your own thoughts, not by your mode of delivering it, [*sic*] you must live or die.[63]

Poetry is then no more than self-conscious artifice, to be abjured by forthright thinkers and honest men. But Carlyle suddenly changes his tack, and advises Sterling against versifying not because it is beneath his abilities but because it is beyond them:

> Besides, I had to observe there was in Sterling intrinsically no depth of *tune;* which surely is the real test of a Poet or Singer, as distinguished from a Speaker? . . . Sterling's verses had a monotonous rub-a-dub, instead of tune; no trace of music deeper than that of a well-beaten drum; to which limited range of excellence the substance also corresponded; being intrinsically always a . . . slightly rhythmical *speech,* not a *song.*[64]

Since Carlyle had begun the debate by attaching pejorative con-
notations to "songs," it is not surprising that his conclusions confused Sterling. Carlyle, it seems, was himself confused—poetry was
either very grand or very false. Sterling, at any rate, rejected Carlyle's advice and continued to tap his "monotonous, well-beaten
drum." The result was two volumes of trifling tales and verses. In
criticizing them, Carlyle makes an abrupt about-face, finding the
poems

> graceful, ingenious and illuminative reading, of their sort,
> for all manner of inquiring souls. A little verdant flowery
> island of poetic intellect, of melodious, human verity; sunlit
> island founded on the rocks.[65]

Odd indeed to hear the rugged moralist talking of "little verdant
flowery" islands of poetry—and such insubstantial islands, after
all. His estimate of the graphic arts also suffers from internal
contradiction. The worship of statues, paintings, and Roman architecture seems to him, at one time, a meaningless, "windy Gospel";
the "temporary dilettante cloudland of our poor Century."[66] It
is a pursuit "which all earnest men, abhorrent of hypocrisy"
should avoid. Yet Carlyle, in a gentler mood, enjoys "fashionable
persons and manners" and welcomes a friend of Sterling's who
"loved art, was a great collector of drawings . . . and was, in short,
every way a very human, lovable, good and nimble man."[67] He
goes so far as to excuse Sterling's highly mannered excesses of
speech: "If perceptibly or imperceptibly there is a touch of ostenta-
tion in him, blame it not: it is so innocent, so good and childlike."[68] In fact Carlyle is not beneath ridiculing men of unrefined
affections, those "Philistines . . . dullards, Children of Darkness"
who occasionally came into his circle of literary friends. At such
times, he passed a not intolerable evening in "borebaiting."[69] In
1838, the Sterling Club was founded to strengthen and formalize
the literary rapprochement that Carlyle and others had achieved.
Despite his strictures on "Talking-Apparatuses" and cliques of

chattering aesthetes, Carlyle speaks with noticeable pride of his charter membership in this organization.[70] In another passage, he reveals a most un-Carlylean love of French elegance, which he finds "a perpetual banquet for the young soul."[71] And finally, although he has elsewhere condemned as "airy Nothingness" the nebulous language of the romanticist, Carlyle employs the same hazy terms to beatify Sterling: "a radiant child of the empyrean, clad in bright auroral hues."[72] The biography closes in a mood of controlled and elevated melancholy, in a country of the soul very far from the cacophony of *Latter-Day Pamphlets*. There is no querulousness or bombast now, only a joy in what is lovely and a delicate sense of loss:

> Poor Sterling, he was by nature appointed for a Poet . . .
> a recognizer and delineator of the Beautiful. . . . A man of
> infinite susceptivity; who caught everywhere, more than
> others, the colour of the element he lived in, the infection
> of all that was or appeared honourable, beautiful and man-
> ful in the tendencies of his Time. . . . Here visible to my-
> self, for some while, was a brilliant human presence . . .
> among the million little beautiful, once more a beautiful
> human soul: whom I, among others, recognized and lovingly
> walked with, while the years and hours were.[73]

In a contemporary review, George Eliot speaks of the *Life* as proof of the continued vitality of Carlyle's "sunny side":

> We no longer see him breathing out threatenings and
> slaughter as in the Latter-Day Pamphlets, but moving among
> the charities and amenities of life, loving and beloved . . .
> the conditions required for the perfection of life writing—
> personal intimacy, a loving and poetic nature which sees the
> beauty and the depth of familiar things, and the artistic
> power which seizes characteristic points and renders them
> with life-like effect,—are seldom found in combination.
> "The Life of Sterling" is an instance of this rare conjunc-
> tion.[74]

Carlyle never manages elsewhere, before or after, such an evocation of the gentler passions, but in *Past and Present* he champions the poet with as much conviction, though without the poignancy of his portrait of Sterling. Again the context reveals a man strangely divided in his loyalties. On the one hand, Carlyle disclaims poetry in favor of "fact," disowning men of serene intelligence for an army of "cloudy-browed, thick-soled workers."[75] On the other hand, he sees literature as a "better . . . perhaps also nobler" profession than the one Abbot Samson has chosen, and defends poets as the greatest heroes in any country: "for what usefuller, I say not nobler and heavenlier thing could the gods, doing their very kindest, send to any tribe or nation, in any time or circumstances?"[76] The poet is, without exception, useful in every era: Carlyle has even discarded his doctrine of heroic "controvertibility." A great man, at least if he is by nature poetical, does not have to adjust his talents to suit the temper of the times. Carlyle assumes such an unequivocal and uncharacteristic position because, at the moment he is writing, poetry constitutes for him the only sacred mission. In 1843, as in 1824, "the fiction of the poet is not falsehood, but the purest truth":

> An inspired Soul once more vouchsafed us, direct from Nature's own great fire-heart, to see the Truth, and speak it and do it; Nature's own sacred voice heard once more athwart the dreary boundless element of hearsaying and cant . . . a voice from the inner Light-sea and Flame-sea, Nature's own heart.[77]

The poet has become the very angel of God, in whose utterance is the sublime confluence of truth and beauty; for Carlyle as for Goethe, reverence for "Art" is still "infinitely enobling."

In the years after 1838, he often looked on poetry with a sympathy that reached almost to preferential esteem. Although he had pleaded guilty, in the *Heroes* lectures, to favoring the soldier-king "beyond all other sorts of men," Carlyle still devoted two of those six lectures to poets and men of letters. In fact, in "The Hero as

Poet," he does more than tolerate great men who cultivate their aesthetic powers: he concedes them the primary place in the moral culture of every nation. As it is true that the refinement of taste and the apprehension of the beautiful are the "highest outcome" of reverence, so also is it true that a sense of what is lovely must precede and inform all other activities, whether philosophical or practical:

> The *Vates* Prophet, we might say, has seized that sacred mystery rather on the moral side . . . the *Vates* Poet on what the Germans call the aesthetic side, as Beautiful, and the like. The one we may call a revealer of what we are to do, the other of what we are to love. But . . . the Prophet too has his eye on what we are to love: how else shall he know what it is we are to do?[78]

The prophet thus grounds all his exhortations on his own poetical faculties; and aesthetic standards are not only the final gloss on civilization but the first step toward it. Carlyle goes as far as Goethe in deriving man's moral nature from his ideas of beauty:

> The lilies of the field,—dressed finer than earthly princes, spring-up there in the humble furrow field; a beautiful *eye* looking out on you, from the great inner Sea of Beauty! How could the rude Earth make these, if her essence, rugged as she looks and is, were not inwardly Beauty? In this point of view, too, a saying of Goethe's which has staggered several, may have meaning: "The Beautiful," he intimates, "is higher than the Good; the Beautiful includes in it the Good."[79]

It seems that if we grant the later Carlyle (of *Heroes* and after) the tone of a zealot and the views of a practical historian, we must also be prepared to grant him, more often than is comfortable, the almost contradictory sentiments of an artist. The evidence of inconsistency after 1840 is sufficient not only to raise strong objections to the cry of "Philistine!" but to indicate a deep and recurrent tension in Carlyle's attitude toward the value of literature. He seems always to mistrust his own judgment, to affirm the efficacy of the poetic intellect with one breath while denying it with the next. In the "Hero as Poet," he qualifies his belief in the supremacy of "the Beautiful" with an immediate suspicion: "The *true* Beautiful; which however, I have said somewhere, 'differs from the *false* as Heaven does from Vauxhall!' "[80] Carlyle apparently feels compelled to make a moral distinction that is not in Goethe and that, coming when it does, reduces the whole passage to circular absurdity.

Such contradictory notions baffled Carlyle's friends as well as his readers. Emerson, during his second visit to England in 1847, came away from his talks with Carlyle in a daze of disappointment and anger. He writes to his wife, comparing the "Sage of Chelsea" to their gardener in Concord:

> Suppose that Hugh Whelan had had leisure enough in addition to all his daily work, to read Plato & Shakespeare, and Calvin and, remaining Hugh Whelan all the time, should talk scornfully of all this nonsense of books that he had been bothered with,—and you shall have just the tone and talk & laughter of Carlyle.[81]

For Emerson, the state of Carlyle's opinions was too confused to make any of his intentions clear: "I find C always cunning: he denies the books he reads; denies the friends he has just visited; denies his own acts & purposes;—By God, I do not know them."[82] Many of Carlyle's literary correspondents, impatient of his testiness, turned to other sources for spiritual guidance. Emerson often put off replying to his letters for as much as a year. Yet however alienated his friends may have felt from his practical views, Carlyle was never far from acknowledging the unique significance of the artist, or the genius of the poet:

> Poetry . . . is *musical Thought*. The Poet is he who *thinks* in that manner . . . it is a man's sincerity and depth of vi-

sion that makes him a Poet. See deep enough, and you see musically; the heart of Nature being everywhere music, if you can only reach it.[83]

In a letter to Robert Browning in 1856, he praises the intermittent eloquence of *Men and Women,* and plainly encourages the poet to cultivate his rhyming talent:

> It is certain there is an excellent opulence of intellect in these two rhymed volumes . . . The keenest just insight into men and things . . . Rhythm there is too, endless poetic fancy, symbolical *help* to express; and if not melody always or often *(for that would mean finish and perfection* [italics added]), there is what the Germans call *Takt*—fine *dancing,* if to the music only of *drums.*
>
> Such a faculty of talent, "genius" if you like the name better, seems to me *worth* cultivating, worth sacrificing oneself to tame and subdue into perfection.[84]

This ambivalence toward literature, which strongly affects Carlyle's criticism during the last forty years of his life, is no less active in his early writing. Just as age is unable to make of him a thorough-going Philistine, so youth does not submerge him utterly in the sometimes flaccid optimism of German poetics. Despite the almost exclusive attention that he gives to Goethe, Schiller, Novalis, and others of the Romantic school in the 1820s, there is a strain of nagging practicality in his evaluation of them. Carlyle's sentiments, in these early years of book reviews and translation, are ultimately on the side of the artist, but he suffers profound doubts along the way. *The Life of Schiller,* his first full-length effort of an original sort, is for the most part (and predictably, perhaps), a eulogy of the literary idealist. With some of the callowness of his adolescent dream of martyrdom, Carlyle descants on the stern glories of a poet's calling:

> If to know wisdom were to practise it; if fame brought true dignity and peace of mind; or happiness consisted in nour-

ishing the intellect with its appropriate food, and surrounding the imagination with ideal beauty, a literary life would
be the most enviable which the lot of this world affords.
But the truth is far otherwise. The Man of Letters . . . is
always hovering between the empyrean of his fancy and the
squalid desert of reality. . . . Yet among these men are to
be found the brightest specimens and the chief benefactors
of mankind! It is they that keep awake the finer parts of our
souls. . . . They are the vanguard in the march of mind.
. . . Such men are the flower of this lower world: to such
alone can the epithet of great be applied with its true
emphasis.[85]

The book impresses one as a paean to Schiller's purity of motive,
to his "refinement of taste" in the "creation of intellectual beauty."
Carlyle sympathizes with the "loftiest thoughts" of his imagination
and the "affecting" graces of his lyricism. The characters in Schiller's dramas may seem unreal, even "staid," but no matter:

He transports us into a holier and higher world than our
own; everything around us breathes of force and solemn
beauty. . . . The enchantments of the poets are strong
enough to silence our scepticism; we forbear to inquire
whether it is true or false.[86]

Carlyle is nonetheless slightly uncomfortable in Schiller's world of
pure forms, and heaps conspicuous praise upon his subject's more
practical literary efforts. Although Schiller's career as a historian
was short-lived and his output meager (one volume and some fragments), Carlyle sees the attempt as a significant advance over his
imaginative writings:

Schiller was, in fact, growing tired of fictitious writing. Imagination was with him a strong, not an exclusive, perhaps not
even a predominating faculty . . . in one so earnest, the
love of truth was sure to be among its stronger passions.
Even while revelling, with unworn ardour, in the dreamy

scenes of the Imagination, he had often cast a longing look
. . . into the calmer provinces of reason . . . the love of
contemplating or painting things as they should be, began
to yield to the love of knowing things as they are.[87]

Somehow Schiller's imagination did not "yield" enough to forestall
the writing of *Wallenstein, Maid of Orleans,* or *William Tell,* and
one suspects that the "longing look" toward actuality is being
taken, not by the poet, but by his critic.

Again, in writing of Novalis in 1829, Carlyle's forbearance is
overtaxed by his subject's uncompromising aestheticism. Although
Novalis "resembles the lofty Dante," and has contrived to live in
the "light of Reason," Carlyle distrusts his passivity and what he
suspects to be an amoral tolerance of nature and man. Carlyle
concedes that in "his belief in Love" Novalis has realized "the
highest and sole duty of man," but he cannot accept the effeminacy
of such an approach to the rigors of life:

His chief fault, again, figures itself to us as a certain undue
softness. . . . There is a tenderness in Novalis, a purity, a
clearness, almost as of a woman, but he has not . . . the
emphasis and resolute force of a man. . . . [he] is too lax in
separating the true from the doubtful, is not even at the
trouble to express his truth with any laborious accuracy.[88]

This charge of moral lassitude is more startling when seen in the
midst of indulgent criticism that surrounds it, for Carlyle has
otherwise defended Novalis's most pacific maxims. The outburst,
apparently a temperamental one, reveals that same tension in Carlyle's early view of the artist that colors all his later judgments.

Unlike his relationship with Schiller and Novalis, which was
purely that of biographer and critic, Carlyle's attachment to
Goethe was cemented by personal friendship. In a correspondence
made warmer and more sentimental by Goethe's extreme age,
the two men exchanged elaborate compliments over a period of
eight years. Carlyle's essays during the 1820s, on Goethe and

Goethe's *Faust,* echo the worshipful tone of his letters to the German poet; and the last of these essays, written in 1832, is unquestionably an attempt to apotheosize its subject.[89] Carlyle describes Goethe's writings as "Pure works of Art" full of "serenely smiling wisdom"; he is the "Wise Man" come into our "Time-element," the "World-Poet" created to lead us back to light![90]

> The true poet is ever, as of old, the Seer; whose eye has been gifted to discern the god-like Mystery of God's Universe, and decipher some new lines of celestial writing . . . he *sees* into this greatest of secrets, "the open secret" . . . thereby are his words in very truth prophetic; what he has spoken of shall be done. . . . The true Sovereign of the world, who moulds the world like soft wax, according to his pleasure, is he who lovingly *sees* into the world; the "inspired Thinker," whom in these days we name Poet.[91]

The torrent of unbridled praise is sustained to the very end, but there is one small crack in Carlyle's regard. He closes with what is purported to be a line of Goethe's: *"Im Ganzen, Guten, Wahren resolut zu leben!"*[92] But Carlyle substitutes, as he continued to do in all later instances, "True" where the poet had written the German for "Beautiful." As in his criticism of Schiller, Novalis, and the "Hero as Poet," he cannot resist inflicting an explicit moral standard on the aesthetic world-view with which he is confronted.

Although Carlyle's public view of Goethe was very much that of a disciple, his private opinion was touched with corrosive doubts. True, he spoke of the poet as "Master" and mourned, in a letter to his brother, the passing of "Venerable, dear Goethe," but as early as 1828 he wrote to John Carlyle:

> You must come round by Weimar as you return, and see this World's-wonder, and tell us . . . what manner of man he is, for daily he grows more inexplicable to me. One letter is written like an oracle, the next shall be too redolent of *twaddle.*[93]

Carlyle's misgivings about the "World-Poet" were matched by a
wavering allegiance to the craft of literature itself. In March, 1831
he advises John: "Neither would I have you quit Literature. . . .
Hold fast to your talent that way as the most precious of your possessions."[94] Only two months later he warns his brother away from
the "idle" pursuit: "I would have you throw out Literature altogether."[95] And Carlyle underscores his disparagement both of
Goethe and of literature in another letter to his brother, two years
later:

> In my own heterodox heart there is yearly growing up the
> strangest crabbed one-sided persuasion, that all Art is but a
> reminiscence now, that for us in these days *Prophecy* (well
> understood) not Poetry is the thing wanted; how can we *sing*
> and *paint* when we do not yet *believe* and *see?* . . . Now
> what under such point of view is all existing Art and the
> study of Art? What was the great Goethe himself? The
> greatest of contemporary men; who however is not to have
> any follower, and should not have any.[96]

Goethe and his kind thus appear, in Carlyle's darker thoughts, as
misdirected leaders with their feet planted, if not in Hell, at least
in a purgatory of moral uselessness.

The early struggle to explain away that "strange crabbed one-
sided persuasion" is painfully detailed in Carlyle's notebooks for
the years 1822 to 1832. To the theories and tendencies of German
aestheticism he raises continual objections, working cautiously to
understand its tenets. Carlyle's honesty in recognizing his own
ambivalence toward art is impressive in these jottings; there is no
doubt that for some years he probed his conscience for a resolution
of the tension. In 1831, for example, he is baffled by the interdependence of the beautiful and the good:

> I wish I could define to myself the true relation of moral
> genius to poetic genius; of Religion to Poetry. Are they one
> and the same, different forms of the same, and if so which is

to stand higher, the Beautiful or the Good? Schiller and
Goethe seem to say the former, as if it included the latter,
and might supersede it: how truly I can never well see.[97]

Even in such a dialogue of the mind with itself, Carlyle achieves
no final answers, although he argues the problem with a directness
and informality that his critical prose does not permit. Contradictions proliferate in the notebooks, as elsewhere: on the positive
side, literary men are the "only Sovereigns of the world," the poet
is "not only a Priest but a High-Priest"; Novalis, for example, is
"a deep man; the most perfect of modern spirit-seekers"; yet, at
the same time poetry is no more than the "jingle of maudlin persons" and Carlyle is "tired to death with [Schiller's] and Goethe's
palabra about the nature of the fine arts."[98] For every intimation
of the sublime, in which art seems "higher than Religion," Carlyle
suffers an offsetting vision of poetry as mere "Stuff and nonsense."[99]
At times literature disgusts him: "A few general ideas . . . a few
descriptions of our feelings—the whole repeated in ten thousand
times ten thousand forms."[100] Carlyle records this last bit of skepticism in 1822, during those days of supposed high optimism that
followed the "Everlasting Yea." For the next ten years, as the notebooks show, he repeatedly put the questions: "What is Poetry?
Do I really love Poetry?"[101] All his later writings indicate that he
never found satisfactory answers. Carlyle may not have resolved
or understood the confusion in his values, but he freely admitted
to the frustration it brought him. In 1830, after a long spate of
criticism and editing, he cried out against the perversity of his own
nature, "Why cannot I be a kind of Artist!"[102]

Certainly Carlyle never tried harder to "be a kind of Artist"
than in *Sartor Resartus,* begun that same year. Of course, the
dramatic effects in *The French Revolution* and part two of *Past
and Present* are of a novelistic sort, but these later "flashes of
lightning" illuminate monastic records and political history. Abbot
Samson, Marat, and Robespierre may assume exaggerated dimen-
sions in Carlyle's portraiture, but Teufelsdröckh is a creature of

pure invention. The "Editor" and his "six paper bags," the town of "Weissnichtwo" and its eccentric professor exist only in a Shandy-world of comic fiction, manipulated by the strings of Carlyle's fancy. Here, as Goethe and Schiller do, he has *created* a context—instead of exploiting an extant one—for the expression of higher truths. Although he lacks the Germans' disciplined artistry, he has nonetheless submitted to the control of his imagination and, in so doing, affirmed the first principle of romantic art.

Yet *Sartor* is not free from that strange contrariety we have seen in Carlyle's other works. In one passage, "Eternity looks through Time" in works of art; poems are windows on "the All"; musical thought reaches to the Platonic substance of "Infinitude itself."[103] But in another passage art's beneficence is illusory; like woman, it is "all Soul and Form," an ocean of weak "Aesthetic Tea."[104] Carlyle says in praise of literature and the power of written language:

> Wondrous indeed is the virtue of a true Book . . . like a spiritual tree . . . it stands from year to year, and from age to age. . . . O thou who art able to write a Book . . . envy not him whom they name City-builder, and inexpressibly pity him whom they name Conqueror or City-burner! Thou too art a Conqueror and Victor, but of the true sort, namely over the Devil: thou too hast built what will outlast all marble and metal, and be a wonder-bringing City of the Mind![105]

And again, recognizing the omnipotence of the "vocables" he admits:

> Greater than all recorded miracles have been performed by Pens. For strangely in this so solid-seeming World . . . it is appointed that *Sound,* to appearance the most fleeting, should be the most continuing of all things. The WORD is well said to be omnipotent in this world.[106]

Here, Carlyle seems to contradict his contention, in *Past and Present* and *Cromwell,* that the "done Poem" is greater than the written one. But there is no need to look ahead ten years to discover the inconsistency, for Carlyle exalts the silent worker to preeminence in the next book of *Sartor:*

> SILENCE and SECRECY! Altars might still be raised to them . . . for universal worship. Silence is the element in which great things fashion themselves together. . . . Speech too is great, but not the greatest. . . . Let not thy left hand know what thy right hand doeth! Neither shalt thou prate even to thy own heart of "those secrets known to all."[107]

Carlyle's argument against literature appears here as distaste for the self-consciousness of writers and speakers who articulate what they already know. In *Characteristics,* finished in the same year as *Sartor,* he amplifies this objection: the rise of "Reviewing" (in which Carlyle played an appreciable part), the conscious structuring of poetry (which Carlyle recommends to Browning and others) are symptoms of modern man's diseased imagination.[108] Carlyle lumps the purest forms of verse with that "mother of Abominations" known popularly as "periodical Literature." All art is full of "Error," "like a sick thing" listening to itself: "Which melodious Singer forgets that he is singing melodiously? We have not the love of greatness, but the love of the love of greatness."[109] Carlyle is seldom more vituperative in treating the literature of his day, yet he prefaces even this attack with what is for him, as prophet, the ultimate flattery: "Literature is but a branch of Religion, and always participates in its character: however, in our time, it is the only branch that still shows any greenness; and, as some think, must one day become the main stem."[110] But what begins favorably, ends opprobriously, for, like other contemporary organisms, the "greenness" of literature soon yellows in the heat of his invective.

Several years after *Sartor* and *Characteristics,* Carlyle gave elaborate form to his ideas of literary self-consciousness in a series of twelve lectures. Denigration of artistic values was probably not intended in the plan of *The History of Literature,* but it turns out,

perversely perhaps, to be a major theme of the course. Although
Carlyle praises almost every important poet from Homer to Goethe
and compliments Cervantes and Johnson along the way, there is
reluctance and suspicion in the eulogies. The "music" of Homer,
the "intensity" of Dante, the "comic vision" of Cervantes, the
"wisdom" of Goethe are offset by a historical perspective from
which Carlyle sees literature as the by-product of cultural decadence. The Romans, whose "whole genius was practical,"[111]
rank above the "dreaming," speculative Greeks; and the Dark
Ages are "healthy" because they are inarticulate, unconscious
times: "In these ages it is not to be expected that there was any
literature. It was a healthy age. We have remarked in the last lecture that the appearance of literature is a sign that the age which
produced it is not far from decline and decay."[112] Again Carlyle
prefers the opaque "Man of Practice," the "Conqueror" and the
"City-builder": "Actions only will be found to have been preserved
when writers are forgotten. Homer will one day be swallowed up
in time. . . . But actions will not be destroyed."[113] Despite its
sincerity and its beauty, apparently the best of European literature
is but a signal of national illness, for art grows out of pride, and
pride out of self-consciousness. Carlyle's exposition of literary history is thus backhandedly sympathetic, since the charms it delin-
eates are fatal.

After surveying the welter of Carlyle's conflicting views on
literature, from *Schiller* to *Frederick* and beyond, one is tempted
to say, with Emerson, "By God, I do not know them!" Only one
thing is certain: Carlyle cared little for balanced evaluation. His
opinions are usually unqualified. Poetry is either "trivial" or "sovereign," prose is either "powerless" or "omnipotent," and art is
either a "superficial film" or "the soul of man." His unconscious
desire to live up to the reputation he was gaining as a "sage" may
partially explain Carlyle's intemperate judgments, but it does
nothing to justify his chronic inconsistency. As we have seen, the
works of his "artistic" youth are riddled with crude pragmatism,
and those "rugged" products of his moralistic old age include the

prettiest kinds of aestheticism. He could say, almost simultaneously, that German Literature was a source of confusion out of which nothing valuable could be got and that he was "endlessly indebted to Goethe" for whatever peace of mind he had.[114] Literature was "little other than a Newspaper," yet it was "all in all to us . . . our Worship and Lawgiving."[115] As he aged, the emphasis in Carlyle's writing did indeed shift from art to ethics, and his strictures on literature grew more severe and more frequent. But the passing of the years answers only the matter of degree or dominance; we are still faced with a strong and unresolved tension in Carlyle's view of the arts which is sustained, in public and in private, throughout the whole of his life.

1. Among the many articles tracing Carlyle's stylistic debt to Richter, see especially J. Smeed, "Thomas Carlyle and Jean Paul Richter."

2. In "Matthew Arnold and Carlyle," pp. 145–46. For a study of the effect of Carlyle's early work on Victorian novels, see Mrs. Tillotson's *Novels of the Eighteen Forties*, especially pp. 150–56.

3. For his poetic treatment, see C. Watkins, "Browning's 'Red Cotton Night-Cap Country' and Carlyle."

4. See Geraldine Jewsbury, *Zoe: A History of Two Lives*; Charles Kingsley, *Alton Locke: Tailor and Poet*; and J. A. Froude, *The Nemesis of Faith*.

5. Quoted in T. Glover, "Carlyle," in *Poets and Puritans*, p. 279.

6. Ibid., and K. Tillotson, "Arnold and Carlyle," p. 135.

7. E. Neff, *Carlyle and Mill*, p. 37.

8. K. Tillotson, "Arnold and Carlyle," p. 133.

9. J. Symons, *Thomas Carlyle*, pp. 222–23.

10. Watkins, p. 362.

11. *Sartor Resartus*, in *Works of Thomas Carlyle*, p. 178 (hereafter cited as *SR*).

12. *Latter-Day Pamphlets*, *Works*, pp. 180–81, 212 (hereafter cited as *LDP*).

13. An earlier work of fiction, *Wotton Reinfred*, was left unfinished in 1827. See *Last Words of Thomas Carlyle*, pp. 1–148, and, for Carlyle's discussion of the work at the time of composition, *Letters of Thomas Carlyle, 1826–1836*. As a term for either *Sartor* or *Wotton*, "novel" should of course be understood in its loosest sense, i.e., full-length prose invention. It helps primarily to distinguish two works of Carlyle fundamentally different from the rest. On this problem of genre (Carlyle himself called *Sartor* a "Didactic Novel"), see G. Levine, *The Boundaries of Fiction* (Princeton, N.J., 1968), pp. 21–23, and G. B. Tennyson, *Sartor Called Resartus*.

14. *Wilhelm Meister, Works,* I, 29 (hereafter cited as *WM*).

15. *WM,* I, 30, 33.

16. *Past and Present, Works,* p. 158 (hereafter cited as *PP*).

17. *PP,* p. 159.

18. *The History of Frederick II of Prussia, Works,* I, 434 (hereafter cited as *HFG*).

19. *HFG,* I, 431–32.

20. "Novalis," *Critical and Miscellaneous Essays, Works,* II, 29, 53 (hereafter cited as *Essays*).

21. *Essays,* II, 29.

22. Ibid., p. 185.

23. *Oliver Cromwell's Letters and Speeches, Works,* I, 78 (hereafter cited as *Cromwell*).

24. *On Heroes, Hero-Worship and the Heroic in History, Works,* p. 209 (hereafter cited as *Heroes*).

25. Symons, *Carlyle,* p. 241.

26. *WM,* I, 22.

27. *Essays,* I, 56.

28. *Carlyle,* p. 166.

29. C. Harrold, *Carlyle and German Thought, 1819–1834,* p. vii.

30. R. Wellek, *The Romantic Age,* p. 337, and G. B. Tennyson, "Carlyle's Poetry to 1840: A Checklist and Discussion, A New Attribution, and Six Unpublished Poems," p. 161.

31. Tennyson, "Carlyle's Poetry," p. 161.

32. B. H. Lehman, *Carlyle's Theory of the Hero,* p. 194. I do not suggest that all critics see the shift from aesthetic to moral preoccupations as a diminution of Carlyle's value– for his contemporaries or for us.

33. Adapted from Goethe's *Generalbeichte, Werke,* I, 140. The line should read: "*Im Ganzen, Guten, Schönen resolut zu Leben!*"

34. C. R. Sanders, "Carlyle, Poetry, and the Music of Humanity," p. 53.

35. From a letter of Sterling's, quoted in ibid., p. 53.

36. Quoted in ibid., p. 54.

37. *Letters to His Wife,* p. 210.

38. Gavan Duffy, *Conversations with Carlyle,* p. 221.

39. Facsimile letter, dated 25 June 1862, and appended to the last pages of *Two Note Books of Thomas Carlyle, from 23rd March, 1822 to 16th May, 1832* (hereafter cited as *Note Books*). The apparent distinction between the needs of "these loud times" and those of another age becomes hopelessly blurred when we consider other similar passages in Carlyle: see below, pp. 192–96.

40. His literary acquaintances included Browning, Clough, Coleridge, Dickens, Emerson, Goethe, Hunt, Geraldine Jewsbury, Kingsley, Lamb, DeQuincey, Allingham. Margaret Fuller, Harriet Martineau, Forster, Espinasse, Ruskin, Sterling, Tennyson, Thackeray, and Wordsworth. He was notably distant toward Gladstone and Disraeli.

41. *Note Book,* p. 184.

42. Among its lighter aspects was the gift of a lock of Jane's hair, which Goethe, pleading baldness, declined to repay in kind. See *Correspondence between Goethe and Carlyle,* pp. 160–61 and 206–7 (hereafter cited as *Goethe Letters*).

43. *Goethe Letters,* pp. 32–33.

44. Ibid., p. 256.

45. Ibid., pp. 34–35.

46. D. A. Wilson, *Carlyle till Marriage,* p. 93 (hereafter cited as Wilson I).

47. *Essays,* IV, 481, 465, 470.

48. J. A. Froude, *Thomas Carlyle: A History of His Life in London: 1834–1881,* II, 307.

49. And surely the same shift in sensibilities that provoked Ruskin to declare *Hard Times* Dicken's greatest novel.

50. *Carlyle: An Anthology,* p. 5 (italics added). See also Arnold's view of Carlyle's style and thought as too morbid, too perverse for genuine greatness or lasting fame (*Discourses in America,* pp. 162–68, 196–202).

51. From the prologue to Schiller's *Wallenstein.* Carlyle distorts the meaning by neglecting to quote the last half of the line: *"heiter ist die Kunst."*

52. *Essays,* IV, 475.

53. Review, quoted in appendix to Bliss, *Letters to His Wife,* p. 404.

54. Nor, one is tempted to infer from the often careless diction of Trollope's novels, does it have a place in contemporary fiction.

55. Bliss, *Letters to His Wife,* p. 381. Again in 1877, Carlyle expressed his sympathy with the aesthetic qualities of Ruskin's prose: "A celestial brightness is in him. His description of the wings of birds the most beautiful thing of the kind that can possibly be. His morality too, is the highest and the purest" (Allingham, *A Diary,* p. 263).

56. Loyalty to Ruskin is no factor here. See Bliss, *Letters to His Wife,* p. 370. Trollope had, admittedly, waged an intermittent, but wholly unilateral, combat with Carlyle since 1855—not on the point of style, however, but of philosophical skepticism. See "Dr. Pessimist Anticant," chapter 15 of *The Warden* (a remarkably slack piece of satire); "Essay on Carlylism" (1868); and an entry in his *Autobiography* for 1876, p. 185. M. Sadlier, in his *Trollope: A Commentary* (1947), confirms Carlyle's charge of philistinism (see pp. 187–89).

57. *HFG,* I, 421–22, 426–28.

58. "Voltaire," *Essays,* I, 436.

59. *HFG,* IV, 465.

60. *Reminiscences,* I, 232.

61. *LDP,* p. 181.

62. *The Life of John Sterling, Works,* p. x (hereafter cited as *Sterling*).

63. Ibid., p. 195.

64. Ibid.

65. Ibid., p. 156.

66. Ibid., pp. 174, 175.

67. Ibid., p. 154.

68. Ibid., p. 46.

69. Ibid.

70. Ibid., p. 159. Among its members were Tennyson and Monckton Milnes.

71. Ibid., p. 26.

72. Ibid., p. 2.

73. Ibid., pp. 266–68.

74. From *Westminster Review*, January 1852, collected in *Essays of George Eliot*, ed. T. Pinney, p. 49. On the manner of the biography, she is equally emphatic: "The style of the work, too, is for the most part at once pure and rich; there are passages of deep pathos which come upon the reader like a strain of solemn music" (p. 51).

75. *PP*, pp. 46–159.

76. Ibid., pp. 104, 86.

77. Ibid., p. 86.

78. *Heroes*, p. 81.

79. Ibid., pp. 81–82.

80. Ibid.

81. *The Correspondence of Emerson and Carlyle*, p. 33 (hereafter cited as *Emerson Letters*). The same passage appears in an article Emerson wrote for an American journal in 1848 entitled simply "Carlyle." See *Miscellaneous Pieces*, p. 230.

82. *Emerson Letters*, p. 38.

83. *Heroes*, pp. 83–84.

84. *Letters of Thomas Carlyle to John Stuart Mill, John Sterling and Robert Browning*, pp. 297–98 (hereafter cited as *MSB Letters*).

85. *The Life of Schiller, Works*, pp. 42–44 (hereafter cited as *LS*).

86. Ibid., p. 78.

87. Ibid., p. 84.

88. *Essays*, II, 51–52.

89. "Death of Goethe," *Essays*, II, 374–84.

90. Ibid., pp. 380, 379, 375.

91. Ibid., p. 377.

92. See above, footnote 33.

93. Quoted in *Goethe Letters*, p. 81. Passage omitted by Norton in letter of 16 April 1828; see *Letters of Thomas Carlyle*, ed. C. E. Norton, I, 149 (hereafter cited as *Letters*). See also letter of 21 September 1823 on Goethe as both genius and "ass" (*Early Letters*, p. 41).

94. *Letters*, I, 273.

95. Ibid., I, 283.

96. 1 October 1833, in J. A. Froude, *Thomas Carlyle: A History of the First Forty Years of His Life: 1795–1835*, I, 385–86 (hereafter cited as *First Forty Years*).

97. *Note Books*, p. 188.

98. Ibid., pp. 184, 180, 140, 151, 41.

99. Ibid., pp. 204, 42. David Masson agrees that these private papers reveal a persistent strain of pessimism in the young Carlyle—an attitude that most of his critics associate only with the embitterment of his last years: "[The early journals] break down, for one thing, that kind of apology for Carlyle's grimness and gloominess which would maintain that, like Timon's misanthropy, it belonged only or mainly to his 'latter spirits,' the final fifteen years of his extreme old age and widowhood. . . . There was certainly an accession of dolefulness in this final period of his life; but essentially the same vein of gloom, grimness, lamentation . . . as the posthumous letters and papers now prove, had been perpetual in his life from the very first" (*Carlyle Personally and in His Writings*, p. 35).

100. *Note Books*, p. 33.

101. Ibid., p. 150.

102. Ibid., p. 226.

103. *SR*, pp. 198, 56–57.

104. Ibid., p. 108.

105. Ibid., p. 138.

106. Ibid., p. 158.

107. Ibid., p. 174.

108. The quoted phrases that follow occur in *Essays*, III, 23–25.

109. Ibid., p. 23.

110. Ibid.

111. *Lectures on the History of Literature*, p. 38 (hereafter cited as *Lectures*); they were delivered April-July 1838.

112. Ibid., p. 69.

113. Ibid., p. 72.

114. Symons, *Thomas Carlyle*, p. 241; and *Reminiscences*, I, 288.

115. *MSB Letters*, p. 192; and *Goethe Letters*, p. 256.

Chapter Two

Tracing the Conflict to Its Source

> Carlyle was one of those who can-
> not conceive of life without a reli-
> gion which should provide him
> with a faith by which he could live.
> —L. Cazamian

Over the years, Carlyle contra-
dicts himself on a variety of issues—social as well as literary. He
dismisses the English aristocracy, like that of eighteenth-century
France, as a self-indulgent anachronism, yet he sees in its cultivated "sweetness" the "seedfield" for great men. Radicalism and
the Reform Bill of 1832 are needed to extend suffrage, to correct
political injustice, but majority rule brings only "blockheadism,"
and despots like Dr. Francia are an excusable expedient.[1] Carlyle
decries Robespierre and Fouquier as heartless executioners, but
he tells Jane he would have felt no pity whatever "if Eyre had shot
the whole Nigger population, and flung them into the sea."[2] His
theory of heroism is especially illogical: on the one hand, great
men are inviolate, and the eras in which they are born must adapt
to them; on the other hand, heroes manifest their leadership in an
idiom appropriate to the particular age. Ordinary men, though
honest and obedient, lack the insight needed to propose reform,
yet it is they who must recognize and promote the true hero when
he comes. The whole idea of a vast political readjustment, which
Carlyle advocates so warmly in *Latter-Day Pamphlets,* seems to

him, at an earlier date, to be a mistaken one: "To reform a world, to reform a nation, no wise man will undertake: and all but foolish men know that the only solid, though a far slower, reformation is what each begins and perfects on *himself*."[3] His political views are thus as much at cross-purposes as his literary opinions.

Some of Carlyle's disciples, in an effort to excuse this "crankiness" and perversity in his view of art and the world, have fastened on a physical cause. Wilson, Froude, and others argue that a man who so vigorously "denies his own acts and purposes" and vilifies the very craft he practices, must have suffered some chronic torment of the body. Carlyle himself offered such an explanation for his moodiness as early as 1819.[4] At that time, and at regular intervals over the next sixty-two years, he complained, in private, of "dyspepsia" and aggravated "biliousness":

> I declare solemnly without exaggeration that I impute nine-tenths of my present wretchedness, and rather more than nine-tenths of all my faults, to this infernal disorder in the stomach. If it were once away I think I could snap my fingers in the face of all the world.[5]

Though friends, wife, and parents sympathized, and physicians examined and advised, none of their palliatives relieved his intestinal discomforts. Carlyle's letters often read like an informal medical history: "rats gnaw" at his stomach, an "excess of bile" puts an end to work for the day, "gastric disorders" interrupt his sleep at two o'clock in the morning; doctors recommend "grey powder" and horse-riding, they forbid him pipe-smoking and ginger-bread—to no avail.[6] The whole range of stomach troubles was compounded by insomnia: according to his own testimony, Carlyle seldom slept more than four hours a night. Street noises, howling dogs, pet birds, and early-morning workmen disturbed his dreams wherever he went. A soundproof study,[7] outfitted with a lounging couch, provided some respite from the "noisy inanity" of London, but no contrivances, it seems, mitigated the pains in his upper abdomen. Carlyle's dyspeptic personality apparently made even his least critical admirers chary of repeated encounters with him. Margaret Fuller, impressed on a first meeting by his good-humored repartee, was dismayed, on a second visit, by his intolerance of "the highest kinds of poetry."[8] Is it then reasonable to consider Carlyle's ill-tempered responses—to contemporary politics, to literature, and to the friends of literature—solely as he suggests, in the light of this physical disability? Carlyle's impatience, his "crabbed" persuasions and his stridency might thus be waved off as temporary "excesses of bile," much as Marley's ghost was thought an "undigested bit of beef," or Matthew Bramble's "peevishness" the effect of "consturpation." Certainly it is a teasing possibility.

Yet notwithstanding his anguished complaints, there is a curious vagueness in Carlyle's description of the disease and a tendency to dismiss medical aid as "useless Quackery." None of the doctors of his day could locate the precise area of his discomforture, and none could determine an organic cause.[9] Although no remedies had any effect on Carlyle's illness, his condition did not measurably deteriorate, and he lived eighty-six years in spite of it. Even his friends privately discounted the importance of these rumored complaints: "We heard of the dyspepsia, and knew it was there; but which of us, in Carlyle's company . . . ever thought of the dyspepsia or ever regarded it as one hundredth of the actual man before us?[10] No one doubts that he suffered actual pain, but most modern critics feel that the evidence points to a psychosomatic disturbance. Dr. J. L. Halliday, in his medical biography of Carlyle, evaluates the symptoms as "largely functional" and concludes that the patient should have been "seen by a psychiatrist."[11] The subsequent Freudian analysis, which occupies most of Halliday's attention, is the purest fancy,[12] but his first conclusion, at least, is not groundless. As a doctor he reviews the medical evidence and concurs with contemporary physicians in finding no physical basis for Carlyle's complaint. Thus, in reaching for an organic answer to Carlyle's contrariety, we are thrown back on some emotional or intellectual tension behind it.

The conflict in his attitude toward literature cannot, of course, be divorced from the physical circumstances in which he lived and wrote. There are a number of elements in the conditions of Carlyle's life which militated against consistency, and which may have contributed to his more irrational antagonisms. Froude, for example, wastes much of his energy attempting to prove Carlyle's sexual impotence with Jane;[13] Wilson and others have as vehemently—and as foolishly—defended his manliness. Neither argument is conclusive,[14] but out of the gossip and often profound absurdities emerges the picture of an unquiet marriage. Both the Carlyles complained of chronic mysterious pains, often vying with one another for sympathy, like sickly antiphonal choirs. Jane was no intellectual lightweight, and could be as caustically incisive in her criticisms as Carlyle was orotund. As Froude admits, Mrs. Carlyle "never flattered anyone, least of all her husband; and when she saw cause for it the sarcasms flashed out from her as the sparks fly from lacerated steel."[15] Mutual resentment forced them to take frequent "vacations" from each other, to Templand, or Scotsbrig, or Germany. During these separations—which lasted for months at a time—they exchanged affectionate, anxious letters, but made no move to reunite. Evidently, the pressures of their highly charged, competitive, and childless relationship could not be met without long intervals for recuperation.[16] There is nothing in Carlyle's private writings to indicate that marital dissonance was a fundamental cause of divisive tensions in his world-view, but such squabbles certainly exacerbated his "rall mental awgony."

It may also be argued that Carlyle's intense work routine inflamed and distorted his opinions. As a student and writer, he applied himself with compulsive zeal, drawing "blear-eyed wisdom out of midnight oil." The self-imposed exile of Craigenputtock, the long hours in the soundproof room in Chelsea and a life of almost exclusively sedentary habits did indeed bring on occasional fits of exasperation and melancholy. But, even if we allow, as Burton does, that self-recrimination is one of the fruits of scholarship, we must also admit that Carlyle's situation was not radically different from that of any highly productive writer. To excuse, on such general grounds, an ambivalence as thoroughgoing as that which Carlyle displays toward literature is to pardon the conflict without regard to its gravity.

In despair of a ready solution to the dilemma, a few critics have settled on an implicitly cynical answer. According to Symons and Harrold, Carlyle never *really* trusted in literary values; in fact, he only exploited "Art" and the canons of German aesthetics to advance himself and his opinions.[17] The ideas expressed in scores of articles should be discounted as "merely profitable by-products of what he truly wished to say."[18] In other words, he wrote in defense of literature not out of principle but out of economic necessity. Once his translations, reviews, and biographies had bought him financial security, Carlyle was free to operate according to his own convictions. And since fame and moderate fortune came with the publication of *The French Revolution* in 1837, it is only after this date that Carlyle's true character emerges in his writing. Released from external pressures (so their economic interpretation runs), he naturally assumed the position of moral zealot and political critic; he lost, in the process, the literary affectations of his youth. Put in harsher, more colloquial language, they assert that in middle life, untempted by the bribe of bread, Carlyle dropped the mask of artist and revealed his essential philistinism. It should be said to the credit of those who suggest Carlyle "used" literature that they do so without self-righteousness and in apparent sympathy with the difficulties Carlyle faced. Moreover, their indictment appears to be impartially arrived at, since they demonstrate no preference for Carlyle either as artist or as moral utilitarian.[19]

Nonetheless, the formulation and grounds of the argument are severely limited: Symons discusses the conflict as a minor critical sidelight to an anecdotal biography, and Harrold, whose investigation is more elaborate, treats only the period 1819–1834. Neither approach is definitive, nor without a wider perspective can it hope to be. In fact, at close range Carlyle's opinions run counter to the tendencies one would expect in an exploitative handling of literature. British reading tastes in the 1820s did not favor an exposition of German poetry and fiction: what little work was known or translated circulated within a fairly narrow group of intellectuals. In these early days, as J. V. Morley declares, "the European movement . . . was little studied in England by even the leading men, much less by the average."[20] Froude also recalls the unpopularity of Carlyle's German criticism: "Neither the Meister nor the Schiller were selling. . . . The booksellers hung back and they judged rightly, perhaps, for their own interests. Carlyle, like all really original writers, had to create the taste which could appreciate him"; "*German Romance* was financially a failure also, and the Edinburgh publishers would make no further ventures."[21] Carlyle would have reaped far greater profits if he had satisfied the public demand for articles on Scott and Gray and Byron.[22] For that matter, nothing prevented him from making his fortune in a reiteration of moral orthodoxy; essays on Milton and Pope would have sold as well as reviews of Schiller and Novalis. Instead, Carlyle chose a vehicle both unfamiliar to his public and philosophically ill-suited to the advancement of Christian evangelism. In doing so he frequently endorsed ideas antithetical to those of which his "true nature" approved. Many of these statements are curiously enthusiastic: "Art is to be loved, not because of its effects, but because of itself; not because it is useful for spiritual pleasure, or even for moral culture, but because it is Art, and the highest in man, and the soul of all Beauty."[23]

Furthermore, if Carlyle's literary recommendations were indeed sheer pretense, one might justifiably expect to find a hint of the ruse or at least some greater consistency in his private writings. Here, with conviction undistorted by necessity, he might have maintained his antipathy toward the arts. Yet in his notebooks Carlyle repeatedly praises the poetic impulse:

> Here, even here [in this world], is the Revelation of the Infinite in the Finite; a majestic Poem (tragic, comic, or epic), couldst thou but read it and recite it! Watch it then;

study it, catch the secret of it, and proclaim the same in such accent as is given thee.[24]

At the same time, he is contemptuous of those who see life unmusically. Even Jeffrey, his early mentor, draws criticism for his dullness and partial vision: "The prose spirit of the world—to which world his kindliness draws him so strongly and so closely—has choked and all but withered the better poetic spirit he derives from nature. . . . Literature! poetry! . . . He knows not what they mean."[25]

Not only was Carlyle an apologist for literature; he also emphatically opposed an economic interpretation of life. No sign of the times distressed him more than the cynicism of contemporaries who preached "cash payment" as "the sole nexus of man to man."[26] As an artist, Carlyle thought himself aloof from the materialism of his age: "Authors are martyrs—witnesses for the truth—or else nothing. Money cannot make or unmake them. They are made or unmade, commanded and held back by God Almighty alone, whose inspiration it is that giveth them understanding. . . . Money cannot hire the writing of a good book."[27] Carlyle lived frugally all his life, and in later years Jane often complained that their circumstances had not improved with the improvement in their fortunes.[28] A pension was refused when it was offered, and a number of lucrative literary adventures were declined as well.[29] Fame and money came or went, but they were always to Carlyle only subordinate considerations—what he scornfully called the "goose goddesses" of ordinary men.

Furthermore, success did not bring anything like consistency to his opinions of literature. As we have seen in the last chapter, Carlyle's late essays and letters continued to reflect an uneasy tension between poetic vision and moral activism. The subjects discussed may have been political, but his treatment of them was stubbornly impressionistic. More than one critic has suggested that *The French Revolution,* for example, ought to be subtitled "A Drama."[30] Carlyle's accounts of the surrender of the Bastille,

Louis's flight from Paris, the howling menace of the mobs in the Place de la Révolution, Charlotte Corday's vendetta, and Napoleon's "whiff of grapeshot" have about them the exaggerated immediacy and conscious shaping of theater pieces.[31] Mill, in a review of the first edition, classed the history as a kind of modern prose epic: a work of scholarship transmuted by genius into art.[32] Whether *The French Revolution* succeeds as document or as drama, there is no question that Carlyle was continuously intrigued by the powers of the creative imagination. He wrote in his journal in July, 1832: "To imagine: *bilden!* That is an unfathomable thing. . . . As yet I have never risen into the region of creation. Am I approaching it? *Ach Gott! sich nähern dem unausprechlichen.*"[33] *Sartor Resartus* and *The French Revolution* were, largely, attempts to articulate that unspeakable, "unfathomable" sense of life.

Years later, in the writing of *Past and Present,* Carlyle tried again to illuminate history with the lamps of imagination. Much of the work's didacticism is relieved, in Book Two, by an inspired portrayal of thirteenth-century monastic life. There Carlyle evokes, as sensitively as in his tribute to Sterling, the strangeness and wonder of a lost time:

> Behold, therefore, this England of the year 1200 was no chimerical vacuity or dreamland, peopled with mere vaporous Fantasms . . . but a green solid place, that grew corn and several other things. The Sun shone on it; the vicissitudes of seasons and human fortunes . . . King Lackland *was* there, verily he; and did leave these *tredecim sterlingi,* if nothing more, and did live and look in one way or the other, and a whole world was living and looking along with him![34]

His history of St. Edmundsbury does, ultimately, have a moral purpose, but Carlyle's immediate concern is with the evanescence and vitality of the past. He reworks Jocelin's narrative into a series of lively scenes, and none is more poignant than the descrip-

tion of Samson unearthing the Abbey's patron saint: "What a scene
. . . John of Dice, with vestry men, clambering on the roof to
look through; the Convent all asleep, and the Earth all asleep,—
and since then, Seven Centuries of Time mostly gone to sleep!"[35]
The drama closes with the kind of contrast that comes hard to the
historian, but easily to the poet: "Jocelin's Boswellian Narrative
. . . *ends* . . . impenetrable Time-Curtains rush down . . . and
there is nothing left but a mutilated black Ruin amid green
botanic expanses, and oxen, sheep and dilettanti pasturing in
their places."[36]

Carlyle's stylistic revisions, as much as any explicit declaration,
betray the conflict in his literary attitudes after 1837. At times he
professes suspicion of the self-conscious artist, admonishing himself to write plainly: "Learn to do it *honestly* . . . *perfectly* thou
wilt never do it. Time flies; while thou balancest a sentence, thou
art nearer the *final* Period."[37] Yet he spent months recasting the
proofs of his works, embellishing purple passages, complicating
syntax, heightening prose rhythms. In a close study of the manuscript changes in *Past and Present,* Grace Calder concludes:

> Carlyle's style was always his own, but the First Draft is
> much less brilliant Carlylean prose than the Printer's Copy.
> The manuscripts serve to show the strokes by which this
> brilliance was achieved. . . . They will ever belie his pro-
> fessions that he cared "little for phrases," for they throw
> open the doors of his workshop and show the artist absorbed
> in his art.[38]

Thus, in later years, Carlyle did more than borrow the language
and spirit of poetry: he shared, as well, the poet's pride in verbal
craftsmanship. Those critics who have dismissed the influence of
literary considerations on the older Carlyle have ignored not only
much of what he said, but also the way in which he said it.[39]

Finally, to make of Carlyle's *early* writings a purely mercenary
venture is to call in question the sincerity of all his literary efforts.
If he wrote, in the 1820s and early 1830s, only to gain freedom to

pursue a more practical course, then why did he not desert the craft of literature when he had won financial independence? In other words, why did he write at all, in the second half of his life, if the methods and aims of literary men were totally abhorrent to him? Two answers suggest themselves: either the early dishonesty of his motives had become habitual, or the assertion of his essential philistinism is simply invalid. The first possibility attracts, in particular, those flamboyant skeptics of the Strachey school who would write off their Victorian fathers as self-seeking dissemblers. In the case of Carlyle, however, the evidence points away from disguise and equivocation. His journals, letters and notebooks reveal a frequency of self-examination that is both earnest and unrestrained. *Sartor Resartus* and *Reminiscences* demonstrate his willingness to put personal trials and shortcomings before the public. Froude, equipped with an intimate knowledge of Carlyle's foibles, affirmed the honesty of his intentions: "He never wrote or spoke any single sentence which he did not with his whole heart believe to be true."[40] No allowance for Froude's extravagance can alter the obvious conclusion: Carlyle was continually at pains to assure his own integrity. If we accept, as the testimony dictates, that his ambivalence toward literature was sincere, then the very fact that he continued to write, in the face of strong misgivings, only serves to enlarge the significance of the conflict.

Froude's treatment of the problem is not radically different from that of many twentieth-century critics. He, too, concentrates on Carlyle's moral pragmatism and virtually ignores any commitment to imaginative literature. Zealot, reformer, political enthusiast— these, for Froude, make up the essential Carlyle: whatever artistic pretensions run through his work are merely eccentricities aggravated by "biliousness." Unfortunately, though he is kinder than modern biographers in attaching the inconsistency to an involuntary cause, Froude does not argue the question impartially. As practical historian and rigid moralist, he has little respect for the "nebulosities" of romantic art. The only extracts he chooses from Carlyle's writing are those that underline his own bias against the ultimate efficacy of literature. After a personal encounter with both men, Leslie Stephen speaks of the difference between Carlyle, and Carlyle as interpreted by Froude: "The wonderful force and vitality of the old man have enabled him completely to conquer Froude, who repeats his doctrines and makes them worse in the repetition."[41] For example, Froude quotes from Carlyle's journal of 1838:

> It often strikes me as a question whether there ought to be any such thing as a literary man at all. He is surely the wretchedest of all sorts of men. I wish with the heart occasionally I had never been one. I cannot say I have seen a member of the guild whose life seems to me enviable. . . . Canst thou alter it? Then act it. Endure it. On with it in silence.

Froude then analyzes the passage in the following pedagogical fashion:

> Let young men who are dreaming of literary eminence as the laurel wreath of their existence reflect on these words. Let them win a place for themselves as high as Carlyle won, they will find that he was speaking no more than the truth, and will wish, when it is too late, that they had been wise in time. Literature—were it even poetry—is but the shadow of action: the action the reality, the poetry an echo.[42]

A more disinterested approach might have led Froude to consider not only Carlyle's contrary moods of self-affirmation, but also the qualifications (such as "often" and "occasionally") in this pessimistic view of literature. For despite recriminations, Carlyle went "on with it," and frequently derived spiritual satisfaction and a strong sense of purpose from his writing. With the exception of a brief public defense of Governor Eyre, Carlyle seldom indulged in that political activism which Froude asserts was his proper domain:

> I have had no concern whatever in their Puseyisms, ritualisms . . . and cobwebberies . . . and no feeling of my own

> except . . . occasional indignation, for the poor world's
> sake . . . with their universal suffrages . . . and scoundrel
> Protection societies. . . . I [have] become independent of
> the world.[43]

Carlyle evidently found greater comfort in his literary habits than
most of his biographers admit.

An alternative source of Carlyle's self-contradiction may lie in
some comic perversity of character. Perhaps he enjoyed the shock
value of voicing precisely those views which were not expected of
him. Margaret Fuller remarks that on one occasion he broke into
laughter at the "gorgeous" absurdity of his own opinions.[44] Certainly the author of *Sartor Resartus,* who could weave fanciful
digressions and ironies into the fabric of a metaphysical creed,
might have treated other subjects just as playfully. He loved anyone whose laugh was "manful," and he often condemned the
solemn attitudinizing of Coleridge and Emerson.[45] Yet the element
of humor is noticeably muted in most of Carlyle's prose after 1831.
Only in *Sartor* and "The Diamond Necklace" does he create anything like the modern idea of comic personae.[46] In general he
attacks his material frontally and with conspicuous seriousness:
Carlyle thought life and writing were a terribly earnest business
in which comedy played a minor role. The headlong "pursuit of
happiness" or mere entertainment always struck him as a mindless
egotism: "The only happiness a brave man ever troubled asking
much about was, happiness enough to get his work done."[47] "We
shall be, if not happy, blessed which is better."[48] There is very
little wryness or light satire in *Heroes, Cromwell,* or *Frederick* and
no levity whatever in the shrill rhetoric of *Latter-Day Pamphlets.*
As an ironist, Carlyle was incapable of maintaining the good-
humored detachment of an Austen or a Thackeray, and his sarcasms are consistently bitter.[49] This very baldness in the tone of his
opinions often exposed him to exquisitely wrought insults from
reviewers and "town wits." For his own part, Carlyle felt only pity
for the deviousness and superficiality of these "word-juggling"

"half-men": "[The fashionable wit's] poor fraction of sense has to be perked into some epigrammatic shape. . . . Such grinning inanity is very sad to the soul of man."[50] They lacked sincerity—to Carlyle the *sine qua non* of ordinary men and heroes, of poets and soldier-kings. He never deviated from his belief that man cannot begin to justify his existence—or perfect it—until he thinks and acts with wholehearted honesty. Like Goethe, he encouraged men to be reverent:

> There is one common word of Carlyle's which continues to express his essential quality: the word *reverence*, not for him, but in him: the governing seriousness of a living effort, against which every cynicism, every kind of half-belief, every satisfaction in indifference, may be seen and placed, in an ultimate human contrast.[51]

If the conflict in Carlyle's view of literature cannot be traced to an economic or a physical cause, what other possibilities are left to us? He does not appear to contradict himself out of mere willfulness or caprice. Julian Symons has suggested another source of tension in his character—one that does not depend so much upon those physical influences Carlyle professed to scorn. At an early age, Symons argues, he refused to take clerical orders because he could not accept the belief-propositions of the church: "For the rest of Carlyle's life a war was to be waged, with varying intensity at different times, between the keen iconoclasm of his intellect and his emotional need for a faith."[52] Thus began "his lifelong struggle to expel with the magic of dogma the hydra-headed monster of doubt."[53] Although the argument is left as a generalization and never applied to the peculiar difficulties of Carlyle's writing, let us assume, for the moment, its potential validity. Quite simply, the problem becomes an antagonism between belief and unbelief, between emotional orthodoxy and intellectual heresy. Carlyle's literary and political inconsistencies, even his psychosomatic disturbances, may then be symptoms of a "life-long" vacillation between the security of dogmatic faith and the uncertainty of enlightened skepticism. Since Symons does not offer direct testimony to the wider significances of the tension, it remains for us to explore the influence, if any, of agnosticism on Carlyle's view of literature.

Perhaps the self-doubt he felt from time to time was a manifestation of his inability to accept a divinely ordered universe. That is, since Carlyle chose literature as a career and found some measure of emotional security in writing, it may be that his distaste for the "vocables" was provoked by religious disillusionment. If so, in advocating more active pursuits, Carlyle ought to have spoken as a skeptic or at least in the secular tones of a pragmatist. The truth is far otherwise. As an opponent of the arts, Carlyle was seldom irreligious. He writes in *Latter-Day Pamphlets:*

> Of Literature, in all ways, be shy rather than otherwise, at present! There where thou art, work, work; whatsoever thy hand findeth to do, do it,—with the hand of a man, not of a phantasm; be that thy unnoticed blessedness and exceeding great reward. Thy words let them be few, and well-ordered. Love silence rather than speech. . . . Learn to *be* something and to *do* something, instead of eloquently talking about what has been and was done and may be! . . . May future generations, acquainted again with the silences, and once more cognisant of what is noble and faithful and divine, look back on *us* with pity and incredulous astonishment![54]

Carlyle's opposition to literature is, after all profoundly moral; he condemns the eloquence of the artist in a context of spiritual affirmation. The foregoing passage employs not only religious diction—"blessedness," "faithful," and "divine"—but at least two biblical paraphrases to reinforce the orthodoxy of his indignation. If anything, the strength of Carlyle's piety increases in proportion to his disenchantment with the value or power of the written word: the silent "Man of Practice . . . has in him what transcends all logic-utterance: a Congruity with the Unuttered"; Cromwell is a "Poet" of "belief, without words"; "Altars" should "be raised to silence for universal worship." For Carlyle, the "Gospel of Work" and the "Doctrine of Silence" are inextricably tied to his faith in God:

> The Practical Labour of England is not a chimerical Trivi-
> ality: it is a fact acknowledged by all the Worlds; which no
> man and no demon will contradict. It is, very audibly,
> though very inarticulately as yet, the one God's Voice we
> have heard in these two atheistic centuries.[55]

Whatever it is that causes him to doubt the efficacy of literature surely does not have its origin in the "keen iconoclasm" of unbelief. He criticizes "the jingle of maudlin persons" from a position of unquestioned conviction and moral assurance.

There is yet another possibility: he may have derided poets and men of letters precisely because they represented the heterodoxy of an intellectual culture. Conversely, if we attribute the tension to a conflict between belief and doubt, perhaps Carlyle's artistic bias is an assertion of his independence from religious commitment. In that case, his defense of literature should reflect a secular turn of mind, just as his strident philistinism appears to signal a retreat into dogma. Again, Carlyle's words belie such a view. He does not endorse poetry as a refuge from religion, or as a sanctuary for the unbeliever. The world of the poet is, for him, as godlike as that of the practical man. He speaks in praise of Goethe:

> To that man, too, in a strange way, there was given what
> we may call a life in the Divine mystery: and strangely, out
> of his Books, the world rises imaged once more as godlike,
> the workmanship and temple of a God. Illuminated . . .
> in mild celestial radiance;—really a Prophecy in these most
> unprophetic times; to my mind, by far the greatest, though
> one of the quietest, among all the great things that have
> come to pass in them.[56]

Carlyle supports an aesthetic that is compatible with, even dependent upon, a "Divine Idea of the World." He observes, on one occasion, that "the taste for Religion and for Poetry go together";[57]
on another that "Art . . . Virtue, and Religion" are the highest
expressions of man's soul.[58] The interdependence of beauty and
truth, of literature and belief in God, are cornerstones of Carlyle's
poetic advocacy:

> He who, in any way, shows us better than we knew before
> that a lily of the fields is beautiful, does he not show it us
> as an effluence of the Fountain of all Beauty; as the *hand-
> writing*, made visible there, of the great Maker of the Uni-
> verse? He has sung for us, made us sing with him, a little
> verse of a sacred Psalm . . . He has verily touched our
> hearts as with a live coal *from the altar*. Perhaps there is no
> worship more authentic.[59]

The best works of the imagination, rightly understood, reveal the
spiritual foundation of our being. There is nothing decadent or
cynical or iconoclastic in Carlyle's admiration of literary genius;
his aestheticism bears no resemblance to the artificiality of the
1880s and 90s. On the contrary, he informs his appreciation of the
arts with as much moral force and religious certainty as he displays
in his disavowals of the poetic method.

In the area of specific literary criticism, Carlyle recoils just as
strongly from positions of theological doubt. In fact, he vilifies
those artists who have lost their faith: Voltaire and his retinue of
skeptics seem to him to have sunk themselves in "the bottomless
abysses of Atheism and Fatalism."[60] Carlyle has no patience with
the barren writers of his own century who hold that "Thought
. . . is still secreted by the brain" and "Poetry and Religion . . .
'are a product of the small intestine'!"[61] Those epochs in which
the emphasis in literature has shifted from inspiration to analysis
shape themselves, to Carlyle, as dark interludes in the history of
art. Cerebral poetry is an "unhealthy" sign of the amorality and
godlessness of a culture. Seasons of belief and unbelief do alternate

with each other, in art as in politics, but Carlyle's sympathies always lie with the ages of faith. He commits himself to a time "full of the richest prospects for all; namely a period of New Spirituality and Belief . . . wherein Reverence is again rendered compatible with knowledge, and Art and Religion are one."[62]

There is then no crisis of faith and denial behind Carlyle's contradictions. He argues for and against literature from a deeply religious point of view. Whatever doubts he had, in 1820, of the existence of God, did not affect his later criticisms of poetry and fiction. The "Everlasting Yea" he achieved in these early years is, for all material purposes, maintained in his literary opinions. Not only did maturity convince him "there's a divinity that shapes our ends"; he also lost his fondness for intellectual gymnastics and systematic thought. Perhaps his most vehement excoriation of "logic-chopping" (which had once briefly intrigued him) occurs at the end of the lecture on "Hero as Prophet":[63]

> Mahomet . . . does not, like a Bentham, a Paley, take Right and Wrong, and calculate the profit and loss, ultimate pleasure of the one and of the other; and summing up all by addition and subtraction into a net result, ask you Whether on the whole the Right does not preponderate considerably? No; it is not *better* to do the one than the other; the one is to the other as life is to death—as Heaven is to Hell. The one must in nowise be done, the other in nowise left undone. You shall not measure them; they are incommensurable; the one is death eternal to a man, the other is life eternal. Benthamee Utility, virtue by Profit and Loss; reducing this God's-World to a dead brute Steam-engine, the infinite celestial Soul of Man to a kind of Hay-balance for weighing hay and thistles on, pleasures and pains on:— if you ask me which gives, Mahomet or they, the beggarlier and falser view of Man and his Destinies in this Universe, I will answer, It is not Mahomet![64]

Clearly he denies the primacy of the intellect; at the same time he affirms his faith in a divine will. There can be no antagonism be-

tween reason and belief because Carlyle's whole nature rejects the
"Steam-engine" mechanics of empirical thought. He strenuously
opposes the "persuasion . . . that, except the external, there are
no true sciences; that to the inward world (if there be any) our
only conceivable road is through the outward; that, in short, what
cannot be investigated and understood mechanically, cannot be investigated and understood at all."[65] The conclusions he reaches
about art, history and contemporary politics have little to do with
a ratiocinative process; they are intuitions, insights, products of the
"Dynamical" forces in man. Carlyle is far more interested in the
impulses of conscience and emotion than in the dictates of formal
logic. This strong intuitive bias underlies his view of literature:
when he is convinced of its worth, poetry originates in the "mystic
deeps of man's soul"; imagination is a "burning light" that lays
bare "the boundless Invisible world." When he is disillusioned
with art he "senses" the ultimate inadequacy of language; or he
"is struck" by the superior valor and nobility of active men. Carlyle's attitude is thus determined by temperament and enforced by
religious conviction.

Lastly, a number of inherent errors are involved in crediting
Carlyle's inconsistency to the oscillations of faith and disbelief in
God. The most salient of these is a too strict dichotomy between
the alternatives. According to Symons, the only choices available
for Carlyle were formal, dogmatic religion and intellectual iconoclasm. It never occurs to him that the rejection of the tenets and
liturgy of the church might not have included the denial of a
divinely ordered universe. Perhaps such a view is rooted in the
clinical analytics of twentieth-century criticism—the very angle of
vision that makes it as difficult for us to understand Arnold's untra-
ditional commitment to spiritual values as it is for us to com-
prehend Carlyle's. The unpredictable element of a spasmodic
temperament further complicates the "untidiness" of Carlyle's
religion. There is no question, however, that the conflict in his
literary opinions takes place in a religious context and is linked
to the structuring of that faith.[66] We have arrived at the chief

source of the tension, and must ask what contradictory beliefs Carlyle held about man's place in a universe ruled by God. What, after all, *was* his religion?

1. Certainly these antinomies are more difficult to reconcile from a twentieth-century perspective that presupposes a political "radical" will exhibit the modern, liberal package of views. Like Dickens, Carlyle's sentiments often conformed to those of an extinct species, the Tory Radical, whose defense of authoritarianism often went cheek-by-jowl with his plea for social reforms. Carlyle, like Ruskin, Morris, and others after him, turned to medieval paternalism as the best alternative to the excesses of laissez-faire. For a thorough discussion of the type, see A. V. Dicey, *Lectures on the Relation between Law and Opinion in England during the 19th Century*.

2. Letter of 11 April 1866 in Bliss, *Letters to His Wife*, p. 388.

3. *Essays*, II, p. 82.

4. Froude, *First Forty Years*, I, 78–79.

5. Extract from Journal, 31 December 1823, quoted in Wilson I, p. 313. All references to Carlyle's journals and diaries are necessarily secondhand. After the controversy over Froude's biography, the Carlyle family reclaimed his personal papers and have forbidden scholars to study them. The only fragments extant are gleanings from the originals that passed through Froude's hands ninety years ago. Carlyle's executors have consistently refused to duplicate or microfilm the journals. (Information courtesy of the Keeper of the Manuscript Room of the National Library of Scotland, Edinburgh).

6. J. Halliday, *Mr. Carlyle My Patient: A Psychosomatic Biography*, p. ix.

7. Built in 1853 atop his Chelsea home.

8. Symons, *Thomas Carlyle*, p. 176. Among those who record similar unpleasant experiences with Carlyle are Browning, Dean Stanley, Geraldine Jewsbury, and, of course, Emerson.

9. Halliday, *Mr. Carlyle My Patient*, p. ix.

10. Masson, *Carlyle Personally and in His Writing*, pp. 44–45.

11. Halliday, *Mr. Carlyle My Patient*, p. xi.

12. The argument rests on two assumptions: first, that all thought and action have a sexual basis; second, that Carlyle's language must be traced to the only vocabulary that has any meaning in and for itself—namely, that which deals with the genito-urinary system. Thus apparently neutral words are actually disguised allusions to the lower torso regions: "coins" and "money" should be read ipso facto as "feces"; "pistols," "lampposts," and so on denote phalli; dark colors are excremental emblems; references to "horses" and "water" demonstrate the subject's preoccupation with sexual potency. Although no direct psychoanalysis is possible, Halliday refuses to be deterred by the paucity of evidence or the ambiguity of those few incidents that he can examine. On one occasion he puts two facts—a vague complaint of Carlyle about constipation and a river journey during which he asked his father about the

dirt on his hands—through the formulaic machinery of Freudianism. After a preposterous discussion of Carlyle as "good-mother-child" and Carlyle's faeces as "equivalent to an interiorised penis," Halliday refreshingly concludes that "further speculation is unprofitable in view of our lack of exact knowledge of all the circumstances" (p. 44).

13. See J. A. Froude, *My Relations with Carlyle,* especially pp. 23–25.

14. Carlyle's impugners quote ambiguous conversations between Jane and Miss Jewsbury, while his supporters point to baby clothes that Jane was thought to have knitted at Craigenputtock.

15. *First Forty Years,* I, 379.

16. Without question, the ubiquitous Lady Ashburton also undermined the Carlyles' rapport, particularly in the 1850s.

17. Symons, *Thomas Carlyle,* p. 123; and Harrold, *Carlyle and German Thought,* pp. 69–85. Albert LaValley, in a recent study, *Carlyle and the Idea of the Modern,* also distrusts the sincerity and persistence of Carlyle's received aesthetic, though from a different perspective. Like some critical Merlin, La-Valley insists that all his works—from the early essays and *Wotton Reinfred* through *Frederick*—must be interpreted in the light of modern derivatives (these include, he assures us, Dr. Strangelove). Unfortunately, this typifies much modern Carlyle criticism that, in promoting the man's originality and emphasizing his "relevance" to twentieth-century readers, ignores the derivative nature of most of his own beliefs.

18. Symons, *Thomas Carlyle,* p. 123.

19. See above, chapter 1, footnote 32.

20. *Recollections,* I, 68. According to Morley, the English were particularly slow to appreciate Goethe, and "serious men" spoke slightingly of him "so late as 1854" (p. 68). There was, of course, some general increase in British attention to things German after the 1815 publication of Madame de Staël's *Germany,* particularly among Coleridge's disciples. See Carlyle's *Unfinished History of German Literature,* ed. Hill Shine, pp. xvi-xviii.

21. *First Forty Years,* I, 392, 401.

22. He did, finally, write an essay on Scott, but not until 1838 and with considerable condescension (see *Essays,* IV, 22–87).

23. *Essays,* I, 56.

24. *Note Books,* p. 211.

25. Journal extract (1830) in Froude, *First Forty Years,* II, 130–31. On Jeffrey's aesthetic instincts, see below, pp. 158–59.

26. *Essays,* IV, 162.

27. Journal extract (July 1832) in Froude, *First Forty Years,* II, 294–95.

28. On the subject of Carlyle's indifference to wealth, Max Muller wrote to his son in May 1881: "'Becoming independent' is one thing, 'becoming rich' another. Everybody ought to try hard to make himself independent, but then a man must learn to be independent with little, such as Carlyle was—one of the most independent and honest men I have ever known" (*The Life and Letters of Frederich Max Müller,* ed. G. Müller, II, 99).

29. These included a lecture series in New England that Emerson repeatedly held out to him.

30. See H. D. Traill's introduction to *The French Revolution*, I, xii.

31. "All those wonderful pictures are so poetical that we can only marvel why the man who painted them could not express himself through the usual vehicle of poetry" (H. Walker, "The German Influence: Thomas Carlyle," in *The Literature of the Victorian Era*, p. 69).

32. He went so far as to call it a "Poem" (Symons, *Thomas Carlyle*, p. 156).

33. In Froude, *First Forty Years*, II, 293–94.

34. *PP*, pp. 44, 46.

35. Ibid., p. 123.

36. Ibid., p. 125.

37. *Note Books*, p. 265.

38. G. Calder, *The Writing of Past and Present*, p. 197.

39. See R. H. Hutton's discussion of Carlyle's self-consciousness in an obituary review included in *Criticisms on Contemporary Thought and Thinkers*, I, 12–13.

40. *Life in London*, I, 5.

41. Letter to Holmes, 24 January 1873, in *The Life and Letters of Leslie Stephen*, ed. F. W. Maitland, p. 231. Murray Baumgarten agrees that Froude edited Carlyle's utterances in order to present him always as a "sage preaching wisdom" ("Carlyle and 'Spiritual Optics,'" p. 503). Whenever possible in publishing Carlyle's commentaries, Froude "omits the reflexive turning of the narrator to his own speaking activity. . . . As is to be expected this is the portion in which the message is not phrased in bugle notes" (ibid., p. 511). Hugh Walker says that Froude was simply insensitive to poetry: "Carlyle, though he could not write verse, was a poet, and, superb artist as Froude was in prose, he had little or no poetic gift" ("The German Influence: Thomas Carlyle," p. 33).

42. *Life in London*, I, 138–39.

43. *Reminiscences*, I, 237–38.

44. Symons, *Thomas Carlyle*, pp. 176–77.

45. On Coleridge, see *Sterling*, pp. 52–62; on Emerson, see letters and conversations after the latter's second visit to England, especially letter to Mrs. Baring, 3 November 1847.

46. "Sauerteig," a fictional German observer of the English scene, is often employed to reinforce Carlyle's opinions in later works. His ideas and manner do not, however, differ appreciably from the author's.

47. *PP*, p. 156.

48. Letter of 24 August 1831, in Bliss, *Letters to His Wife*, p. 62.

49. Louis Cazamian speaks of Carlyle's humor as "crude and brutal": it "is akin to Swift's, setting force above sweetness, subtlety or delicacy. . . . So intense . . . is Carlyle's humor that it is not amusing so often . . . as it is . . . dominating" (*Carlyle*, pp. 243–44).

50. *PP*, p. 151.

51. R. Williams, *Culture and Society, 1780–1950*, p. 86.

52. Because it is a dilemma that plagues many modern English prose writers (Hardy, Virginia Woolf, Graham Greene, and others), Symons probably found

it a ready, plausible answer to Carlyle's querulous disposition. Like LaValley, he consistently superimposes his own *Zeitgeist* on the early Victorian world.

53. Symons, *Thomas Carlyle*, pp. 30–31.

54. *LDP*, pp. 212–13.

55. *PP*, pp. 168–69.

56. *Heroes*, p. 157.

57. *Note Books*, p. 189.

58. *Essays*, I, 56.

59. *Heroes*, p. 163.

60. *Essays*, II, 65.

61. Ibid.

62. *Goethe Letters*, pp. 190–91.

63. As Carlyle finished, Mill rose to his feet and shouted, "No!"

64. *Heroes*, pp. 75–76.

65. *Essays*, II, 66.

66. H. D. Traill, in his introduction to *Sartor Resartus*, agrees that Carlyle is primarily concerned with the "didactic purpose" of literature, especially when that purpose assumes religious or prophetic significance. Traill goes on to disparage Carlyle's insensitivity to "literature pure and simple,—literature as literature," by which Traill seems to imply the existence of a literature dissociated from its meaning (*SR*, pp. vi-viii). It is true that Carlyle had little patience with such academic distinctions, but it is certainly not true that he was incapable of enjoying the manner in which art presented its truths. As he says in the 1828 essay on Goethe's *Helena*: "The grand point is to *have* a meaning, a genuine, deep and noble one; the proper form for embodying this . . . will gather round it almost of its own accord. We profess ourselves unfriendly to no mode of communicating Truth; which we rejoice to meet with in all shapes, from that of the child's Catechism to the deepest poetical Allegory" (*Essays*, I, 149). And certainly, if we consider *Past and Present* as didactic art, affinities between Carlyle's aesthetic and medieval theories of the value of literature (derived from St. Paul and St. Augustine) are germane.

Chapter Three

Carlyle's Religious Development

> . . . I, turning, call to thee, O
> Soul, thou actual Me,
> And lo, thou gently masterest
> the orbs,
> Thou matest Time, smilest content
> at Death,
> And fillest, swellest full the vast-
> nesses of space.
> —Walt Whitman

Just as there is manifest a sharp division in Carlyle's literary attitude, so too do there appear antipathetic strains in his religious nature: the one essentially personal, dynamic, and parallel to his intellectual development; the other received, static, and for the most part instinctive. The first of these strains submits more easily to a chronological dialectic, despite its heterodoxy, and it is at the growth of such a body of individualized convictions in Carlyle that we ought first to look.

FROM BURGHER FAITH TO "EVERLASTING NO"

His parents, Margaret and James, enforced, almost in equal measure, the piety of his childhood. Both were orthodox Calvinists, unshakable in their strict adherence to "Scriptures" and the creeds. Carlyle describes his mother as a descendent "of the pious, the just, and the wise."[1] Froude says of his father's reputation among the Ecclefechan townsfolk, "It was well known that he was strictly temperate, pure, abstemious, prudent and industrious."[2] In the case of James Carlyle, this was no hastily acquired paternal image: from boyhood he had acted toward his contemporaries with the studied gravity of a God-fearing moralist. Carlyle records an incident from his father's youth in which James and his friends, meeting to play cards, had begun to argue: "My father spoke out what was in him about the folly, the sinfulness, of quarreling over a perhaps sinful amusement. . . . They threw the cards in the fire, and . . . not one of the four ever touched a card again through life."[3] James owed the tenets and dogma of his faith to the teachings of his uncle, Robert Brand, a "vigorous religionist, of strict Presbyterian type."[4] Through him, James had joined a dissenting sect known as "Burghers," a group dedicated to the most rigorous kind of Christian commitment. Their Puritan worship, they believed, was of a purer sort even than that practiced in St. Giles. As Carlyle points out in his *Reminiscences*, "All dissent in Scotland is merely stricter adherence to the National Kirk in all points."[5] Margaret Carlyle supported her husband in his arch Calvinism, and, together with their children, they attended weekly services at the Burgher meetinghouse. Carlyle recalls, sixty years later, the sincerity and plainness of that Dumfriesshire congregation: "This peasant union, this little heath-thatched house, this simple evangelist, together constituted properly the 'church' of that district. They were the blessing and the saving of many. On me too their pious heaven-sent influences still rest and live."[6] The average Scottish Burgher of that time was a practicing Stoic without the slightest knowledge of ancient philosophy and a believer in a Miltonic universe without the smallest taste for poetry:

> His was not a creed for cowards and weaklings. According to its articles, life was a hard, ungracious bargain between man and his Maker, the great Task-Master. As a partial expression of the Scotch with a meagre soil, of their centuries of oppression under Church and State, the creed naturally exalted labor and suffering as the chief realities of life.[7]

Although the Carlyles were relatively prosperous, James was careful to preserve in his family those habits of parsimony and hard work he thought to be in keeping with a godly life:

Frugality and assiduity, a certain grave composure, an earnestness (not without its constraint, then felt as oppressive a little, yet which now yields its fruit) were the order of our household. We were all particularly taught that work (temporal or spiritual) was the only thing we had to do, and incited always by precept and example to do it well.[8]

The young Carlyle was seldom permitted to forget these stern Puritan realities and they bred in him a lifelong distrust of pleasurable experiences: "It was not a joyful life (what life is?) yet a safe, quiet one; above most others . . . a wholesome one."[9] As to the precepts (or "principles," as they were called) of his parents' faith, they rose, as in other species of Calvinism, from a belief in the terrible immanence of God, the reality of sin, the corruption of the world, and the literal truth of the Bible. Carlyle was daily fed a diet of scriptural lessons, particularly from the Old Testament. His parents, untutored in the doubts and qualifications that accompany intellectual training, accepted much in the Bible as actual and miraculous that theologians, even then, spoke of as metaphor or parable.[10] Their dogmatic interpretation of Christianity, doubtless fostered by the parochialism of village life, was, as Carlyle later said, one of the last examples of the Burghers' uncompromising system of belief.[11] It was as a product of this "old system" that Carlyle left Annan for Edinburgh University in the fall of 1809.

Almost at once his convictions were challenged. At best, professors and students were far less earnest about religion than his father had been, and many of them openly questioned the commandments of the Bible. They did not, at first, sway Carlyle from his catechisms, since much of the student skepticism seemed to him unthinking and sophomoric. To reinforce a defense of his father's doctrine, he read *Evidences of Christianity* and debated the problem of miracles and divine immanence. But soon his own maturing intellect protested against what is recognized as a largely emotional allegiance to Calvinism. He later admitted that he was then supporting orthodox Christianity "with the greatest desire to be convinced, but in vain."[12] After his first year at the university he came home full of questions, none of which he dared put to his un-bending father. Instead he asked his mother, "Did God Almighty come down and make wheelbarrows in a shop?"[13] And, "What can be the meaning of the Song of Solomon? How is it known that it is symbolical, representing Christ and the Church?"[14] The anguish such blasphemy caused her compelled him thereafter to "shut up" his thoughts in the presence of his parents.

In spite of, or perhaps because of, the ban on religious specula-tion at home, Carlyle pressed his inquiries with greater urgency in Edinburgh. His parents had always spoken of their religious principles as if they were demonstrable laws, so it was not surpris-ing that their son read, at first, with an eye to empirical proofs of God. Out of the "chaos" of the University Library he "succeeded in fishing up more books than had been known to the keeper thereof,"[15] but none of them quelled his rising doubts. In fact, he began to cultivate a sarcastic manner in treating the facile beliefs and cynicisms of his colleagues. The more he read, the less he was able to tolerate conviction, either positive or negative; he filled the breach in his certainties with ridicule of others and acquired, among his associates, the pseudonyms "Jonathan" and "Dean" (after his Swiftian temper).[16] Carlyle also found consolation in his talent for mathematics—but even this small pleasure was "due mainly to the accident that Leslie [his instructor in that science] alone of my Professors had some genius in his business."[17] These diversions kept Carlyle, during his college days at least, from the emotional crisis of an absolute rejection of Calvinism.

When, in 1814, he had completed his undergraduate study, Carlyle was still sufficiently indulgent of his parents' wishes to be-gin training for the ministry. Election to clerical office seemed to them the natural fruit of an eldest son's education; indeed, it had always been the particular hope of Margaret Carlyle's life. Thomas struck a compromise between his own misgivings and his parents' fervor by agreeing to a six-year course of schoolmastering and occasional sermonizing. It was probably his hope that over so many years either he would resolve his doubts or his family's ambitions would die of attrition. Carlyle's inclination for teaching was no stronger than his enthusiasm for the church, yet for two years he maintained a tutorship at Annan and delivered annual papers in theology before his Edinburgh examiners. He nevertheless set limits to filial duty: between mathematics lessons at the schoolhouse, he read books of a different character—a few of which were profoundly heterodox. They included works of Voltaire, Diderot, and Rousseau. The independence of mind that led Carlyle to their writings had immediate rewards: with some relief he recognized, in *Confessions* and the life of Diderot, many of the elements of his own religious dilemma.[18] But perhaps the writer who did the most to promote his doubts and hasten an eventual apostasy was David Hume.

Hume, unlike the French *philosophes,* made an appeal not only to Carlyle's intellect but also to his sense of decorum. Hume's skepticism appeared more deliberate and thus better suited to the high seriousness of the questions it raised—certainly it was stripped of any consciousness of fashion or volatile self-pity. Of the essays, "Superstition and Enthusiasm" and *An Enquiry Concerning Human Understanding* particularly interested Carlyle. They treated ultimate problems, as he had been trying to do, in the light of common sense; they avoided the contemporary extremes of careless exegesis and abstruse analysis. Philosophy and religion had, according to Hume, slipped out of touch with man and his immediate concerns—formal thought was now exclusively academic; formal belief was rooted in superstition.[19] No one better expressed the frustration Carlyle felt between the alternating irrelevancies of village life and university life. To a friend he admitted that he "liked the Essays of the infidel 'better than anything I have read these many days. I am delighted with the book.' "[20] The *Enquiry* dismissed those "disjointed notions and nondescript ideas" of Carlyle's professors and theologians as phantasms of the cerebellum. Moreover, Hume incorporated into his argument a clear distaste for complexity of method—a prejudice that at times reached almost to anti-intellectualism:

> The only method of freeing learning, at once, from these abstruse questions is to enquire seriously into the nature of human understanding, and show, from an exact analysis of its powers and capacity, that it is by no means fitted for such remote and abstruse subjects.[21]

For Hume, the power of that understanding was limited by sensations, or "impressions." All ideas were, to him, merely "feeble perceptions" or copies of sense experience.[22] Carlyle understood the prosaical bias behind such an assumption, but at the time it seemed to him a far more plausible hypothesis than those offered by Burgher divines.[23] Hume summarily denied meaning to whatever was inexplicable or innate: every idea, he said, could be traced to an impression or combination of impressions; only ideas that could be so traced were meaningful; therefore, any idea to which it was impossible to assign an antecedent impression must be dismissed as meaningless.[24] This rapid and obviously tautological chain of reasoning excluded from the *Enquiry* any impartial discussion of a supersensible reality—a fact that did not escape Carlyle. Given Hume's premise, God became extraneous, or worse, He became an illusion created from the echoes of sense experience:

> The idea of God, as meaning an infinitely intelligent, wise and good Being, arises from reflecting on the operations of our own mind, and augmenting, without limit, those qualities of goodness and wisdom. We may prosecute this enquiry to what length we please; where we shall always find that every idea we examine is copied from a similar impression.[25]

Carlyle saw at once the consequences of such a view. He later wrote of this period in his development: "I began with Hume and Diderot, and as long as I was with them I ran at Atheism, at blackness, at materialism of all kinds."[26] Carlyle was perhaps too careless in grouping Hume with the *philosophes*—the Scotsman stopped short of the fanatical temper of atheism—but he was certainly correct in marking the anti-Christian sympathies of both schools. Once again, as in the case of Diderot, Carlyle must have drawn parallels between his own intellectual development and that of Hume: both were brought up in strict Calvinist households; both rejected the doctrines of their parents during adolescence; both adopted mildly abusive attitudes toward organized religion in the early years of their adult lives.[27] Yet despite Hume's disaffection with the church, the *Essays* were far too good-naturedly optimistic to breed in Carlyle that kind of thoroughgoing existential despair which was later to overtake him. Instead, they encouraged him to postpone an answer to the problem of God and pursue his "more relevant" secular interests.

Thus admonished, Carlyle temporarily suspended religious considerations in order to explore the tidier world of science. During the winter of 1816 he read Newton's *Principia*, Wood's *Optics*, Delambre's *Astronomie* and passed what he later recalled as the "happiest time" of these early years.[28] Here, in the region of empirical law and discovery was a certainty and direction denied to priests and metaphysicians. For a time, Carlyle held all wider speculation in contempt, assuming the stoical view that "Heaven and Hell are for knaves and fools to talk about."[29] Yet Carlyle could not avoid the admission that by refusing to think about thought he was operating in an ontological vacuum; that, in fact, he was repressing the urgent demands of his own unconscious by escaping into the deadliest kind of actuality. Soon enough he turned back to those first-order questions, this time with redoubled frustration: "When *will* there arise a man who will do for the science of mind what Newton did for that of Matter—establish its fundamental laws on the firm basis of induction—and discard for ever those absurd theories that so many dreamers have devised?"[30] Carlyle owed such phrases as "firm basis of induction" to Hume and the *philosophes,* and it was on such a basis, and such a basis only, that he was then determined to decide ultimate issues.

Late in 1816 he accepted a teaching appointment at Kirkcaldy to replace the somewhat headstrong Edward Irving. Carlyle and the former schoolmaster became immediate friends; more importantly, Irving made available to his curious and rather unsettled companion the whole of his extensive library. Among the books Carlyle found there, one in particular—Gibbon's *Decline and Fall*—put the coup de grace to his flagging trust in a Christian God: those "winged sarcasms" finally convinced him of the hypocrisy of priests and the foolishness of belief in miracles. With heavy irony, Gibbon hammered away at the superstitious intolerance of the early church:

> The condemnation of the wisest and most virtuous of the pagans, on account of their ignorance or disbelief of the divine truth, seems to offend the reason and the humanity of the present age. But the primitive church, whose faith was of a much firmer consistence, delivered over, without legislation, to eternal torture, the far greater part of the human species. A charitable hope might perchance be indulged in favour of Socrates, or some other sages of antiquity, who had consulted the light of reason before that of the gospel had arisen. But it was unanimously affirmed, that those who, since the birth or death of Christ, had obstinately persisted in the worship of the daemons, neither deserved nor could expect a pardon from the irritated justice of the Deity.[31]

Many years later Carlyle confessed, "I then first clearly saw that Christianity was not true."[32]

Earlier, in the winter of 1817, he had allowed his enrollment as a divinity student to lapse,[33] and now, with doubt hardening into denial, he refused even to attend church with his family. He told Irving of his loss of faith[34] and of the wretchedness it brought him, but Irving, as an ordained minister who believed not only in miracles but, later, in the "gift of tongues," could offer little help.

James Carlyle, although he held his temper in the face of his son's irreverence, said nothing to comfort him. Only Carlyle's mother gave religious counsel, and that was doctrinaire and uncomprehending. She wrote to him in 1819:

> Seek God with all your heart; and oh, my dear son, cease not to pray for His counsel in all your ways. Fear not the world; you will be provided for as He sees meet for you. . . . I beg you do not neglect reading a part of your Bible daily, and may the Lord open your eyes to see wondrous things out of His law![35]

It was, after all, just at this point that Carlyle broke with his parents: where, he asked, were the evidences of moral consciousness in the conduct of the world? Where was the immanent God of which the Bible spoke? Where, in a random clutter of things, was the token of divine wisdom? In *Sartor*, Carlyle records the anxiety and disillusionment he then felt: "A desert this was, waste, and howling with savage monsters. Teufelsdröckh gives us long details of his 'fever-paroxysms of Doubt'; his Inquiries concerning Miracles, and the Evidences of religious Faith; and how . . . with audible prayers he cried vehemently for Light."[36] But the God of Carlyle's father would not answer; the church, it seemed, worked everywhere against the current of history and his own senses. To help him put off "the dead Letter of Religion," Carlyle read Hume again and attempted a new career, more in keeping with the conscience of a skeptic. In December 1818, he left Kirkcaldy for Edinburgh and resolved, rather tepidly, to take up law.[37]

This time Carlyle found slight comfort in a preoccupying worldliness; he attended a series of law lectures, but could not generate in himself any enthusiasm for the intricacies of the juridical code. The palliative simply would not serve: Carlyle's despair had matured too far to dissipate in the face of diversions. Mathematics and legal quibbling were now games far too feeble to hold back the dark; those unanswered final questions, left in the wake of Christian disillusionment, could not be treated by "various dull

people of the practical sort." Carlyle execrated his Edinburgh colleagues, calling them "mere denizens of the kingdom of dulness,
[who worked] towards nothing but money as wages."[38]

During the next three years, Carlyle continued, ostensibly, to
study law; but in fact, his reading was undisciplined by the pursuit of any practical ambition. No book answered his needs, no
one pointed the way toward certainty, no activity seemed relevant
to the demands of his spirit. Carlyle operated under a single imperative: he must unravel the metaphysical dilemmas that obsessed him, for without some sense of the ultimate ground of
"this time-element" he believed that no labor was possible for a
man of "earnest nature."[39] Intellectually, as well as emotionally,
he sought a final cause. Carlyle was, in these years, a most unwill-
ing skeptic, almost childlike in his determination to regain conviction. To him, it was inconceivable that an intelligent being
could fashion his life and his work upon doubt alone.[40] Only in
the sense that a life so fashioned is conceivable and acceptable to
the twentieth-century thinker can we scoff at Carlyle's early
wretchedness as the "emotional need for a faith." Among most of
his contemporaries, such thoughts were part of a common and
rational demand for truth. He looked into French and Italian authors, but was not persuaded to any new beliefs. Again his mother
proffered her advice to him to make "the word of God" his "great
study," but Carlyle was too honest to retreat into catechisms
either:

> One circumstance I note . . . after all the nameless woe that
> Inquiry, which for me was genuine love of Truth, had
> wrought me, I nevertheless still loved Truth, and would
> bate no jot of my allegiance to her. Truth! . . . though the
> Heavens crush me for following her: no Falsehood! though
> a whole celestial Lubberland were the price of Apostasy.[41]

This scrupulous intensity presaged a mental crisis in Carlyle's development. By 1820, it was clear to him that as a man of "moral
nature, the loss of his religious Belief was the loss of everything."[42]

Disquietude and impatience gave way to trauma as Carlyle confronted the depth of his ignorance:

> Shade after shade goes grimly over your soul, till you have
> the fixed, starless, Tartarean black. . . . A feeble unit in the
> middle of a threatening Infinitude, I seemed to have nothing
> given me but eyes, whereby to discern my own wretchedness.
> . . . The men and women round me, even speaking with
> me, were but Figures: I had practically forgotten that they
> were alive, that they were not merely automatic.[43]

When his mood was blackest, Carlyle lost even the sense of evil—the sense that indifference to moral values was in any way sinful. The devil became as meaningless to him as God: "To me the Universe was all void of Life, of Purpose, even of Hostility: it was one huge, dead, immeasurable Steam-engine, rolling on in its dead indifference, to grind me limb from limb."[44] Thus Carlyle documents the full agony of his "Everlasting No." His Calvinist dogmas had been exploded by skeptical analysis, and he had no belief-propositions to replace them. Conventional Christianity seemed no longer to justify moral behavior: because of its rigid literalism, in Carlyle's mind, it would always be exposed to the prick of common sense. In such mental circumstances, there were open to Carlyle, at the age of twenty-five, only two courses of action: either to surrender to intransigent self-pity or to renew the search for a radical theology from which to launch his energies. He did, in fact, do both.

From sympathetic references to Byron in letters and essays,[45] and especially from Teufelsdröckh's admonition to "close thy Byron," we may presume that for a short time at least, Carlyle entertained the more extravagant sentiments of that poet. The ferocity of his later repudiation of Byronic attitudes only lends credence to the view that he once indulged the same weaknesses. About this time, he was also introduced to *The Sorrows of Young Werther*, a novel that appropriately dwelt on the despair of an intelligent and sensitive youth. There is much in his "Everlasting

No" (even in its peculiar German character) that echoes the histrionic agony of Wertherism.[46] This is not to say Carlyle enjoyed either his melancholy or his inactivity; on the contrary, he complained to his brother:

> It is a shame and misery to me at this age to be gliding about in strenuous idleness, with no hand in the game of life where I have yet so much to win, no outlet for the restless faculties which are thus up in mutiny and slaying one another for lack of fair enemies.[47]

He was clearly anxious for a way out, and, soon enough, one offered itself. In 1818, Carlyle's curiosity about German ideas and culture had been piqued by reading Madame de Staël's *Germany,* and he shortly set himself the task of learning the language of that country. With little difficulty, he found a tutor willing to instruct him in German in return for lessons in French; he was further encouraged in his studies by the "advice of a man who told him he would find in that language what he wanted."[48] What he wanted, of course, was a body of positive principles upon which he might construct an unassailable new religion, and through which he could discern the work he was to do.

GERMAN LITERATURE AND TRANSCENDENTAL FAITH

There is no question that Carlyle, at this time of life, approached German literature as he had recently approached French, Italian, and every other: with an eye to his spiritual needs. The "love of truth" was with him (as perhaps it is with all of us) not altogether disinterested: he had begun to pursue in his reading that aspect of the truth which would satisfy both his emotions and his intellect. British "common sense" philosophy and French "persiflage," despite their direct appeal to his logical faculties, had undermined all of Carlyle's deeper props.[49] Whether intentionally or not, their insistence upon the primacy of external evidence conjured up, in Carlyle's developing consciousness, the

picture of a mechanical and wholly amoral world. Without the
"Hebrew old-clothes" of Christian dogma, Carlyle felt himself reduced to slow, material suffocation: he had become a "feeble
unit," pining "in the imprisonment of the Actual."[50] The "Everlasting No" was, after all, essentially the experience of a man over-
whelmed by concretions and his own physicality. History, science,
and "logic-chopping" had begot a "steam-engine" universe that,
it appeared to Carlyle, man was not only reluctant but powerless
to change. Certainly, the Bible, as a source of spiritual energy and
a refuge from nihilism, had proved itself exhausted and barren.
It was in this mood of profound depression and religious longing
that Carlyle began his study of German art.

Of particular importance in considering the connection between
religion and Carlyle's view of the arts is the fact that in the days
before 1820 he had exhibited no marked predilection for imaginative literature. With the exception of a native fondness for Burns
(the poet died only a few miles from his birthplace) and some admiration for the "passion" of Byron, Carlyle had focused his reading largely on intellectual and historical subjects. That is not to
say he was ignorant of, or prejudiced against, "creative" writers,
but merely that, before his introduction to German, he had shown
no preference for artists above other thinkers.[51]

One of the earliest and most significant contacts Carlyle made
with German literature was in the works of Goethe. As had often
been the case in his appreciation of other authors, Carlyle was
first aroused to sympathy by the writer's intense pessimism.
Werther and *Faust* convinced him that another, wiser man had
undergone the terrors of "Unbelief": later, and more importantly,
Wilhelm Meister assured him that after despair, there was a road
back toward affirmation. One of the characters in *Meister* describes a mental crisis that closely parallels the morbid selfishness
of Carlyle's "Everlasting No":

> Wrapped up in himself, he has looked at nothing but his
> own hollow empty *Me*, which seemed to him an immeasur-

able abyss. . . . "I see nothing . . . here there is no height, no depth, no forwards, no backwards; no words can express this neverchanging state. . . . No ray of a divinity illuminates this night: I shed all my tears by myself and for myself."[52]

But Goethe was not content simply to express unhealthy emotions —he saw them as a necessary part of enlightenment, asserting that without some experience of these pains no true belief was possible:

> Who never ate his bread in sorrow,
> Who never spent the darksome hours,
> Weeping and watching for the morrow,
> He knows ye not, ye heavenly Powers.[53]

Somehow, in spite of recriminations and apparent familiarity with the world, Goethe displayed precisely the sense of purpose and tranquility of mind for which Carlyle was searching.[54] In contrast to the sustained pessimism that characterized most of his other reading, Carlyle found in *Wilhelm Meister* a surprising amount of confidence and hope: the novel's hero works slowly out of his difficulties and his prejudices until, in the end, he looks upon his own prospects with tolerance and faith. Carlyle did not immediately understand the source of Meister's optimism, but he did see that it involved one radical renunciation. Before all else, Meister disowns any claim to sensual happiness. After his travels (in Part Two) he understands the pointlessness of dependence on external circumstances:

> Emigration takes place in the treacherous hope of an improvement in our circumstances; and it is too often counterbalanced by a subsequent emigration; since, go where you may, you still find yourself in a conditional world, and if not constrained to a new emigration, are yet inclined in secret to cherish such a desire.[55]

There is perhaps here an echo of *Rasselas,* but Goethe, unlike Johnson, finds ground for hope in man's dissatisfaction with material delights: "Let a man learn, we say, to figure himself as without permanent external relation; let him seek consistency and sequence not in circumstances but in himself: there will he find it: there let him cherish and nourish it."[56] Indeed, life is everywhere to be enjoyed, if one can first dismiss those preoccupying external manifestations of "self" that inhibit deeper joys. True life begins with *Entsagen,* with the renunciation of animal appetites as ultimate concerns and with the quiet admission that you are your own world. Encouraged in part by his recent Leith Walk experience, Carlyle assented enthusiastically and dated his spiritual renewal from that moment:[57]

> There was one thing in particular which struck me in Goethe. It was in his *Wilhelm Meister.* . . . No man has the right to ask for a recipe of happiness: he can do without happiness. There is something better than that. . . . Spiritual clearness is a far better thing than happiness. Love of happiness is but a kind of hunger at the best: a craving because I have not enough of sweet provision in this world.[58]

That "spiritual clearness" of which Goethe spoke did not come at once to Carlyle, but at least he had made a beginning. Years later, in *Sartor,* he acknowledged the debt:

> Foolish soul! What Act of Legislation was there that *thou* shouldst be Happy? A little while ago thou hadst no right to *be* at all. . . . Art thou nothing other than a Vulture, then, that fliest through the Universe seeking after somewhat to *eat:* and shrieking dolefully because carrion enough is not given thee? Close thy Byron: open thy Goethe.[59]

Perhaps one confusion that may arise in translating *Entsagen* should be cleared up at once: by "self-denial" and renunciation of happiness Goethe did not mean asceticism; on the contrary, the "self" to be denied was the self as object and not the self as subject. Mechanical relationships and rewards, matter considered as an end in itself, personal happiness as "appetite" alone—these, not the individual consciousness or spirit, were the elements of our nature to be repressed.[60] Thus Goethe advised men to "annihilate" their materially preoccupied selves in order to promote their moral, aesthetic selves. Carlyle obviously understood the double significance Goethe attached to "self" when, speaking of *Wilhelm Meister,* he said, "the Ideal is in thyself, the impediment too is in thyself."[61] For Carlyle, the impediment to wisdom and faith had been exactly what Goethe suggested it was, namely, an imprisonment in his own senses and a total dependence, brought about by his reading of Hume and the *philosophes,* upon the pleasures of the phenomenal world.

It was only upon rereading *Wilhelm Meister* that Carlyle began to understand the direction this rededication of his energies ought to take. The hope that Goethe first raised of transcending the senses could be of little lasting value to Carlyle unless it carried with it the promise of a goal toward which he might work. In *Meister,* that action which spiritual clearness and self-abnegation most naturally encouraged was the impulse toward Art. Man and nature, once stripped of their implacable externality, become for Goethe's hero derivatives of the spirit and metaphors of the unseen truth behind the universe. As an advocate of that spiritual redefinition of life, Meister feels bound to interpret the beauty of natural objects through the faculty of his expanding imagination:

> To see this lordly world lying round one day after day. . . .
> What delight, in figures and tints, to be approaching the
> Unspeakable! . . . The surrounding world also was opened
> to his sight. . . . And while Nature unfolded the open
> secret of her beauty, he could not but feel an irresistible at-
> traction towards Art, as toward her most fit expositor.[62]

Nature, then, is the symbol of truth—a symbol that yields its secret to the liveliest apprehension of its beauty. Aesthetic aware-

ness and the individual's refinement of the symbolic truth he sees
—that is, Art—are passive and active sides of the same coin; together they comprise the highest duty of a reverent man. Thus,
for Goethe, Nature and Art pointed the same ultimate meaning:

> As all Nature's thousand changes
> But one changeless God proclaim;
> So in Art's wide kingdom ranges
> One sole meaning still the same:
> This is Truth, eternal Reason,
> Which from Beauty takes its dress,
> And serene through time and season
> Stands for aye in loveliness.[63]

Many of these ideas anticipated Carlyle's understanding—he
did not immediately grasp the relationship between beauty and
truth or the function of the external world as a key to spiritual
elevation. In order to follow a systematic development of such
Goethean ideas, Carlyle would have needed to consult Kant's *Critique of Aesthetic Judgment*—a treatise that Goethe admired for
its contribution to the theory of romantic poetry,[64] and that contained a formal argument of the steps from *Entsagen* to the sentiments of an artist. Lacking this, Carlyle nevertheless caught the
thrust of Goethe's argument: from a renunciation of pure materialism, one gained the qualities of reverence, balance, and tranquility necessary for constructive labor; and from the nature of
that change of attitude, art suggested itself as the fittest career for
the convert. Because Carlyle's skills were of the verbal sort, he took
Goethe's exhortation as a call to develop his talent for literature
and poetry. He confessed to Froude many years later that German
writers, especially Goethe, had made him "impatient of the trod-
den ways which only led to money or to worldly fame," and the
example of their quiet faith had convinced him that "literature
was the single avenue which offered an opening into higher regions."[65] *Wilhelm Meister* had not supplied him with all the arguments necessary for a sound and workable religion—that would

come later—but it had taught him to admire, above all else, the "profound sentiment of beauty, [and the] delineation of all its varieties."[66] Without the antidote of Goethe in these early years, Carlyle owned that he would have "pistolled his way through" his difficulties.[67] As it was, he grew eager to be up and working at some original expression; whether in the form of novel, poem, or essay he could not yet determine. Over the next five years, he made attempts at all three genre, with varying success. He wrote to his brother in March 1822: "It is in fact certain that I must write a book. Would to Heaven that I had a subject which I could discuss, and at the same time loved to discuss. . . . My condition is rather strange at present. I feel as if I were impelled to write."[68] As if to emphasize his indebtedness to Goethe for the inclination toward literature, Carlyle ended the same letter with an epigram from *Wilhelm Meister:* "Therefore, Jack, I mean to try if I can bestir myself. Art is long and life is short."[69]

Goethe may have been the strongest, but he was certainly not the only recuperative influence on Carlyle. About this time, equipped with his new facility for German, Carlyle read extensively in Schiller. He found there ideas pleasingly similar to Goethe's; more importantly, he encountered in Schiller another artist who spoke with sincerity and spiritual conviction. Like Goethe, Schiller argued for the renunciation of happiness as the prelude to wisdom, since "A boundless duration of Being and Well-being simply for Being and Well-being's sake, is an Ideal belonging to Appetite alone, and which only the struggle of mere animalism longing to be infinite, gives rise to."[70] Such "animalism" was, for Schiller and Goethe, the chief characteristic of the modern "Philistine": above all, the *Philister* equated his welfare with a happiness of "agreeable sensations."[71] Carlyle quite properly saw in the convictions of these German artists an indictment of utilitarianism as well. Experience measured merely in quantities of pleasure and pain was a gospel suitable to the insensitivity of lower animals; the human spirit, Carlyle and Schiller agreed, demanded something closer to its own potentialities: "Strictly considered, this truth, that man has in him, something higher than a love of Pleasure, take pleasure in what sense you will, has been the text of all true Teachers and Preachers, since the beginning of the world."[72] Of false preachers, dedicated to utility and "stomach-philosophy," Carlyle saw too much in his own country. He began to look toward Schiller and Goethe as toward the principal advocates of spiritual values in an age of philistinism, and to hope that their opposition might "one day inspire a universal battle of Mind versus Matter."[73] Schiller certainly conceived of his own role as part of a crusade against triviality and unbelief: "The artist comes [into this world] . . . not . . . to delight it by his presence, but dreadful like the son of Agamemnon, to purify it!"[74] In this respect he was far more zealous than Goethe: Schiller's commitment to Art as truth informed his work and his life with an almost unrelieved earnestness. As Carlyle said, "he is the gravest of writers," renouncing all "outward, honour, pleasure, social recreation, [even] friendly affection" in favor of his poetry:

> To Schiller the task of the Poet appeared of far weightier import to mankind, in these times, than that of any other man whatever. It seemed to him that . . . when the noise of all conquerors, and demagogues, and political reformers had quite died away, some tone of heavenly wisdom that had dwelt even in him might still linger among men, and be acknowledged as heavenly and priceless, whether as his or not; whereby, though dead, he would yet speak, and his spirit would live throughout all generations, when the syllables that once formed his name had passed into forgetfulness forever. . . . He lived for it: and he died for it; "sacrificing," in the words of Goethe, "his life itself to this Delineating of Life."[75]

It was precisely this single-mindedness of Schiller's that gave Carlyle further hope of personal salvation. Schiller's world-view, though narrower than Goethe's, was more intensely religious, and it pointed, with greater specificity, to the literary man as the possessor of "heavenly wisdom." Again, Schiller's religious development resembled Carlyle's: he had endured his own "Everlasting No."

> I have looked at men, at their insect anxieties and giant projects—their godlike schemes and mouselike occupations, their wondrous race-running after Happiness . . . this whirling lottery of life, in which . . . blanks are the whole drawing. . . .
>
>> And all our conquest in the fight of Life
>> Is knowledge that 'tis Nothing.[76]

And he passed beyond it into religious affirmation. Moreover, he apparently sustained and deepened his faith by the refinement of his literary skills:

> Literature was his creed, the dictate of his conscience; he was an apostle of the Sublime and Beautiful, and this his calling made a hero of him. . . . As Schiller viewed it, genuine Literature includes the essence of philosophy, religion, art. . . . The treasures of Literature are thus celestial, imperishable, beyond all price. . . . Man may have lost his dignity, but Art has saved it.[77]

But Carlyle did not limit himself to an admiring exposition of Schiller's ideas; impressed by the poet's religious fervor, he soon adopted the Literary Man as his own ideal. In the *Life of Schiller*, begun in 1823 as a short essay and finally issued as a book, Carlyle says as much:

> Among these men of letters are to be found the brightest specimens and the chief benefactors of mankind! It is they that keep awake the finer parts of our souls; that give us better aims than power or pleasure. . . . Such men are the flower of this lower world: to such alone can the epithet of great be applied with its true emphasis.[78]

Three elements combined in the nature of these German artists to inspire Carlyle's praise: for him, they were at once "noble souls" able to withstand the "Sovereignty of Mammon," leaders in "the war of Mind against Matter," and, above all, religious men, planting spiritual values in a world of sense. Imbued with the rudiments of a new faith, Carlyle began to proselytize, recommending Schiller and Goethe to his wife and friends, often over the objections of more conventional companions.[79] His eagerness to carry the message of the new Germany to English readers led him into the "journey-work" of translating *Wilhelm Meister's Apprenticeship*. With its publication in 1824 and the completion of the biography of Schiller in 1825, Carlyle launched his own literary career.[80]

Yet he was not altogether happy as the purveyor and critic of other men's ideas, however noble. Carlyle longed to create an original work—to match those of Schiller and Goethe—but as yet he had no exact sense of the religious principles that underlay their eloquence. Goethe had not cited a specific source for his doctrines, and from metaphysical theories, current or traditional, he remained steadfastly aloof.[81] He had, however, spoken with enthusiasm of Kant's *Critique of Aesthetic Judgment* and appeared, to Carlyle, to share with a number of other Germans a basic allegiance to the precepts of transcendentalism.[82] In the *Philosophical and Aesthetic Letters of Schiller*, Carlyle again came up against the influence of Kant, this time more directly.[83] Although Schiller's chief concern with idealistic philosophy was in its poetical application, he went a good deal farther than Goethe toward adopting its cosmological ground-plan:

> The Transcendental Philosophy, which arose in Schiller's busiest era, could not remain without influence on him: he had carefully studied Kant's system, and appears to have not only admitted but zealously appropriated its fundamental doctrines. . . . Schiller . . . appears to have been well contented with his Philosophy; in which, as harmonized

with his Poetry, the assurance and safe anchorage for his
moral nature might lie.[84]

Carlyle, of course, was anxious to find a similar "anchorage" for
his own moral nature, and it seemed to him that his best hope of
a fully articulated and intellectually acceptable religion lay in the
labyrinthine structure of transcendentalism. The path Carlyle had
taken through German literature led inevitably to Kant and Fichte
as sources of moral and aesthetic conviction.[85] But he was not
immediately prepared to tackle what rumor held to be the immensely difficult task of comprehending German idealism at first
hand.

Instead, Carlyle sought an interpreter of "Kant & Co." The new
German system had not gained wide acceptance in England; in
fact, only Coleridge was known to have mastered its principles.[86]
To him, Carlyle first went for enlightenment. Twenty-five years
after the visit, in his well-known portrait of "Coleridge at High-
gate," Carlyle recalls both his own eagerness and his disappointment at the sage's unintelligibility: Coleridge sat, surrounded by
admirers, an old man nodding and mumbling about "om-m-ject"
and "sum-m-ject," lost in a "tide of ingenious vocables, spreading
out boundless as if to submerge the world."[87] Carlyle took him
aside in an effort to obtain a definition of *Vernunft* and *Verstand*
—key terms in the transcendental system—but could get nothing
sensible from the "meandering discourse" of the man. Some of
Carlyle's scorn in this account is undoubtedly a later interpola-
tion (perhaps the exaggerated reaction of a rival warming to the
joys of caricature), but a passage from the *Life of Schiller* suggests
both that in 1825 Carlyle had not yet read Kant on his own and
that he was indeed frustrated by Coleridge's obscurity: "The
Philosophy of Kant is *probably* combined with errors to its very
core; but . . . *may* bear in it the everlasting gold of truth!", and
in a footnote, "Are our hopes from Mr. Coleridge always to be
fruitless?"[88]

It is difficult to believe that Carlyle dismissed the aid of Coleridge without reading his published studies, or that from them he did not gain valuable, albeit occasional, insight into transcendentalism.[89] Most of the major tenets of Coleridge's beliefs were included in *The Friend, Biographia Literaria,* and *Aids to Reflection* (written between 1809 and 1825), but nowhere did he arrange ideas in anything like a logical sequence. Another obstacle for Carlyle, as an opponent of orthodox theology, seems to have been the tendency of Coleridge, especially in his later years, to obscure the differences between transcendental faith and Christian dogma. As he aged, Coleridge grew more conventional (in politics as well as religion) and probably, in consequence, lost much of the young Carlyle's respect.[90] Nonetheless, transcendentalism had been for Coleridge an important first step to intelligent belief, and his popular adaptations of Kantian principles surely gave Carlyle at least a rough outline of the new system.

Yet whatever glimpses Carlyle got into transcendentalism through his appeal to Coleridge were insufficient: he understood, by the end of 1826, that full comprehension of the Kantian and Fichtean structure required a direct confrontation with the original writings. There is some doubt about the extent to which Carlyle carried his investigation of these primary sources—a few critics claim that he filled the gaps in his understanding through the expedient of critical expositions.[91] However that may be, Carlyle's own records during the period testify to his having studied the major works of Kant, Fichte, and Schelling.[92] Moreover, his writings, after the winter of 1827, indicate a thorough familiarity with the metaphysical and aesthetic outline of transcendentalism, despite a clear disregard for the formal methods of the philosophers in question.[93] From this moment onward, Carlyle was apparently satisfied that he had a working knowledge of the fundamentals of transcendental religion. Yet before we can understand precisely how these basic principles of German idealism affected Carlyle's opinion of literature (our prime objective), we must first attempt a brief analysis of the doctrines themselves. For purposes of clarity and relevance, I shall limit exposition to four basic treatises: Kant's Critiques of *Pure Reason, Practical Reason,* and *Aesthetic Judgment,* and Fichte's *Science of Knowledge.*

The rationale of the *Critique of Pure Reason* must have seemed to Carlyle the scientific equivalent of Goethe's *Entsagen;* for it, too, denigrates man's hopes of ultimate happiness through an adjustment of external circumstances. More strictly, it recommends a refutation of empiricism as the necessary antecedent to the apprehension of truth. In order to justify such a refutation, Kant had first to investigate the limits of sense experience and of the reasoning faculty. Other philosophers had been approaching the problem of God, morality, the limits of the universe in space and time, and so on, in the belief that their instrument—reason—was sufficient to resolve these questions, either positively or negatively. In particular, Kant was dismayed by the assumptions underlying Hume's skeptical empiricism.[94] The Scottish philosopher claimed to be denying "knowledge in order to make room for faith," but what he really advocated was practical atheism. Kant made the same claim to faith in his preface to the first *Kritik*[95]—the difference being that, unlike Hume (who intended the remark only as a ruse to prevent the censure of his books by Edinburgh divines), Kant meant what he said.[96] Carlyle obviously caught the significance of this split between the motives of the two philosophers. He wrote in January 1827: "I begin to see some light through the clouds in Kantism . . . empiricism, if consistent, they say, leads direct to Atheism!—I am afraid it does."[97]

Kant begins the first *Kritik* by defining the bounds of sense. The general limiting features of the empirical consciousness, without which we could have no experience as we know it, seem to him to rest on six principles. These principles—temporality, unity of consciousness, objectivity, spatiality, spatio-temporal unity, permanence, and causality—depend upon a further condition, the principle of significance.[98] According to that principle, for our ideas of the world to be empirically intelligible, there must be experiences that correspond to those ideas; that is, for every concept there must be an example—in Kant's language, sensibility and understanding, "intuition" and "judgment" are interdependent.[99] To this extent, he agrees with Hume's reasoning in the *Enquiry* and Carlyle's speculations prior to 1821. But it is at this point that Kant breaks with the arguments of materialistic philosophers. Since systematic inquiry itself conforms to the principle of causality, Kant asserts that we are compelled by that principle to pursue, in our inquiries, an ever greater generality of explanation. This serial process eventually leads us to entertain the idea of totality, and that idea may assume one of two forms: either our inquiries are ultimately limited, i.e., by the beginning of time or matter or the outward limit of space; or they are infinite and unlimited.[100] If we then invoke the principle of significance to prove either possibility, we are left in an empirically untenable position. Thus the nature of systematic investigation inevitably leads us to posit its totality—what Kant calls "the demand of reason for the unconditioned"—and that idea, whether finite or infinite, *transcends* all possible experience. In other words, reason ultimately confounds itself. And since reason cannot tell us either how, what, or where we are, we must own that the objects we perceive are merely appearances that may or may not correspond to things as they are in themselves. Even space and time are relative concepts upon which we can hang no certainties at all. Thus the interpretive value of experience is wholly subjective, and we must take care to differentiate between the apprehended Actual and the unknown Real—what Kant calls the disjunction between phenomena and noumena.[101] The practical value of this first *Kritik* is substantially negative: by dismissing reason as a standard for absolute judgments, and by affirming that the problem of ultimacy is a vital one,[102] it constitutes no more than a prelude to transcendental faith. Carlyle, prepared as he was by his own experiences of the fruitlessness of "logic-chopping" and by the bracing example of Schiller's accomplishment as a Kantian, had no qualms in following Kant through these initial stages in the establishment of a new spiritual doctrine. As Carlyle puts it in 1827: "The Germans

. . . assail Hume, not in his outworks, but in the centre of his citadel. They deny his first principle, that sense is the only inlet of knowledge, that experience is the primary ground of Belief."[103]

Kant's second *Kritik,* that of *Practical Reason,* argues back to a positive position.[104] Having already put the interpretive value of experience in the subject, he holds further that the form of the intuition of external things does not depend on them, but on the human mind.[105] And among the human mind's concepts is the idea of morality—the faculty of desire to live according to the good. This originates with what Kant calls the Categorical Imperative; that is, with the demand that one "act so that the maxim of thy will can always at the same time hold good as a principle of universal legislation."[106] Thus he points to the existence of an innate reason higher than, and distinct from, the understanding. From this moral law, he eventually works outward to a belief in divine realities and the immortality of the soul. The moral consciousness, when dominant, allows us "a prospect into the supersensible" though "only with weak glances."[107] Kant concludes that if God *could* be proved with the aid of empirical data, our behavior would be determined by fear and necessity—we would become "virtuous mechanisms."[108] But since our behavior is self-determined and our morality disinterested, transcendental faith is at least as valuable as transcendental knowledge might be: "Thus what the study of nature and of man teaches us sufficiently elsewhere may well be true here also, that the unsearchable wisdom by which we exist is not less worthy of admiration in what it has denied than in what it has granted."[109] The inner moral sense, the thought of freedom, God, immortality, all constitute some higher Reason and demonstrate the probability of God (and for the Kantian transcendentalist, they are sufficient for his faith—he says, after all, that God *must* be, not that he *is*), but they do not make up a rational proof. It is in this sense, despite all the formidable machinery of formal argument, that Kant's system must be considered mystical doctrine rather than strict philosophy. Nonetheless, it goes a great deal further than Christianity in its appeal to the intellect, and it is this, coupled with the encouragement he received from German romantic writers, that probably won Carlyle as a disciple.

The third, and for Carlyle (since it complemented so much of the thinking of Goethe and Schiller) the most pertinent of Kant's major statements, was the *Critique of Aesthetic Judgment*. It is here that Kant attempts to define the direction and practical force of transcendentalism. In essence, he argues that the faculties of Understanding and Reason can function together to bring about the moral perfection of the individual. He contends that behind our ideas of the beautiful and the sublime there operates a crucial union of these faculties, and that this synthesis is capable of producing, in the abstract, aesthetic principles, and in their application, Art.[110] Our consciousness of beautiful objects, whether in nature or Art, is a "presentation" of the "morally good," and those symbols in turn provide a "foot-hold" for our *a priori* concepts.[111] This interaction permits a reconciliation between the sensuous and the good:

> We call buildings or trees majestic or stately, or plains laughing and gay; even colors are called innocent, modest, soft, because they excite sensations containing something analogous to the consciousness of a state of mind produced by moral judgments. Taste makes, as it were, the transition from the charm of sense to habitual moral interest possible without too violent a leap, for it represents the imagination, even in its freedom, as amenable to a final determination for understanding, and teaches us to find, even in sensuous objects, a free delight apart from any charm of sense.[112]

Thus in a sensible world where a disparity exists between Reason and Understanding, *beauty* is truth, but in the ideal world, truth is its own manifestation. Again, Kant sees exquisite compensation in those "weak glances" which nature and Art allow us into the supersensible, and goes on to suggest that Fine Art ("the rendering of moral ideas in terms of sense")[113] presents us most often with the "prototypes of excellence" that our Reason demands: "For only when sensibility is brought into harmony with moral feeling can genuine taste assume a definite unchanging form."[114] Kant is not so much interested in objective aesthetic criteria, which he admits cannot be deduced rationally, as he is in the faculty of judgment itself and the moral efficacy of the artist's creations.

Another source to which Carlyle turned for an exposition of transcendental doctrine was Fichte. In the 1790s as one of Kant's first disciples, Fichte had dedicated himself to the task of simplifying and strengthening the system of the *Kritiks* so that it might reach beyond the province of the German lecture hall. In doing so, he naturally altered Kantian idealism at many points, but he retained what was the essential excitement of it: the sense that here was a higher philosophy for this world, a release from the paradoxes of space and time and the understanding. In the *Science of Knowledge*, first published in 1794, Fichte made his crucial contribution to transcendentalism.[115] The work begins with an essentially romantic premise extrapolated from Descartes: the simple identity "I am I" is Fichte's root, and in the peculiar reality of the "I" lies the foundation of his argument.[116] Like Kant, Fichte believes that the world of objects is one of appearances; he calls it the "Nicht Ich," or Not I, and thinks it merely the projected habitation in which the I conceives of itself.[117] Transcendental Reason (among the elements of which is the moral sense) is for Fichte the I's innate demand for freedom from the Not I; that is, the I's urge for absolute independence.[118] What the individual's Reason desires is to be wholly subject, to be a creative awareness that produces its own object without itself being the object of sense—in other words, what Fichte calls the "Divine Absolute" or God. Although this desire involves a contradiction—individuality and thus I-ness would be lost as the I approaches the Absolute—yet it is, for Fichte,

> the ideal which should be the aim and the inspiration of every life, and a life is glad and triumphant as it draws near to this. This approach is indeed in appearance only . . . yet

nonetheless is every advance a gain. Thus there is open to the soul a career of joy and victory that shall know no limit.[119]

Later Fichte restates this upward progress in Hegelian terms:

> It is by the Divine Life within it that the spirit presses on toward the Divine Ideal. . . . And the ideal to which the soul aspires is infinite. So soon as one form has been attained another and higher takes its place. In the fact of its impulse to attain to this ideal, the spirit finds the pledge of its own immortality.[120]

In the realm of metaphysics, Fichte is obviously less of the formal philosopher and more of the religious enthusiast than Kant, and Carlyle had difficulty in following the steps of the argument. He wrote in his notebook in January 1827: " 'the subject and the object as absolutely identical,' etc.—to this I can attach next to no meaning."[121] Yet a few years later, in an essay on Novalis, Carlyle appears to have assimilated Fichte's concept of the "I" and the "Not I" and acknowledges the profound value of that distinction:

> To a transcendentalist, Matter has an existence, but only as a Phenomenon: were *we* not there, neither would it be there; it is a mere Relation, or rather the result of a Relation between our living Souls and the great First Cause; and depends for its apparent qualities on our bodily and mental organs; having itself *no* intrinsic qualities; being, in the common sense of the word, Nothing. . . . There is, in fact, says Fichte, no Tree there; but only a Manifestation of Power. . . . This, we suppose, may be the foundation of what Fichte means by his far-famed *Ich* and *Nicht-Ich*.[122]

Both Kant and Fichte, despite methodological differences, draw what was for Carlyle the same essential conclusion, namely, that time and space do not exist objectively and that the phenomenal world is somehow dependent upon the activity of man's mind and

God's.[123] In 1829, he spoke of what was to him the inestimable importance of transcendentalism:

> It is the most serious in its purport of all Philosophies propounded in these latter centuries; has been taught chiefly by men of the loftiest and most earnest character; and does bear, with a direct and comprehensive influence, on the most vital interests of men. . . . [For] if Time and Space have no absolute existence, no existence out of our minds, it removes a stumbling-block from the very threshold of our Theology. For on this ground, when we say that the Deity is omnipresent and eternal, that with Him it is a universal Here and Now, we say nothing wonderful; nothing but that he also created Time and Space, that Time and Space are not laws of His being, but only of ours. Nay . . . the whole question of the origin and existence of Nature must be greatly simplified; the old hostility of Matter is at an end, for Matter is itself annihilated; and the black Spectre, Atheism, "with all its sickly dews," melts into nothingness forever.[124]

As Carlyle said of Kant, so might he also have said of Fichte, that in reading them he was bound to entertain the view "that all the world was spirit . . . that there was nothing material at all anywhere."[125]

In Fichte's aesthetics, Carlyle again found strong parallels with Kant's doctrine. Both philosophers saw beauty as a manifestation of good, and Fichte particularly emphasized aesthetic perception as the antecedent to ethical behavior: "In the contemplation of beauty, the limitations of the material and the sensuous are broken through and the spirit returns to itself. The enjoyment of beauty is thus not virtue—it is the preparation for virtue."[126] To Fichte as well as to Kant, Art and nature were keys to unlock the door between the actual and the ideal. To both thinkers the poetical sense preceded and informed all others, since the very nature of our being seemed to demand that we proceed through the sensuous and the articulate to an understanding of the supersensible and the unuttered. These ideas quite understandably reassured a generation of German poets and artists: Richter welcomed Kant's *Critique of Judgment* as a "whole solar system" of thought;[127] Schiller and Novalis accepted the "antithesis between the physical and the moral, the natural and the ideal, the phenomenal and the noumenal" and like Kant and Fichte saw "in the aesthetic experience the bridge that spans the abyss between them."[128] Carlyle was faced with one inescapable fact: German Art and German Transcendentalism were inseparably linked; and this new religion to which he had pinned his hopes thrived on nothing so much as on the consciousness of beauty. As Kant said:

> All other forms of perception divide the man, because they are based exclusively in the sensuous or the spiritual part of his being. It is only the perception of beauty that makes him an entirety, because it demands the co-operation of his two natures. . . . Beauty alone confers happiness on all, and under its influence every being forgets that he is limited.[129]

Carlyle understood that for the transcendentalist, Art's intangible values stood far in advance of any practical concern: "The Earth and all its glories are in truth a vapour and a Dream, and the Beauty of Goodness the only *real* possession. Poetry, Virtue, Religion, which for other men would have but, as it were, a traditionary and imagined existence, are for him the everlasting basis of the Universe."[130] Moreover, Carlyle found in Fichte a specific defense of the Literary Man,[131] and thus a moral justification for his own activities. It is on the authority of Fichte that Carlyle can say "Literature is an 'apocalypse of Nature' . . . a 'continuous revelation' of the God-like in the Terrestrial and Common."[132] Goethe and Schiller had exalted the poet, but Fichte was the first of Carlyle's mentors to emphasize the equivalent importance of Men of Letters and to speak of them as the "supreme moulders of an age."[133] In such manner did Carlyle's religious inquiries come full circle: imaginative literature encouraged him to explore and accept the tenets of transcendental faith, and that faith, in its turn, led him back to literature as to its practical complement.

But transcendentalism did more than predispose Carlyle toward the arts. It also allowed him to experience, for long periods of time, that enviable sense of serenity that belongs to the man who has become "independent of the world." Unlike the matter-of-fact fundamentalism of his father, Carlyle's new theology discounted the appearance of evil in the face of events. As one orthodox critic put it: "Goethe and the philosopher of Chelsea tell us to dismiss our fear, because reverence, not fear, is the proper feeling, and the only one which the true religion permits us to entertain."[134] To the follower of Kant and Fichte, all that was, was ultimately spiritual and functioned only as emblems of divine truth. Thus, since "our Me" was "the only Reality," the idealist felt no need to tie his hope to the fortunes of "this so solid-seeming World." In place of warfare, punishment, hysteria, and sorrow, the transcendentalist held his duty to be a tranquil delineation of the truth he reverenced behind phenomena. Fichte in particular exhorted Carlyle to set a tolerant optimism between his moral ideal and the apparent failure of the world to match it.[135] Under the influence of transcendentalism, Carlyle escaped the depressing contradictions of religious orthodoxy and intellectual iconoclasm and was encouraged to cultivate his own indwelling divinity. As he said himself, in interpreting the message of Goethe's *Faust:*

> Joy ye in the living fullness of the beautiful (not the logical, practical, contradictory, wherein man toils imprisoned); let Being (or Existence), which is everywhere a glorious birth into higher Being, as it forever works and lives, encircle you with the soft ties of Love; and whatsoever wavers in the doubtful empire of appearance (as all earthly things do); that do ye by enduring faith make firm.[136]

To exhaust oneself attempting material reforms in this "doubtful empire of appearance" or to despair at their apparent failure was, for the transcendentalist, a foolish profligacy, since all we see is but the reflex of our inward attainments.[137] Thus, in his commitment to German idealism, Carlyle found himself committed not only to literature but also to a highly pacific, often contemplative world-view.[138]

While he was still occupied in unraveling the exact purport of transcendental doctrine, Carlyle continued his work as translator and editor of German literature. By the end of 1826, he had compiled a group of essays and German stories to be published under the title *German Romance*.[139] The anthology included critical appraisals of the authors (among whom were Musaeus, Tieck, Hoffman, and Richter); and these editorial judgments understandably contained a number of ideas borrowed from the Kantian aesthetics Carlyle was then studying.[140] In particular, Carlyle evaluated the contribution of these romantic writers in accordance with the degree of religious awareness they displayed: those who were witty, sentimental, and superficially comic drew Carlyle's censure for putting talent ahead of genius; those who revealed strong moral affections, and a profound faith in the life of the spirit were praised as "pure" poets.[141]

But the business of literary criticism, however educative, did not satisfy Carlyle's needs as a writer. He was not, he said, content simply "to Germanize the public." In fact, the discovery of the achievements of Tieck, Richter, and later, Novalis, only whetted his appetite for a personal triumph in the field of letters. In his anxiety to be about some original work, he again suffered from dyspepsia and sleeplessness. He wrote to his mother in December 1826: "If I could heartily commence some *book of my own,* of the sort I wished, it could do more for me than any mere publishing or editorial engagement."[142] By the beginning of 1827, he felt the confidence necessary for such an effort. German writers, especially Goethe, had urged him to find an outlet for his convictions;[143] and now, with transcendental faith as an anchor for his ideas, Carlyle was prepared, finally, to test his own artistic powers.[144] That he had not done so earlier (the desire to write a novel had been one of Carlyle's preoccupations since 1822), may be in part attributable to his intellectual honesty, that is, to his recognition of the inchoate nature of his religious beliefs. Not until he had reinforced the literary impulse (that followed on that first reading of *Wilhelm Meister*) with a broader understanding of German idealism was Carlyle willing to give his own ideas single prominence. Masson agrees that Carlyle's slow start on an original composition was rooted in his reluctance to speak before he was sure of his ground. "It was not enough that he should be able to write fluently and eloquently in a general way, by the exercise of mere natural talent, on any subject turned up. He had to provide himself amply with *matter*, with systematized knowledge of all sorts."[145] After January 1827 he was fairly certain that he had extracted from Kant and Fichte what in them was of essential value; at least he was sure enough of what he believed to undertake the writing of *Wotton Reinfred*.[146]

Needless to say, *Wotton* has received slight critical attention in the 140 years since it was written—largely because Carlyle left it unfinished and unrevised, and because it did not find its way into print until 1892.[147] Whatever technical faults it may have as a novel, *Wotton* is nonetheless extremely valuable as an indicator of Carlyle's religious convictions in the months immediately following his exposure to German philosophy. Perhaps because artistically it represents a false start on the road to *Sartor Resartus*, *Wotton* ought, rightly, to be left in obscurity. Certainly, as Froude says, it lacks inventiveness;[148] and as a fictional vehicle for Carlyle's views, it is often embarrassingly frail. Characterization and plot are wooden throughout, and the dialogue, when it is not baldly philosophical, is generally insipid. The hero thinks nothing of "internally" exclaiming "in Doric words" or of beating his breast in Latin:

> "*O causa causarum, miserere mei!*" cried Reinfred, looking upwards, with the tears almost starting to his eyes. "*Miserere*

mei!" repeated he, throwing himself down on the table, and
hiding his face in his hands.

His cousin looked at him sympathizingly, but spoke not.[149]

If we concede (as we must) that dramatic bathos of this sort dooms
Carlyle's novel from the outset, we are still left with *Wotton* as an
accurate history of the author's religious education—second only
to *Sartor* itself.

The novel's hero is introduced to us in a state of extreme depression, closely resembling the "Everlasting No" of the Teufelsdröckh
saga. This crisis in his development has arisen from his immersion
in skeptical philosophies, particularly those of Hume, Gibbon,
the *philosophes,* and various scientific materialists. Like Carlyle in
1820, Reinfred has been "intellectualized" out of his sense of
purpose.

After two chapters of "soul-agonizing," the remaining five
chronicle a kind of ungainly resurrection—and are disturbingly
similar to *Wilhelm Meister.* The hero and his friend set out on a
journey that functions in the same metaphorical sense as Meister's
travels. Along the way, Wotton encounters men and circumstances
that slowly convert him to a new spirituality and optimism. The
travelers meet a "sociably frank" stranger who advises them, in
what might pass for a paraphrase of Goethe's warning in *Meister,*
against a reliance on material happiness:

> True goodness of all sorts must have its life and root within
> ourselves; it depends on external appliances far less than we
> suppose. The great point is to have a healthy mind, or, if I
> may say so *a right power of assimilation,* for the elements of
> beauty and truth lie round us on all sides, even in the mean-
> est objects, if we could but extract them.[150]

In the speaker's idea of internal truth and external symbols of
that truth, he is already hinting at Kantian concepts. Wotton's
interest is aroused by these remarks in much the same way Carlyle's
had been by the conclusion to *Wilhelm Meister's Travels,* and he

agrees to follow the stranger to a house where it is promised that "refreshment and rest are waiting for us."[151] Once there, Wotton is astonished to find a company of devout, intelligent men who have apparently kept their faith without losing their intellectual honesty. Wotton's feelings must come very close indeed to representing Carlyle's own mood when, in 1821, he first viewed the enormous vitality of German idealism:

> That air of candour and goodness, those striking glimpses of man's nature and its sufferings and wants, had his sympathy and hearty approval; but he sought in vain for the basis on which these people had built their opinions; their whole form of being seemed different from his. Men equally informed and cultivated he had sometimes met with, but seldom or never had he seen such culture of the intellect combined with such moral results, nay, as it appeared, conducing to them. Here were fearless and free thinkers, yet they seemed not unbelievers, but, on the contrary, possessed with charity and zeal.[152]

And from the far side of transcendentalism, Carlyle can look back dispprovingly at Wotton's initial distrust: "It is not always that originality, even when true and estimable, pleases us at first; if it go beyond our sphere, it is much more likely to unsettle and provoke us."[153] Soon the more articulate members of the company offer clues to the tenets of their unique religion. Wotton is first presented with what amounts to a summary of Kant's *Kritik der reinen Vernunft:* "Demonstrability is not the test of truth; logic is for what the understanding *sees;* what is truest we do not *see* for it has no form, being infinite; the highest truth cannot be expressed in words."[154] Wotton's hosts go on to condemn the antagonists of Kant, especially Hume, who, as the current "ruler of the world," has carried a herd of ambitious utilitarians and epicureans in his train:

> Was man made only to feel? Is there nothing better in him than a passive system of susceptibilities? Can he move only

like a finer piece of clockwork? . . . Is his spirit a quality, not a substance? has it no power, no will? . . . O philosophy! . . . what hast thou been made to teach! In thy name cozeners have beguiled us of our birthright and sold us into bondage, and we are no longer servants of goodness, but slaves of self.[155]

Like Kant, Carlyle's company of enlightened philosophers discriminates between the faculties of Reason and Understanding: "Understanding perceives and judges of the images and measures of things . . . reason perceives and judges of what has no measure or image. The latter only is unchangeable and everlasting in its decisions, the results of the former change from age to age."[156] But perhaps most significantly, Wotton's new teachers emphasize the applied transcendentalism of Kant's *Critique of Judgment*. The hero asks, reasonably enough, how their divine idea of the world can be expressed, and Dalbrook, the chief among them, answers: "Expressed? . . . in the still existence of all good men. Echoes of it come to us from *the song of the poet;* the sky with its azure and its rainbow and its beautiful vicissitudes of morn and even show it forth. . . . It is an open secret . . . woe to us if we have no vision for it."[157] Although the "open secret" belongs to Goethe, even the nonconverted guests are quick to recognize Kant's influence behind the words, and to protest: "Kantism! Kantism! German mysticism! mere human faculties cannot take it in."[158] Carlyle in fact highlights two major corollaries of German transcendentalism: that the poet is the "high priest" of the noumenal universe, and that the essence of his message is unification, clarity, and love. Carlyle makes very clear both what he takes the role of the poet to be and what our estimate of his value ought to be:

The first poets were teachers and seers, the gifted soul, instinct with music, discerned the true and the beautiful in nature, and poured its bursting fulness in floods of harmony, entrancing the rude sense of men; and song was a

heavenly voice bearing wisdom irresistibly . . . into every
heart . . . [Let us] Look with their eyes on man and life!
All its hollowness and insufficiency are there; but with them,
nay by them, do beauty and mercy and a solemn grandeur
shine forth, and man . . . is no longer little or poor, but
lovely and venerable; for a glory of Infinitude is round him.
. . . Life with its prizes and its failures . . . were a poor
matter iself; [to the poet] it is baseless, transient and hollow,
an infant's dream; but beautiful also, and solemn and of
mysterious significance. Why should he not love it and reverence it? Is not all visible nature, all sensible existence the
symbol and vesture of the Invisible and Infinite? Is it not in
these material shows of things that God, virtue, immortality
are shadowed forth and made manifest to man? Material
nature is as a *fatamorgana*, hanging in the air; a cloud-pic-
ture, but painted by heavenly light; in itself it is air and
nothingness,[159] but behind it is the glory of the sun. . . .
It is only the invisible that really *is*, but only the gifted sense
that can of itself discern this reality![160]

Carlyle could in no way enter more fully into the spirit of idealism
or paraphrase more closely the essence of the aesthetic theories of
Kant, Schiller, and Fichte.[161] But in order to make the interde-
pendency of literature and religion thoroughly explicit, Carlyle—
through one of his characters—puts the obvious question: "What
is all this? Must a poet become a mystic, and study Kant before he
can write verses?"[162] The transcendental philosopher replies that
"Kantism" is "but the more scientific expression of what all true
poets and thinkers, nay, all good men, have felt more or less distinctly, and acted on the faith of, in all ages."[163] That is to say,
Kant merely formulates the doctrines of a transcendental faith
that has always operated behind the poetic consciousness of true
artists. The belief in beauty as sensible truth, the sense of tranquility and optimism in the face of material hardship, which together sustain the disciples of Kant, have been the property, so
Carlyle asserts, of the literary genius in every epoch.[164] For Wotton
and, of course, for Carlyle, transcendentalism is an acquired rather

than a native faith. Nonetheless, from this fragmentary novel, it is evident that by 1827 Carlyle had familiarized himself with German idealism, adopted it as his own faith, and accepted the commitment to literature which it implies.

Unfortunately, he was not yet as skillful as he was convinced. For obvious reasons, among them lack of humor and the inability to integrate the philosophical and romantic strands of the story, Carlyle discontinued *Wotton* at the end of the seventh chapter.[165] Instead he took up the work of criticism again, turning out, over the next four years, nearly twenty essays on German writers and the history of German literature.[166] All of the them reflect the critic's adherence to transcendental doctrine: Carlyle continued to look at poetry and prose as organs of mystical religion, condemning, where he found it, worldly and sensational writing, and reserving his praise for verse and fiction of an expressly spiritual sort.[167] The systems of Kant and Fichte and the examples of Goethe and Schiller had convinced Carlyle that "not brute Force, but only Persuasion and Faith is the king of this world."[168] As a result, he became an ever more fervid advocate of Goethe's new "World-Literature," which he agreed should be "all in all to us":[169]

> The more cheering is the one thing we do see and know: That [Literature's] tendency is to a universal European Commonweal, that the wisest in all nations will communicate and co-operate; whereby Europe will again have its true Sacred College . . . wars will become rarer, less inhuman, and in the course of centuries such delirious ferocity in nations . . . may be proscribed and become obsolete for ever.[170]

Thus the literary man, devout and peace-loving, assumed for Carlyle an exaggerated significance in a world that was otherwise inhabited by skeptics and *Kraftmänner*. But German idealism shaped more than his view of literature: Carlyle's first political tract, "Signs of the Times," (1829) also owed many of its articles to Kant. The division of human faculties into "mechanical" and "dynamical" is clearly analogous to Kant's discrimination between Understanding and Reason, and Carlyle's final appeal for self-cultivation derives, in equal measure, from *Wilhelm Meister* and *The Critique of Practical Reason*. This bias toward subjective, internal values animates most of his criticism written before 1832, and can be traced to transcendental principles in almost every case. Year by year, Carlyle was becoming the most respected English spokesman for the ideas of modern Germany, yet, as his confidence and his reputation grew, so too did his impatience with the secondhand nature of his own accomplishments. Once more the wish to be "a kind of artist" obsessed him, and in the early months of 1831, he began another fictional self-portrait—*Sartor Resartus*.

This time he brought to the writing of his novel a surer grasp of the dramatic and technical elements of narrative prose. Like *Wotton, Sartor* was conceived, in outline, as a religious autobiography, but of a far subtler sort. From Richter he had learned the art of comic digression[171] and the value of fully realized personae. More importantly, he understood now what he could not appreciate in 1827: that *double entendre,* when incorporated with didactic purpose, made the harshest truths more entertaining, if not more palatable.[172] In fact the manner of *Sartor* displays the playful, even amoral aspect of parody and satire as much as the matter of it chronicles the growth of spiritual conviction in the author.[173] In contrast to *Wotton,* Carlyle's second novel has received a vast amount of critical attention in the last 130 years— much of it focused, naturally enough, on the tenets of the hero's religion.

Certainly, that Carlyle derives Teufelsdröckh's professed faith from Kantian sources is firmly established in each of the three sections of *Sartor*. In the first, his "humour of looking at all Matter and Material things as Spirit" constitutes a "clear logically-founded Transcendentalism," of the sort that opposes "Reason" to "vulgar logic." The professor from Weissnichtwo paraphrases Fichte's

Ich–Nicht Ich distinction as well: "Think well, thou too wilt find that Space is but a mode of our human Sense, so likewise Time; there *is* no Space and no Time . . . this so solid-seeming World, after all, were but an air-image, our me the only reality: and Nature, with its thousandfold production and destruction, but the reflex of our own inward Force . . . *the living visible Garment of God.*"[174] In the second, autobiographical part, Teufelsdröckh is rescued from despair by reading *Wilhelm Meister,* accepts literature as his "calling," and reconciles himself to a "life of Meditation" by the Kantian practice of looking "through the show of things into things themselves." Here, as in *Wotton,* the process of self-discovery parallels the author's own. In the final section, especially "Natural Supernaturalism," Teufelsdröckh joins Fichte in dismissing custom, science and the Understanding as criteria for truth, since our physical being is but "dust and Shadow; a Shadow-system gathered round our Me; wherein, through some moments or years, the Divine Essence is to be revealed in the Flesh."[175] As in Kant's third *Kritik,* the hero believes Art to be "the rendering of moral ideas in terms of Sense," an aesthetic recognition that "the Universe is but one vast Symbol of God."

Of course, *Sartor* contains a number of elements that have only tangentially to do with transcendentalism: the comic digressions on clothes, history, and politics; the "phoenix" theory of society; the amusing crotchets of diction and plotting. In consequence, it is an infinitely richer and more original work than *Wotton,* and the fact that its hero is a professor rather than a student gives evidence of Carlyle's increased confidence in his own powers. Yet both novels are the result of a single impulse: to articulate the new spirituality to which Carlyle had been converted, and to persuade others to follow his example.

Throughout the rest of his life, Carlyle apparently remained faithful to the metaphysical convictions he formed in these years: he seldom attended church and certainly never took an active interest in the ecclesiastical movements of his day, yet he never ceased to believe in Fichte's "Divine Idea of the world."[176] As Espinasse puts it, "He used to say that he never felt spiritually at ease until he left the church behind him and went out into the 'bare desert' where there was a temple not made with hands."[177] And as late as 1879, transcendental principles—the categorical imperative, time and space as appearances, nature as the symbol of the divine—still formed the nucleus of Carlyle's heterodox faith.[178] The history, then, of Carlyle's religious development amounts (if we except the transitional stages of doubt and atheism) to a substitution of transcendental theology for dogmatic, Calvinist theology.[179] Further, it is clear that the nature of his adopted religion stirred Carlyle's sympathy for the arts in general, and for literature in particular. Among men, Carlyle, like his hero Teufelsdröckh, recognized only one supreme example—the man who, in his external labor, is "endeavoring towards inward Harmony": "Highest of all, when his outward and his inward endeavor are one: when we can name him Artist; not earthly Craftsman only, but inspired Thinker, who with heaven-made Implement conquers Heaven for us!"[180] Carlyle was especially attracted by the poet's peculiar ability to evoke that "awful sense of the mystery of existence" which is at the heart of transcendentalism.[181]

Lastly, there is no question that as an idealist philosopher Carlyle had enormous influence on his contemporaries.[182] Emerson, intrigued by his German essays, visited Carlyle at Craigenputtock and later arranged for the Boston publication of *Sartor*.[183] The American had some prior knowledge of the systems of Kant and Coleridge, but Teufelsdröckh's *Clothes-Philosophy* undoubtedly acted as the catalyst for his own initial statement of transcendental faith in 1836.[184] Years later, Walt Whitman—perhaps the greatest of transcendental poets—acknowledged that, without the inspiration of Carlyle, he and others like him would probably never have written at all.[185] T. H. Green, in evaluating the religious contribution of Wordsworth, Carlyle, and Fichte to nineteenth-century thought, argues that his contemporaries found in them "the congenial idea of a divine life or spirit pervading the world, making nature intelligible, giving unity to history . . .

and inspiring individual men of genius."[186] R. H. Hutton compares Carlyle's transcendental utterances to those of Emerson and concludes that they have justly enjoyed greater currency than the American's.[187] In 1855, George Eliot anticipates these eulogies in a review of Carlyle:

> There is hardly a superior or active mind of this generation that has not been modified by Carlyle's writings; there has hardly been an English book written for the last ten or twelve years that would not be different if Carlyle had not lived. . . . The extent of his influence may be best seen in the fact that ideas which were startling novelties when he first wrote them are now become common-places. And we think few men will be found to say that this influence on the whole has not been for good.[188]

In the same vein, James Martineau remarks that it was not unusual, in the 1840s and 50s, to hear young, earnest Englishmen declaring, "*Carlyle* is my religion!"[189] Like the rest of Carlyle's contemporaries, Martineau looks at "the vast influence of Carlyle's writing on the inmost faith of our generation," as upon one of the "essential facts" of Victorian culture.[190] Many critics feel, even now, that his introduction of transcendental ideas into the mainstream of British thought was his primary contribution: "To convince the English mind that there is an alternative to the garb of Hebrew old-clothes on the one hand, and the nakedness of Atheism on the other, was the main part of his function in literature."[191]

Carlyle was no less renowned as a friend of literature: Goethe honored him with gifts and medals;[192] Goethe's associates thought so highly of his talents that they entreated him to translate *Faust* for the English-speaking world;[193] Tennyson, Hunt, Thackeray,[194] Dickens,[195] Browning,[196] Sterling, Forster, Ruskin, and a score of other poets and writers cherished their acquaintance with the "sage of Chelsea": on his eightieth birthday, many of them were among the 119 signatories of a scroll declaring Carlyle the "embodiment of the 'Hero as Man of Letters.' "[197] Leslie Stephen, who saw Car-

lyle frequently in his last years, writes in 1873 that "he is by far
the best specimen of the literary gent we can at present produce. . . . He is indeed a genuine poet and great humorist."[198]
Louis Cazamian declares that Carlyle will be remembered as "one
of the most spirited poets of modern England" whose imaginative
genius was nourished on transcendentalism:

> His vision of the world is that toward which the poets of the
> romantic generation had striven: a perception of the spiri-
> tual in the material. But the universality, the might and the
> lofty vistas of German idealism gave to Carlyle's vision . . .
> a breadth and clearness beyond comparison. His imagina-
> tion lived so freely under the sense of the unreality of time
> and space, that every spectacle he pictured had its double
> aspect of reality and dream. . . . No poet has had in a
> higher degree, sublimity of imagination; no poet has with
> greater power evoked the infinite, or the eternal silences
> which lie behind the transitory sights and sounds of life
> . . . the quality which will best assure the duration of Car-
> lyle's work is . . . that energy which is capable of . . .
> eliciting from the world and from the soul fragments mar-
> velous in their beauty.[199]

Yet his idealistic convictions and his advocacy of literature notwithstanding, Carlyle often entertained ideas contrary to the tenor
of these commitments. His closest friends recognized—and we
have seen in earlier chapters—that despite the inherent mildness
of his faith and his profession, Carlyle continually acted in "the
most curious opposition to himself."[200] In such an unsettled mood,
he confessed to his brother in 1833 his "crabbed one-sided persuasion that all Art is but a reminiscence now," that "*Prophecy
. . .* not Poetry is the thing wanted," that "Goethe . . . is not
to have any follower, and should not have any."[201] We must now
turn our attention from transcendentalism to another religious
prejudice behind Carlyle's view of literature—namely, to that
force that, in the main, dictated his antagonism toward the arts.

1. *Reminiscences*, I, 53.

2. *Firsty Forty Years*, I, 7.

3. *Reminiscences*, I, 39.

4. *First Forty Years*, I, 7.

5. *Reminiscences*, I, 82.

6. Ibid., I, 51–52.

7. C. Harrold, *Carlyle and German Thought, 1819–1834*, p. 26.

8. *Reminiscences*, I, 55.

9. Ibid.

10. Margaret Carlyle's education was so limited, in fact, that she only learned to write late in life in order to correspond with her eldest son.

11. *Reminiscences*, I, 83.

12. W. Allingham, *A Diary*, p. 232.

13. Ibid., p. 253.

14. Ibid., p. 268.

15. *SR*, p. 91. Although reliable as a history of Carlyle's early thought, *Sartor* is not always to be trusted for autobiographical details. It has thus been consulted, in every instance, with the author's caution in mind: "Nothing in 'Sartor Resartus' is fact; symbolical myth all" (*First Forty Years*, I, 103).

16. *First Forty Years*, I, 29.

17. Ibid., p. 26.

18. In 1833, Carlyle told Emerson that in his early years "Rousseau's *Confessions* had discovered to him that he was not a dunce" (Emerson, *English Traits*, p. 20). See also "Diderot," *Essays*, III, 193: like Carlyle, Diderot preached sermons and taught mathematics in his younger days—neither with any conviction.

19. Carlyle was apparently unaware of Hume's work as an extension of Berkeley's speculations.

20. Wilson I, p. 109.

21. D. Hume, *An Enquiry Concerning Human Understanding*, in *Theory of Knowledge*, ed. D. C. Yalden-Thompson, p. 10.

22. Ibid., p. 17.

23. As early as 1814, Carlyle spoke of the "bigoted scepticism" and "blind prejudice" of Hume (letter to Mitchell in Wilson I, p. 99).

24. *Enquiry Concerning Human Understanding*, p. 20.

25. Ibid., p. 17.

26. *Lectures*, p. 205.

27. "Hume on Religion," in *David Hume: A Symposium*, ed. D. F. Pears, p. 80.

28. Wilson I, p. 116.

29. Ibid., p. 115.

30. Letter to Mitchell, 1816, ibid., p. 117.

31. Edward Gibbon, *The Decline and Fall of the Roman Empire*, I, 479–80.

32. Allingham, *A Diary*, p. 232.

33. For the journal account, see Froude, *First Forty Years*, I, 54.

34. See *Reminiscences*, I, 177.

35. Froude, *First Forty Years*, I, 59.

36. *SR*, p. 92.

37. "He appears, though in dreary enough humour, to be addressing himself to the Profession of the Law" (*SR*, p. 93).

38. Froude, *First Forty Years*, I, 64–65.

39. It was about this time (1819) that Carlyle first complained of dyspepsia —a fact that adds weight to the prevailing theory of its psychosomatic origin.

40. On Carlyle's need for a religion, see Cazamian, *Carlyle*, p. 19.

41. *SR*, p. 131.

42. Ibid., p. 129.

43. Ibid., pp. 129, 132–33.

44. Ibid., p. 133.

45. See *Wotton Reinfred, Last Words*, p. 92, and the letter of 19 May 1824 to Jane Welsh in Wilson I, p. 327 (on the death of Byron), and "State of German Literature," *Essays*, I, 69. For a thorough treatment of Byron's influence on Carlyle, both early and late, see C. R. Sanders, "The Byron Closed in *Sartor Resartus*."

46. He later said of this period: "I was then in the very midst of Wertherism —the blackness and darkness of death" (*Lectures*, p. 186). For Carlyle's comments on the novel itself, see *Essays*, I, 211–24.

47. Letter of 9 March 1821, in Froude, *Firsty Forty Years*, I, 99.

48. Emerson, *English Traits*, p. 20. The "man" was probably Mr. P. Swan of Kirkcaldy, who also supplied Carlyle with a number of German texts. See Froude, *First Forty Years*, I, 91. Cazamian agrees that Carlyle was led to study German from rumors of its new answers to spiritual dilemmas (*Carlyle*, p. 32).

49. "Hume's philosophy, which had attracted him briefly in the beginning phase of his own religious scepticism, afforded him little or no positive aid in his personal difficulties as he passed through the more wretched years" (Shine, ed., *Unfinished History of German Literature*, p. 90).

50. *SR*, p. 156.

51. Carlyle's 1814 apostrophe to the glories of "literary fame" (see above, p. 13) should be ranked with similar early comments on the law ("It seemed glorious to me for its independency") as an example of the impetuous and understandably fickle temper of adolescence.

52. Spoken of, and by, the Harper, *WM*, II, 16.

53. *WM*, I, 167.

54. Carlyle was immensely curious. He wrote in an early essay on Goethe, "How has this man, to whom the world once offered nothing but blackness, denial and despair, attained to that better vision which now shows it to him not tolerable only, but full of solemnity and loveliness?" (*Essays*, I, 210).

55. *WM*, II, 370.

56. Ibid., p. 415.

57. June 1821? This date is given by Froude for Carlyle's reading of *Wilhelm Meister* as well as for his Leith Walk "conversion"—an assertion disputed by Alexander Carlyle and others since. There survives little evidence to argue a preference for June 1821 or July-August 1822 in the Leith Walk matter, although signs of Goethe's influence appear as early as October 1821: from this date Carlyle's articles take for their subjects, not chemistry and geometry, but metrical romances, Milton, and, in an April 1822 review, Goethe's *Faust*. The larger question—of the validity and completeness of his mystical conversion—can be answered less equivocally. From a firsthand knowledge of Carlyle's letters and notebooks from 1822 forward, one is compelled to agree with Carlisle Moore's verdict that Leith Walk represented, at best, an initial successful skirmish with the "mud-gods" of the Everlasting No. Despite Carlyle's retrospective view of the issue—which telescoped a protracted rise from despair into a single, cataclysmic leap—his journals during the 1820s indicate that "there were . . . other awakenings, other illuminations, which, with the help of Goethe, of Kant and Fichte [enabled] him gradually to leave the Everlasting No farther and farther behind" (C. Moore, "*Sartor Resartus* and the Problem of Carlyle's Conversion," p. 669). I do not agree with Moore, however, that the process of rebirth begun with Leith Walk and the reading of *Wilhelm Meister* was not finished until 1830 and the writing of *Sartor Resartus*. That work was, in fact, the highly wrought outward sign of a conversion inwardly confirmed and completed in the early months of 1827 (see below, p. 99).

Nonetheless, there are nagging difficulties about the Leith Walk incident: first, Carlyle later spoke of it as the only autobiographical parallel in Sartor (under the alias Rue Saint-Thomas de l'Enfer) that the reader ought to take "quite literally" (*Love Letters*, II, 380); and second, the conversion *precedes* the Goethe-inspired Everlasting Yea and even the Centre-of-Indifference stage of Teufelsdröckh's spiritual growth. For that reason it seems to me whatever happened on that summer day in Edinburgh was largely a proto-conversion, a spontaneous revolt of the instincts that gave Carlyle some hope of a more unified, permanent restoration to follow. He tells us he outstared his fear of death and supplanted "whining Sorrow" with "Indignation and grim, fire-eyed Defiance"; finally he affirms that he "directly thereupon began to be a man." Such an emphasis upon the effort of will involved and upon the manliness of his triumph suggests that the impetus for this initial "New-birth" derived from his native, Puritan stoicism rather than from any vision of a new metaphysics. Frederick Roe, Werner Leopold, and J. H. Muirhead all take similar views (*Carlyle as a Critic of Literature*, p. 19; *Die religiöse Wurzel von Carlyles literarisher Wirksamkeit*, pp. 45–46; *Platonic Traditions in Anglo-Saxon Philosophy*, p. 130). The experience amounted, then, to a kind of visceral convulsion that, without the deeper reassurance of transcendental faith that followed, would soon have lost its force for lack of a directing epistemology.

58. *Lectures*, p. 187. See also Allingham, *A Diary*: "Goethe . . . pointed out to me the real nature of life and things—not that he did this directly; but incidentally, and let me see it rather than told me. This gave me peace and great satisfaction" (p. 253). For other testaments to his reaction to *Wilhelm Meister*, see Froude, *First Forty Years*, I, 135, and Adrian Arthur, "Dean Stanley's Report of Conversations with Carlyle," p. 74.

59. In the chapter on his mental crisis in the Autobiography, J. S. Mill makes much the same comment on the inefficacy of Byron's poetry: "In the worst period of my depression, I had read through the whole of Byron. . . . As might be expected, I got no good from this reading, but the reverse." Instead he turned to Wordsworth, who offered "real, permanent happiness in tranquil contemplation," and to Goethe, who argued for "the maintenance of a due balance among the faculties." Both poets reject the external happiness that Mill had recently found so unsatisfying (see *Autobiography*, chap. 5).

60. *Entsagen* "was an aesthetic ideal. . . . It pointed to the harmonious outflowering of all one's energies, the lower subordinated to the higher. . . . It has no similarity to the ascetic ideal; it is fundamentally a creative act, an effort at a constant envisaging of the whole" (Harrold, *Carlyle and German Thought*, pp. 216–17).

61. *SR*, p. 156. He defined *Entsagen*, in the 1827 essay on Richter, as "a harmonious development of being" (*Essays*, I, 20). See also *Essays*, IV, 39.

62. *WM*, II, 315, 305.

63. *WM*, II, 329.

64. See the Introduction, I. Kant, *Kritik of Judgment*, p. xiii.

65. Froude, *First Forty Years*, I, 132.

66. Wilson I, p. 202.

67. Ibid.

68. Froude, *First Forty Years*, I, 151–52.

69. The passage in *Meister*, from the Abbe's Indenture, reads, "Art is long, life short, judgment difficult, opportunity transient" (*WM*, II, 75).

70. From *Aesthetic Letters*, as translated by Carlyle in "Schiller," *Essays*, II, 192.

71. Although Arnold gave it currency, Carlyle should rightly be credited with the introduction of the term *Philistine* into English literary criticism. See his 1824 preface to *Wilhelm Meister's Apprenticeship*, I, 22n. (quoted above, p. 10); George Eliot's supporting opinion in *Essays of George Eliot*, ed. T. Pinney, p. 296n.; and David DeLaura's discussion "Arnold and Carlyle," p. 107.

72. *Essays*, II, 191.

73. Ibid., p. 193.

74. Ibid., p. 197.

75. Ibid., p. 196.

76. From *The Robbers* and *Maid of Orleans*, as translated in part in *Essays*, II, 204, 208.

77. *LS*, pp. 200–202.

78. Ibid., pp. 43–44. According to Cazamian, it is in the *Life of Schiller* that Carlyle established his religious view of literature: "The bias of Carlyle's mind is revealed . . . the moral basis attracts him most . . . for him literature is a religion . . . swiftly and surely he seizes upon the pure idealism of the creative mind" (p. 87).

79. Irving, upset by the "subversive" German lessons Carlyle was giving Jane, tried on numerous occasions to "put in a word for Jesus" with the young girl (Wilson I, p. 212).

80. That is, if we except the "small . . . unsatisfactory" articles that he wrote for *Brewster's Encyclopedia* in 1820 (see Froude, *First Forty Years*, I, 91).

81. See *LS*, p. 110.

82. "Unconscious of any illegitimate identification of Goethe's teachings with those of the philosopher, Carlyle regarded Fichte and Goethe as two exponents of one general doctrine" (Harrold, *Carlyle and German Thought*, p. 14).

83. "Carlyle's study of Schiller's aesthetics based upon Kantian thought had for some time beckoned the young Scot toward German transcendental philosophy" (Hill Shine, *Unfinished History of German Literature*, p. xxiii).

84. *Essays*, II, 211–12.

85. "The year 1825–26 was of great importance to Carlyle. It marked his emergence from the ethnic or purely humanistic phase of intellectual development, into the phase of transcendental thought. . . . Largely through the aesthetic writers in Carlyle's humanistic period he had gradually approached the tenets of transcendentalism" (Hill Shine, "Carlyle and the German Philosophy Problem during the Year 1826-27," p. 807).

86. "He was thought to hold, he alone in England, the key of German and other Transcendentalisms" (*Sterling*, p. 53). Norman Fruman, in a recent study, *Coleridge, the Damaged Archangel*, contends that S. T. C.'s philosophy was almost wholly derived from "Kant and Co.": "For we *know* that Coleridge read, avidly read, the German school and annotated their works, and used their ideas, their technical vocabulary, and sometimes page after page verbatim. . . . Studies of Coleridge's philosophy are not likely to be very much advanced by further insistence on the primacy of his English heritage, but rather by still more intensive study of the pervasive influence of Germany" (p. 120).

87. Ibid., p. 55.

88. *LS*, p. 114 (italics added). Carlyle also expressed his disappointment in a letter to his brother of 24 June 1824. In it, he reckons Coleridge "a man of great and useless genius" (Froude, *First Forty Years*, I, 228–29).

89. Although his notebooks for these years contain scattered references to Coleridge, only one recorded comment derives directly from S.T.C.'s published material (see *Notebooks*, pp. 46–47, and *Biographia Literaria*, chap. 15, on "talent" and "genius"). For a closer assessment of Carlyle's debt to Coleridge, see Shine, *Unfinished History of German Literature*, p. 100.

90. Gavan Duffy paraphrases Carlyle's opinion of the matter in 1849: "Whatever Coleridge had written was vague and purposeless, and, when one came to consider it, intrinsically cowardly. . . . He had reconciled himself to believe in the Church of England long after it had become a dream to him" (*Conversations with Carlyle*, pp. 59–60).

91. See Shine, "Carlyle and the German Philosophy Problem," p. 612. See also Shine, *Unfinished History of German Literature*, p. 111. In addition to Shine and Harrold, M. Storrs (*The Relation of Carlyle to Kant and Fichte*) and R. Wellek (*Immanuel Kant in England, 1793–1838*) have discussed the problem of determining the extent of Carlyle's firsthand intimacy with Kant's critiques. For Carlyle's report of having read 150 pages of the first *Kritik* by September 1826, see *Love Letters*, II, 234. I have examined Carlyle's edition

of the *Kritik der reinen Vernunft* (Leipzig, 1818) in his study in Chelsea, but have found no marginalia to indicate where, or whether, he cut short his reading of it.

92. This dating of Carlyle's exposure to transcendental philosophers is supported by the *Note Books*, pp. 112–13. See also Shine, "Carlyle and the German Philosophy Problem," p. 815, and James Martineau: "In 1827, he defended the *Kritik der reinen Vernunft* against ignorant objectors" (*Essays, Philosophical and Theological*, I, 390). From a letter he wrote to Espinasse in 1841, it is also clear that Carlyle held Kant to be the principal figure among the German philosophers and that he thought the first *Kritik* quite intelligible: "After all the Fichteisms, Schellingisms, Hegelisms, I still understand Kant to be the grand novelty, the prime author of the new spiritual world, of whom all the others are but superficial transient modifications. If you do decide to penetrate into this matter, what better can you do than vigorously set to the *Kritik der reinen Vernunft*, a very attainable book and resolutely study it and restudy it until you understand it? You will find it actually capable of being understood, rigorously sequent, like a book of mathematics; labour that pays itself; really one of the best metaphysical studies that I know of. Once master of Kant, you have attained what I reckon most precious: namely, deliverance from the fatal incubus of Scotch or French philosophy, with its mechanisms and its Atheisms, and be able, perhaps to wend on your way leaving both of them behind you" (Espinasse, *Literary Recollections*, p. 59). See also *Essays*, I, 75.

93. "Though he never proceeded in his philosophic interests far enough to satisfy a systematic student of that subject, he did read some of Kant, and much of Kant's interpreters" (Shine, *Unfinished History of German Literature*, p. xxiii).

94. See P. F. Strawson, *The Bounds of Sense*, p. 19.

95. *Critique of Pure Reason*, trans. N. K. Smith, p. 19.

96. See "Hume on Religion," in *David Hume: A Symposium*, p. 78.

97. *Note Books*, p. 102.

98. Strawson, *The Bounds of Sense*, p. 16.

99. Or, as he says in the preface, "reason cannot progress with *a priori* concepts alone in a scientific manner" (*Pure Reason*, p. 24).

100. What Kant calls the "categories of pure understanding" (see *Pure Reason*, pp. 71–74).

101. Ibid., p. 149.

102. Hume would argue that the question is practically, if not intellectually, irrelevant.

103. *Essays*, I, 81.

104. Unamuno sees *Practical Reason* as an emotional reaction to the void left after the first *Kritik*, an expression of the philosopher's "longing not to die" (*The Tragic Sense of Life*, p. 28).

105. *Critique of Practical Reason*, trans. T. K. Abbott, p. 100.

106. Ibid., p. 119.

107. Ibid., p. 246.

108. Ibid., p. 245.

109. Ibid., p. 246.

110. See *Critique of Aesthetic Judgment*, trans. J. C. Meredith, p. 39.

111. Ibid., pp. 222, 223.

112. Ibid., p. 225.

113. Ibid., p. 227. Among artists, Kant particularly favors the poet: "Of all the arts *poetry* . . . maintains the first rank. It expands the mind by setting the Imagination at liberty" (*Critique of Judgment*, trans. J. H. Bernard, p. 215).

114. *Critique of Aesthetic Judgment*, p. 227.

115. Again the question of whether Carlyle read this work in the original German is unanswerable. He certainly read *The Nature of the Scholar* (see *Letters*, I, 53, and Storrs, *The Relation of Carlyle to Kant and Fichte*, pp. 83–90) and *Outlines of the Science of Knowledge* (a condensed version of the *Wissenschaftslehre*) in *The Popular Works of J. G. Fichte*, a second edition (1848) of which can still be seen in his private library.

116. Kant would have questioned the substance of this "I," saying that Fichte had confused the unity of experience with the experience of unity; that, in other words, we cannot be sensibly certain of the I as an immutable quantity (see Strawson, *The Bounds of Sense*, p. 38). For a summary of Fichte's premises, see C. C. Everett, *Science of Knowledge: A Critical Exposition* (Chicago, 1892), pp. 77–84.

117. *Science of Knowledge*, pp. 129–35. Fichte makes the same observation in Lecture II of *The Nature of the Scholar*: "Nature itself is . . . the sphere of that activity and outward expression of power in which human life eternally unfolds itself" (*Popular Works of J. G. Fichte*, I, 260). Compare *Science of Knowledge*, p. 273: "The world is the projection of human spirits and represents the stage which they have reached."

118. *Science of Knowledge*, p. 191.

119. Ibid., p. 192.

120. Ibid., p. 273.

121. *Note Books*, p. 112.

122. *Essays*, II, 24–25.

123. He writes in the same essay, "Time and Space are not external, but internal entities . . . they are mere *forms* of man's spiritual being, under which his thinking nature is constituted to act" (pp. 25–26). See also Harrold, *Carlyle and German Thought*, p. 90.

124. *Essays*, II, 26.

125. *Lectures*, p. 205.

126. *Science of Knowledge*, p. 286.

127. Epigraph opposite page one of the prefaces to Kant's *Theory of Ethics*.

128. I. Knox, *The Aesthetic Theories of Kant, Hegel, and Schopenhauer*, p. 69.

129. *Critique of Judgment*, trans. J. H. Bernard, p. 117.

130. *Essays*, II, 29.

131. See Fichte's *Vocation* and *Nature of the Scholar*, especially Lectures I–III, IX, and X, in *Popular Works*, I, 245–363. Carlyle interpreted *Gelehrte*

as a designation for all serious prose writers: "It was in Fichte's conception of the nature of the scholar . . . that Carlyle found, or thought he found, his conception of the Hero as Man of Letters" (Shine, "Carlyle and the German Philosophy Problem," p. 822).

132. *Heroes*, p. 187.

133. Harrold, *Carlyle and German Thought*, p. 192.

134. S. L. Wilson, "The Theology of Thomas Carlyle," in *The Theology of Modern Literature*, pp. 152–53.

135. Transcendentalism made possible, so Fichte said in *Science of Knowledge*, "a peace such as I never knew before"; for "if it lost the help that comes from the *a posteriori* argument, it escaped the difficulties that are involved in this . . ." (p. 8). "God is practically recognized as an ideal, and may thus be seen in absolute beauty and completeness. One can doubt His reality, and his perfection no more than one can doubt his own being" (p. 273).

136. *Frazer's Magazine* 7 (1833): 539–40.

137. According to Masson, the tranquility of the trancendentalist position was usually reasoned to in the following manner: "If the world of space, time, and history is but a fabrication of our present thinking, a phantasmagory of the present human spirit, what does it matter how much our present thinkings may change, or how many aeons of so-called time and imagined processes and marches of events we may find it necessary to throw into our phantasmagory?" (*Carlyle Personally and in His Writings*, p. 75).

138. Orthodox "religion represents . . . the Good as *infinitely* . . . different from the Evil, but sets them in a state of hostility (as in Heaven and Hell)—Art likewise admits and inculcates this quite infinite difference; but *without* hostility, with peacefulness. . . . In this way is Goethe's morality to be considered as a *higher* (apart from its comprehensiveness, nay universality) than has hitherto been promulgated" (*Note Books*, p. 204).

139. See his comments in a letter to John, 24 October 1826, *Letters*, I, 9. The four volumes appeared at the same time as his translation of *Wilhelm Meister's Travels*, i.e., January 1827.

140. For a full exposition of the transcendental elements in these essays, see below, pp. 160, 166–68, 173.

141. See especially *GR*, I, 16–17, 264–66; II, 18–19, 126–28.

142. *Letters*, I, 18.

143. "There is just one man unhappy: he who is possessed by some idea which he cannot convert into action, or still more which restrains or withdraws him from action" (excerpt from Goethe recorded by Carlyle in his journal, 7 December 1826; see Froude, *First Forty Years*, I, 384).

144. "In 1825–1826 his own doubts were settled . . . and he emerged, with Goethe and Schiller, upon an ethical and aesthetic approach to German transcendentalism" (Shine, *Unfinished History of German Literature*, p. 90).

145. *Carlyle Personally and in His Writings*, pp. 62–63.

146. At this time his meditations were those of a convinced Kantian; he condemns Herder as a materialist, Pope as a pedagogue, and says: "Yes, it is true. The decisions of reason (*Vernunft*) are superior to those of understanding (*Verstand*)" (journal entries for December 1826, in Froude, *First Forty*

Years, I, 386–87). See also Shine, *Unfinished History of German Literature*: "By 1827 . . . he had found—largely through the Germans—much of the ethical aesthetic, philosophical, religious, and historiographical insight that was to make him an important figure in his generation. The German writings, he firmly believed, had led him out of his early darkness and had literally saved his life. And missionary that Carlyle essentially was, he proceeded in his attempt to show the light to others" (p. xxiv).

147. In addition to W. S. Johnson's early study (cited below, p. 113), two recent works include criticism of Wotton: G. B. Tennyson's *Sartor Called Resartus* (1965) and A. LaValley's *Carlyle and the Idea of the Modern* (1968). Neither isolates the full range of transcendental borrowings in the novel, but, rather, concentrates on its stylistic and autobiographical elements.

148. *First Forty years,* I, 385.

149. *Wotton Reinfred,* in *Last Words of Thomas Carlyle,* ed. R. Preuss, p. 2. W. S. Johnson declares that *Wotton* is interesting "if for no other reason . . . as evidence of Carlyle's entire unfitness for fiction" (*Thomas Carlyle: A Study of His Literary Apprenticeship, 1814–1831,* p. 77).

150. *Wotton,* p. 51.

151. Ibid., p. 55.

152. Ibid., p. 59.

153. Ibid., p. 60.

154. Ibid.

155. Ibid., pp. 69–70. His companion seconds their renunciation of external happiness: "We would have a paradise of spontaneous pleasures; forgetting that in such a paradise the dullest spirit would and must grow wearied, nay, in time unspeakably wretched" (p. 68).

156. Ibid., p. 63.

157. Ibid., p. 61.

158. Ibid.

159. Carlyle was especially fond of that aspect of poetic vision; he quotes Prospero's remark that we "are such stuff as dreams are made on" on some five separate occasions in his collected essays.

160. *Wotton,* pp. 96, 98.

161. He restates the Kantian concept of time and space at the end of another long paean to the poet: "Time and space are modes not things; forms of our mind, not existences without us; the shapes in which the unseen bodies itself forth to our mortal sense; if we were not, they also would cease to be" (p. 97). See also *Essays,* II, 25–26.

162. *Wotton,* p. 98. On this point, G. B. Tennyson agrees that for the rest of Carlyle's life "poetry and German philosophy" were linked in his mind (*Sartor Called Resartus,* p. 90). Tennyson also discusses Carlyle's dismissal of systematic differences between Goethe's "open secret" and Fichte's "Divine Idea," and his insistence that the legitimate poet is he who *sees* and deciphers spiritual truth behind phenomena (pp. 91–92).

163. *Wotton,* p. 99.

164. A view that afterward prevented Carlyle from sympathizing with the

work of artists whose *Weltanschauung,* however moral, was essentially pessimistic.

165. According to a letter of 4 June 1827, he ceased work on the novel in May of that year (*Letters,* I, 62).

166. They were published mostly in *Fraser's Magazine* and the *Edinburgh, Foreign,* and *Foreign Quarterly* reviews.

167. For a more detailed discussion of the transcendental elements in these essays, see below, pp. 158–76.

168. "Historic Survey of German Poetry," *Essays,* II, 369.

169. See Carlyle's letter of December 1829 on this subject in his correspondence with Goethe (*Goethe Letters,* p. 163).

170. *Essays,* II, 370.

171. Parallels with *A Tale of a Tub* and *Tristram Shandy* suggest themselves as well.

172. Carlyle's style in *Sartor* compares closely with that of Richter: "abounding, without measure, in obscure allusions, in the most twisted phraseology; perplexed into endless entanglements and dislocations, parenthesis within parenthesis; not forgetting elisions, sudden whirls, quips, conceits and all manner of inexplicable crotchets: the whole moving on in the gayest manner, yet nowise in what seem military lines, but rather in huge, parti-coloured mob-masses" (Carlyle on Richter's style, *Essays,* II, 98).

173. As Cazamian puts it: "His imagination clothed with life the abstract conclusions of Kant, developing from the doctrine of the subjectivity of sensory images a poetic vision of the universe" (*Carlyle,* p. 35). In that sense, *Sartor* is the finished portrait for which *Wotton* was the sketch.

174. *SR,* p. 43.

175. Ibid., p. 212.

176. In a letter of December 1841, George Eliot admires the "solid, original" character of Carlyle's spirituality: "His soul is a shrine of the brightest and purest philanthropy, kindled by the coal of gratitude and devotion to the Author of all things. I should observe that he is not 'orthodox'" (*Letters,* ed. G. S. Haight, I, 123). David Masson emphasizes Carlyle's unyielding opposition to formal Christianity: see *Carlyle Personally and in His Writings,* pp. 82–83; also p. 86. Often Carlyle was patronizing in his attitude toward orthodox principles: see Espinasse, *Literary Recollections,* p. 199; and Allingham, *A Diary,* p. 217. Hugh Walker remarks as well upon Carlyle's independence of dogma, despite his being "one of the most religious men" ("The German Influence: Thomas Carlyle," p. 76). J. Tulloch speaks of the permanence and strength of Carlyle's "peculiar, personal" faith: see "Thomas Carlyle as a Religious Teacher," in *Movements of Religious Thought in Britain,* p. 202.

177. Espinasse, *Literary Recollections,* p. 196.

178. See Allingham, *A Diary,* pp. 203, 256, 264, 273. On the question of the maintenance of his beliefs, Cazamian concludes that Carlyle "always conceived of [the German idealists] primarily as transcendentalists, as men whose reflection bore upon the supreme realities, transcending the field of sensible appearances. The transcendental movement . . . was to be the constant rhythm of his thinking, the scheme of his doctrine" (*Carlyle,* p. 105).

179. Despite Froude's temperamental opposition to mysticism, even he grudgingly agrees that this was the case with Carlyle (H. Paul, *The Life of Froude*, p. 293). Hugh Walker sees Carlyle's reliance on transcendentalism in the same light and sets it in contrast to Coleridge's: "Carlyle valued German idealism because he found in it the basis of a religion still possible to men of the nineteenth century . . . while Coleridge uses the distinction [between *Verstand* and *Vernunft*] to bring back by an intellectual jugglery an impossible past, Carlyle uses it to build up a new world out of the ruins of the old" ("The German Influence: Thomas Carlyle," p. 43).

180. *SR*, p. 182.

181. Shakespeare's *Tempest* and Goethe's *Faust* seemed to him to convey best this mystery (*SR*, pp. 212–14). For a time at least, Carlyle appears to have enjoyed his own reputation as a mystic. He wrote to Eckerman in December 1828: "I mean to write on Novalis, and not in the style of mockery, but in the true 'mystic vein' which is thought to be peculiar to me. For you must know that I pass here generally enough for a "Mystic' or man half-drowned in the abysses of German speculation: which, considering everything, is all, in my opinion, exactly as it should be" (*New Letters of Thomas Carlyle to Eckermann*, ed. W. Speck, pp. 4–5).

182. "The Germany of Kant, Fichte and Goethe . . . and the mighty stream of philosophical doctrine upon which these masters launched Carlyle, in giving a new depth to his ideas, gave a new depth to the intellectual life of England, and brought about one of the principal transitions in the history of British thought" (Cazamian, *Carlyle*, p. 55).

183. In 1835, three years before the British hard-cover edition appeared.

184. Carlyle himself believed that "Emerson had, in the first instance, taken his system out of 'Sartor' and others of my writings, but he worked it out in a way of his own" (Duffy, *Conversations with Carlyle*, p. 93). In Emerson's case, Platonic and Christian antecedents (imperfect actuality, the deceitfulness of this world, and so on) have also to be considered. Consult the appendix for a comparison of the essay "Nature" and *Sartor*.

185. See F. Roe, *Victorian Prose*, p. 3. With more humor than Froude, Whitman also blames most of Carlyle's contrariety on dyspepsia: It "is to be traced in every page, and now and then fills the page . . . behind the tally of genius and morals stands the stomach, and gives a sort of casting vote" ("Death of Carlyle," in *Essays from the Critic*, p. 32).

186. R. L. Nettleship, *Memoir of T. H. Green*, pp. 25–26.

187. "Ralph Waldo Emerson," in *Brief Literary Criticisms*, pp. 238–39. On the question of his impact and popularity, David Masson remarks: "In and from 1840 Carlyle's name was running like wildfire through the British Islands and through English-speaking America: there was the utmost avidity for his books especially among the young men; phrases from them were in all the younger men's mouths and were affecting the public speech" (*Carlyle Personally and in His Writings*, p. 67). With his successful adaptation of German idealism, he appeared to his readers to have "knocked out his window from the blind wall of his century" (R. H. Horne, quoted in K. Tillotson, *Novels of the Eighteen Forties*, p. 151).

188. *Essays of George Eliot*, pp. 213–14. High praise indeed from a woman who knew full well that Carlyle refused, categorically, to read her novels. Ac-

cording to a letter from Mary Sibree, Miss Eliot's own religious position in
1843 had been partly determined by Carlyle's teachings: "She . . . seemed to
be leaning to the doctrine of Carlyle and Emerson when she remarked that
she . . . considered herself a revelation of the mind of the Deity" (*Letters*, I,
162n). Another letter—from Miss Eliot to Harriet Beecher Stowe in July 1869
—indicates her belief in Goethe's "open secret" (*Letters*, V, 49).

189. *Essays, Theological and Philosophical*, I, 393.

190. *Essays*, I, 338. See also Neff on Carlyle as one of the two poles of nineteenth-century thought (*Carlyle and Mill*, pp. 184–200).

191. Walker, "The German Influence: Thomas Carlyle," p. 49.

192. See letter of 20 July 1827 in *Goethe Letters*, p. 263.

193. See letter from Eckermann of 6 December 1830 and Carlyle's reply
of 22 January 1831, in which he states his intention to translate *Faust* (*Goethe
Letters*, p. 108). Also discussed in *New Letters of Thomas Carlyle to Eckermann*. This later edition includes Carlyle's letter of 6 May 1834, in which he
tells Eckermann that he can no longer consider such a feat of translation
among his literary plans (p. 9).

194. See his *Punch* review of 1850 and his criticism of the *French Revolution* in the *Times* for August 1837, as quoted in K. Tillotson's *Novels of the
Eighteen Forties*, pp. 79n, 153n. Carlyle found Thackeray's novels, particularly
Vanity Fair, far less pleasant reading than Dickens's: Amy Cruse, in her
valuable study *The Victorians and Their Books*, pp. 261–62, paints an
amusing picture of Carlyle's reaction to the "terrible cynicism" of *Vanity Fair*.

195. Mrs. Tillotson remarks: "He considered it 'indispensable' to try out
The Chimes on Carlyle before publication, dedicated *Hard Times* to him,
and long before he wrote *Tale of Two Cities* was reading 'that wonderful
book,' *The French Revolution*, 'for the 500th time' " (*Novels of the Eighteen
Forties*, p. 153).

196. For Browning's comments on the death of Carlyle, see entry for March
1881, in Allingham, *A Diary*, pp. 310–11.

197. The plaque still hangs on the wall of Carlyle's attic study in Cheyne
Row. His popularity among writers of fiction is not so inexplicable as it may
seem. Despite occasional contemporary charges of "didacticism," Mrs. Tillotson concludes that Carlyle's insistence upon the religious orientation of
literature was welcomed by most serious-minded novelists: "The 'novel
proper' as distinct from the novel as the product of an 'amusement-industry'
was helped by Carlyle to a status in literature and life which it has hardly
lost" (*Novels of the Eighteen Forties*, p. 156). Partly because of Carlyle,
novelists were once more led to acknowledge religion "as a powerful element
in all life—in art, in speculation, in every intellectual growth. . . . Many saw
that no human product, least of all literature, can be divorced from religion"
(J. Tulloch, *Movement of Religious Thought in Britain*, pp. 194–95).

198. *Life and Letters of Leslie Stephen*, ed. F. W. Maitland, p. 231.

199. *Carlyle*, pp. 285–86.

200. Harriet Martineau, *Autobiography*, I, 387.

201. Letter of 1 October 1833, in Froude, *First Forty Years*, I, 385–86.

Chapter Four

Puritan Reaction

> Idealism can be talked and even
> felt; it cannot be lived.—C. S.
> Lewis

Without question, transcenden-
tal doctrine encouraged Carlyle's trust in the power of an aesthet-
ically based morality. The positive influence of Kant and Goethe
figured as strongly in a comment he made to Espinasse in 1868 as
it had in the early German essays: "[Carlyle] talked to me of the
ultimate supremacy of the beautiful. . . . In time, he prophesied,
beauty would be all-in-all." In later life he remembered, with particular affection, his association with the writers of German romance: "Those were among my happiest hours spent in the
company of poetic, genial men."[1] Not surprisingly, such sentiments won Carlyle the friendship and respect of the contemporary
reading public. As late as 1885, one critic, unconscious of any hy-
perbole, declared Carlyle to be "the venerated Patriarch of British
Literature, an acknowledged sovereign among the British men of
letters."[2]

Yet in spite of his professions of benevolent aestheticism—which
naturally ingratiated him among the *literati*—Carlyle was often
vilified by writers and poets. Swinburne, after a visit to Cheyne
Row, remembered only "the dung-dropping mouth of Carlyle."[3]

The Sage of Chelsea seemed, to men with an ear for consonance and harmony, to be at best an "inarticulate poet"; at worst, "a virulent old sophist."[4] According to Allingham, Tennyson was frequently put off by Carlyle's disdainful opinion of poets: "[He] said he had read part of Carlyle's *Frederick* till he came to, '*they did not strive to build the lofty rhyme*,' and then flung the book into a corner. . . . [Tennyson] referred to Carlyle's contemptuous way of speaking of poets, saying, 'We are all tadpoles in a pool, one a little larger or smaller than others.' "[5] Goldwin Smith remembered him only as crabbed and peevish, without any of the sympathy or mildness that idealism should have fostered in his views: "Carlyle . . . was a universal cynic; he criticized everything and everybody, he criticized a person for taking up a certain position, he criticized him for changing it."[6] Dr. Garth Wilkinson, in a letter of February 1850 to Henry James, Sr., repudiates Carlyle's behavior with as much vehemence:

> Carlyle came up here on Monday. . . . He was suffering dreadfully from malaise and indigestion and gave with his usual force his usual putrid theory of the universe. All great men were miserable; the day on which any man could say he was not miserable, that day he was a scoundrel. . . . All this was interpolated with convulsive laughter, showing that joy would come in to him were it even by the path of hysteria and disease. To me he is an unprofitable man, and though he gave me a kind invitation, I have too much respect for my stomach to go much into his company. . . . By the next boat I will endeavor to send you over my thoughts on his recent pamphlet, the first of a series of Latter-Day-Tracts. He is very rapidly falling out with all his present admirers, for which I like them all the better.[7]

Harriet Martineau was baffled by the paradox of his restiveness: he was "the most woeful complainer while glorifying fortitude,— the most uncertain and gloomy in mood, while holding forth serenity as the greatest good within the reach of Man."[8] To Leslie

Stephen, Carlyle's advice seemed a strange mixture of sublimity and irrationality: "I see the prophet pretty often myself, and . . . I am almost equally repelled and attracted by him . . . he talks a good deal of arrant and rather pestilent nonsense."[9] After listening to one of Carlyle's blustering diatribes, in which he had reviled Keats for "wanting a world of treacle,"[10] and Keats's achievements as "fricassee of dead-dog,"[11] Allingham concluded sadly that "His is the least judicial of minds. . . . If equanimity be the mark of a Philosopher, he is, of all great-minded men, the least of a Philosopher."[12] Allingham was sufficiently unnerved by the frequency of these splenetic outbursts to speak of him elsewhere as "Carlylus Tyrannus."[13] Espinasse, too, found Carlyle's antagonism toward the arts out of keeping with his literary orientation: "Against metre and fiction he waged perpetual war, although Goethe had been a poet, dramatist and novelist, Schiller a poet and dramatist much more than a historian, and Jean Paul, from first to last, a writer of fiction chiefly."[14] To this same friend and observer, Carlyle's imprecations against poetry seemed not only rash, they were symptoms of an ungenerous spirit. Despite his charitable pretensions, Carlyle continually displayed "an antiphilanthropic temper of mind."[15]

Clearly then, against the current of transcendental optimism in Carlyle's character, there ran an equally forceful stream of virulence and melancholy that seems to have dictated his antipathy toward literature. David Masson recalls that "strange constitutional grimness and gloominess of his through all the external changes of his life,"[16] and Emerson, distressed on a second visit to England by "Carlyle's vehement denunciations of authorship,"[17] notes as "depressing any spiritual influence that Carlyle exerted on those who sat at his feet."[18] As early as 1843, in a review of *Past and Present*, Emerson spoke of its author as a "sick giant."[19] In an aside to Emerson at their 1848 meeting, Carlyle admitted the extent of his disillusionment when he described his "feeling towards his fellow men as 'abhorrence mingled with pity.' "[20] How does one explain such a carping, intolerant strain in Carlyle's thought? In Chapter Two, we considered and discarded a number of possible sources for what in Carlyle amounted, at times, to outright misanthropy. The only credible suggestion left in abeyance was that of a religious dilemma. Touching on that neglected possibility, at least one of his critics has declared it to be the source of Carlyle's gloomy temperament: his "melancholy, even in its fiercest rages and paroxysms . . . was essentially a religious melancholy, touching the metaphysical on all sides."[21] If such is indeed the case, the question next arises, What sort of religious creed to which Carlyle was exposed might have exerted so "depressing" a spiritual influence on his view of literature and the world?

Calvinism, most of his biographers suggest, or Knoxian Puritanism, quickened Carlyle's intemperate dislikes. Even though he lost his childhood belief in the literal truth of the Bible and the miraculous theology of Christianity, Carlyle apparently retained until death the instincts and prejudices that accompany and reinforce the dogmas of the Scottish Puritan. Cazamian sees his religious development as at least in part retrogressive:

> The march of his mind brought Carlyle far beyond the precise particulars of his parents' faith; but the impress of their spirit was never effaced from his. . . . The shape and quality of his moral being, if not all of its traits, were those of Scottish Puritanism. . . . The influences which engraved the deepest marks upon his spirit were those of his childhood, the home in which he grew up, the severe, peculiar ways of his parents, the temper of life in his native village.[22]

Froude says that Carlyle's religion was simply "Calvinism without the theology,"[23] and Frederick Harrison, with something less than compassion, elaborates on that definition: "Discarding the creed, the practice, and the language of Puritanism, Carlyle still retains its narrowness, its self-righteousness, its intolerance, and its savagery."[24] One twentieth-century critic goes so far as to assert that "no one familiar with the character of the two men will doubt that John Knox had much to do with the shaping of Carlyle."[25]

Allingham implies that Carlyle's excoriations were not so much the result of Puritanism alone, as of the tension between that inbred faith and the more sophisticated world-view that his intellect had led him to adopt: "Carlyle's Scottish dogmatic breeding . . . was burned and branded into his youthful conscience and imagination—It could not be made to fit in with facts—Hence, what sufferings! what rages! He was contemptuous to those who held to Christian dogmas; he was angry with those who gave them up."[26] A similar idea about the inner conflict of religious sentiments seems to operate behind Masson's verdict: "the real misery, so far as there was misery, was wholly of internal origin. It was the fretting of such a sword in such a scabbard . . . it was that 'rall mental awgony in my ain inside' about which Carlyle and his wife used to jest with each other to the last as his sole incurable ailment."[27] Clearly, most of his contemporaries agreed that Calvinist prejudices contributed as much to Carlyle's outlook as transcendentalism had, and some even suggested this early training was the source of his intermittent quarrel with literary values. A dialogue between Tennyson and Allingham on James Carlyle's view of literature represents that attitude fairly: "A: 'Carlyle declares his father was the strongest-minded man he knew, yet he would admit no poetry into his house. . . . Nor fiction of any sort.' T: 'There he was wrong. But I suppose he was an old Puritan.'"[28] Cazamian, too, adheres to this popular assumption of hostility between Carlyle's Calvinism and his dedication to literature: "despite his sense of the beautiful . . . his Puritanism was too insurgent against the sacred sensuousness of art."[29]

It is possible then, in view of these critical asseverations, that in the doctrines and temper of Calvinist Scotland, we may find the prime source for Carlyle's contemptuous opinion of literature. Let us therefore proceed with what none of his critics and biographers have undertaken, namely, an analysis at close range, of those principles set out in Calvin, Knox, and the mainstream of Puritan preaching that may have—through the authority of his father—colored Carlyle's view of the arts.

No belief figures more prominently in Calvin's *Institutes of the Christian Religion* than the doctrine of original sin. Other Christian sects, following Saint Augustine's example, incorporate the concept in their theologies, but none give it the critical emphasis of Calvin. For him, it is *the* crucial event in the history of mankind—far more significant, in fact, than the incarnation of the Son of God. The single inescapable fact about man as he sees him is the corruption he has inherited from Adam; each of us is necessarily tainted, as it were, to his very boot-soles with evil:

> Every descendent . . . from the impure source is born infected with the contagion of sin; and even before we behold the Light of life, we are in the sight of God defiled and polluted. . . . From a putrefied root . . . have sprung putrid branches. . . . Original sin, therefore, appears to be an hereditary pravity and corruption of our nature, diffused through all the parts of the soul, rendering us obnoxious to the Divine wrath. . . . [Adam] involved us in guilt.[30]

Much of the gloom and pessimism that attached itself to later generations of Puritans arises here, in Calvin's sense of the omnipresence of evil. But Calvin is not satisfied with an acknowledgement of the darker side of man's nature; he is personally convinced that, of our own accord, we are incapable of behaving virtuously; that, in effect, we are totally depraved: "Man, having been corrupted by his fall, sins voluntarily, not with reluctance or restraint . . . with the strongest propensity of disposition, not with violent coercion . . . such is the pravity of his nature, that he cannot be excited and biased to anything but what is evil."[31] Unlike Kant, who sees our salvation in the desire for good, Calvin denies to man even the wish to act rightly: "The will . . . is fettered by depraved and inordinate desires, so that it cannot aspire after anything that is good."[32] Thus, because of the permanence of sin and our total impotence in the accomplishment of divine truth, we ought to mistrust all our affections—even what we take to be genuine reverence or moral striving. Poets and philosophers who mar-

vel that man is "in apprehension . . . like a god," have forgotten
what is crucial and obvious to the radical Christian; namely, the
inherent weakness of every human soul. We cannot, by any sublime insights or energy of will, partake of divine glory; considered
as individual intelligences, we are under contract to the devil.

It follows naturally from such a conviction of human depravity
that Calvin would counsel his brethren to deny the self in all its
manifestations, whether internal or external: "We are not our
own; therefore neither our reason nor our will should predomi-
nate in our deliberations and actions . . . therefore let us, as far
as possible, forget ourselves and all things that are ours."[33] In so
far as Calvin admonishes man to deemphasize the value of his material possessions, transcendentalists would have shared his view;
but the Genevan reformer carries his asceticism beyond the self
as an object, to a renunciation of the inner self as thinking being.
Introspection for the purpose of cultivating the moral and aesthetic faculties is to Calvin fruitless and perhaps blasphemous;
there is but one legitimate excuse for self-examination, one reason for considering our own consciousness, and that is to quicken
our "due sense" of personal unworthiness and sin:

> We should contemplate our miserable condition since the
> fall of Adam, the sense of which tends to destroy all boast-
> ing and confidence, to overwhelm us with shame. . . . The
> truth of God directs us to seek in the examination of our-
> selves . . . a knowledge that will abstract us from all
> confidence in our own ability . . . and reduce us to sub-
> mission.[34]

And since he denies the existence of an indwelling divinity in
man, Calvin takes immediate issue with the pantheists of his day
(in many ways, forerunners of German idealism). The error of
these spiritual thinkers, he contends, is their ignorance of the un-
bridgeable distance between man's corrupt nature and God's perfection:

> They supposed that the soul was an emanation from the

substance of God; as though some portion of the infinite Deity had been conveyed into man. But . . . if the soul of man be an emanation from the essence of God, it will follow that the divine nature is not only mutable and subject to passions, but also to ignorance, desires, and vices of every kind. Nothing is more inconstant than man, because his soul is agitated and variously distracted by contrary notions; he frequently mistakes through ignorance; he is vanquished by some of the smallest temptations; we know that the soul is the receptacle of every kind of impurity;—all of which we must ascribe to the Divine nature, if we believe the soul to be part of the essence of God, or a secret influx of the Deity.[35]

The transcendentalist does not, of course, as Calvin claims, neglect the vagaries of human thought and behavior; but he does divide them from that inviolable part of the soul, namely, the "higher Reason" or the "mind of the supersensible." Idealists do acknowledge the existence of the "Understanding" or the "mind of the flesh," but they choose to concentrate upon what is lovely in the spirit of man; Calvin, on the other hand, convinced of the pervasiveness of sin, distrusts self-consciousness in any form whatever, and particularly when it involves an assertion of personal divinity. He would argue that to construct religious belief upon the assurances we derive from our individual consciences and imaginations is to put more faith in the corrupted mind of man than in the received word of God. Calvin is altogether intolerant of poets, pantheists, and anyone else who builds his images of God out of his private fancy:

> The office of the Spirit . . . which is promised to us, is not to feign new and unheard of revelations, or to coin a new system of doctrine, which would seduce us from the received doctrine of the Gospel, but to seal to our minds the same doctrine which the Gospel delivers. . . . [Beware] those proud fanatics, who think themselves possessed of the only valuable illumination, when, neglecting and forsaking the

Divine word, they, with equal confidence and temerity, greedily embrace every reverie which their distempered imaginations may have conceived.[36]

The exercise of man's spiritual imagination is, for Calvin, an assertion of that pride and confidence in self that the sin of Adam has made unsightly in the eyes of God.

Again, because our perceptions are clouded with evil thoughts, the world of nature affords us no intelligible clue to divine glory. Calvin agrees with the pantheist that natural phenomena are symbols of Godhead, but to the founder of Puritanism—lacking faith in the interpretive powers of man—they are insufficient signs:

> Notwithstanding the clear representations given by God in the mirror of his works . . . we derive no advantage from them. . . . Vain, therefore, is the light afforded us in the formation of the world to illustrate the glory of its Author, which, though its rays be diffused all around us, is insufficient to conduct us into the right way. . . . For as soon as a survey of the world has just shown us a deity, neglecting the true God, we set up in his stead the dreams and phantasms of our own brains; and confer on them the praise of righteousness, wisdom, goodness, and power due to him.[37]

Thus, because our natural perversity will always intervene, there is nothing of profound spiritual value to be gained by a refinement of taste or an accumulation of aesthetic experience. On the contrary, we have much to fear if we covet the unencumbered self-consciousness of the artist.

Since, of ourselves, we are blind to the manifest will and glory of God in the works of nature, Calvin argues further that man must rely wholly upon the Bible as a literal guide in matters of divine enlightenment and in the regulation of his conduct:

> The Scripture, collecting in our minds the otherwise confused notions of Deity, dispels the darkness, and gives us a clear view of the true God. . . . God, foreseeing the ineffi-

cacy of his manifestation of himself in the exquisite structure of the world, hath afforded the assistance of his
word. . . . We must come, I say, to the word, which contains a just and lively description of God as he appears in
his works. . . . If we deviate from it . . . we shall never
reach the goal.[38]

It is not so much Calvin's attachment to the Scriptures (which,
after all, contain a good deal of poetry) that prejudiced his followers against the generality of imaginative literature, as it is his belief in their exclusive and literal truth.

Another corollary of this allegiance to the Bible removes the
dogmatic Puritan one step farther from the sentiments of the
literary artist. Because of Calvin's preoccupation with man's unworthiness, he tended to emphasize the Old Testament stories of
punishment, fear, and obedience rather than the milder, more
compassionate lessons of Christ. Theoretically, of course, the God
of the Puritans is to be loved as well as feared: "Our knowledge
of God should rather tend, first, to teach us fear and reverence. . . . The nature of pure and genuine religion . . . consists
in faith, united with a serious fear of God."[39] But the fact of our
sinfulness convinces Calvin that the uncomfortable emotions of
guilt and terror are more acceptable to an outraged Deity than
the complacency of love:

> We represent repentance as proceeding from a serious fear
> of God. For before the mind of a sinner can be inclined to
> repentance, it must be excited by a knowledge of the Divine
> Judgment. . . . Fear denotes that trepidation with which
> our minds are penetrated whenever we reflect upon our de-
> merits, and on the terrible severity of the Divine wrath
> against sinners.[40]

The Calvinist God enters most often into the affairs of men to
punish their wickedness or to try their faith; seldom, if ever, can
one expect His reassurance or the blessing of a tranquil life. We

should, in fact, welcome a world of torment and struggle, since it illustrates the immanence of God and the unsettled destiny of our spirit:

> The Lord, by continual lessons of miseries, teaches his children the vanity of the present life, that they may not promise themselves profound and secure peace in it . . . frequently disquieted and infested with tumults. . . . We learn that this life, considered in itself, is . . . adulterated with a mixture of many evils; and in consequence of this at once conclude, that nothing can be sought or expected on earth but conflict.[41]

This endless battle is undoubtedly a moral one, a war of good and evil forces, and a lesson can be read from the conclusion of each skirmish, however unjust the result may appear: if, for example, the Philistines are defeated, God's justice has carried the day; if the soldiers of the true faith have fallen, the Lord has punished their halfheartedness. There is always, for the Calvinist, a literal meaning in the face of events, a reenactment in modern history and the present age of those righteous wars and clear judgments of the Old Testament. Unlike the transcendentalist, who is content to contemplate the "weak glances" into the supersensible that the beauty of nature and his own imagination afford him, the Puritan is an active moralist, spurred on by his guilt and his fear of the terrible vengeance of God. In this sense he is profoundly Hebraic; that is, he prefers, as Matthew Arnold says, "doing to thinking."[42] And because his faith stems from the doctrine of original sin rather than any gentler or more positive persuasion, Calvin himself believes the surest way to serve God is to expose and vilify the wickedness of man: "Every one should study to admonish his brother, whenever occasion shall require. . . . [And] it is the duty of the Church, on the occasion of any notorious scandal, immediately to summon the offender, and to punish him in proportion to his crime."[43] Most of Calvin's disciples unfortunately understood him to mean that "it is the main business of our lives to hate and oppose."[44] Hence the severity of utterance and the studied strictness of conduct in Calvinist communities.

Finally, the antinomian doctrine of election, set out in the *Institutes of the Christian Religion,* enforced the Hebraic temper of Puritanism. Already favoring an active, blindly obedient worship of God and disavowing the reflective approach of idealists and poets, the followers of Calvin and Knox were bolstered in their mindless toiling after righteousness by the concept of predestination. God, they were taught to believe, had elected certain of their brethren to everlasting life, but upon a basis so arbitrary and so incomprehensible to man that their "distempered imaginations" could not hope to find the key. Thus did election by grace contrive to double man's sense of awe, "true humilitie" and submission before the will of his Creator. As Knox said in a defense of predestination: "No other doctrine maketh man carefull to obey God according to his commandement, but that doctrine only which so spoileth man of all power and vertue, that no portion of his salvation consisteth within himself."[45] It served, then, as a further justification for that radical asceticism which makes Calvinism so hostile to the arts. But what of the Hebraic principle of work and action as the central fact of Puritan life? Superficially, it appears that predestination freed man from the necessity of good works; but in fact, it has the opposite effect on Calvin's disciples. According to the formulators of the doctrine, those who are the elect of God give evidence of their salvation in the performance of good works, and those who are damned exhibit their unholiness in their idleness and disobedience of Scriptural commands: "After man be made just by Faith, and possesseth Jesus Christ in his hart, then can he not be idle. For with true Faith is also given the Holie Spirite, which suffereth not man to be idle, but moveth him to al godly exercise of good workes."[46] Thus the industry of the Puritan in the service of his God, although it could not, of itself, save him, was nonetheless the surest sign of his having been saved.[47]

From this brief look at the *Institutes,* it is obvious that Calvin deduced a set of principles diametrically opposed to the aesthetic and literary values of religious idealism: he condemns man, his imagination, and every manifestation of self-consciousness; he belittles the revelatory power of natural beauty; he distrusts passivity, reflection, contentment, and spiritual joy, believing instead that "the life of man is a perpetual batell upon earth," in which we are best employed in censuring sin, reading Scripture, obeying without question the authorities that God has set up over us, and renewing daily our sense of personal guilt in the suffering and conflict that plague the world.

As these precepts came out of sixteenth-century Geneva, they were already such as would discourage a follower from attendance upon contemporary literature, but through the vigorous expansion of Calvin's severe principles in John Knox's ministry, generations of Puritans, particularly in Scotland, took an increasingly sour view of the uses of the imagination. For a number of reasons, an analysis of the character and writings of Knox should help us to understand important aspects of Carlyle's make-up: first of all, because Knox established the temper of that Scottish Calvinism in which Carlyle was exclusively schooled until the age of fourteen; second, because Carlyle often wrote of him as the heroic ideal of priesthood and the saviour of Scotland;[48] third, because many of Carlyle's biographers have suggested strong parallels between the natures of the two men.

Knox embraced, unquestioningly, the doctrine of man's depravity and meanness: "Of nature we ar so dead, so blynd and so perverse, that neather can we feill when we are pricked, see the lycht when it schynes, nor assent to the will of God when it is reveilled. . . . Of our selves we ar nott sufficient to think ane good thought."[49] And because he believed so strongly in the corruptibility of men's minds, Knox became an active opponent of individualism in religion, whether pantheistic, Anabaptist, or Catholic. Only Calvinism, he said, was founded on the objective commandments of God; all others were tricks of Satan to flatter our vanity. The Anabaptist and even the Lutheran—certainly the

artist—were guilty in Knox's eyes of "fylthy lustes" and "insatiable
covetousnes" since they relied on their own consciences and spiritual aspirations for a revelation of God's truth: "Many maketh an
idoll of thair owne wisdome or fantasye: more trusting to that
which thay thinke good, nor unto God, who plainly sayeth, not
that things which seameth good in thy eyes, do unto thy God, but
what thy Lord hath commanded."[50] Thus Knox, like Calvin, en-
joined men to act and to obey rather than to think; to suppress their
personal visions and self-consciousness, since "All wirschipping,
honoring, or service inventit by the braine of man in the religioun
of God, without his own express commandment, is Idolatrie."[51]
There was, of course, no more contemptible sin in Knox's lexicon
than "idolatrie"; against every branch of the "false Kirk" built on
men's "vain imaginations" the Scottish Reformer directed his
wrath. As Carlyle says in an 1875 essay, Knox manifested "complete incompatibility with whatever is false in word or conduct;
inexorable contempt and detestation of what in modern speech is
called *humbug*."[52] Knox's energies, more than Calvin's, were of
the destructive, denunciatory sort; he advocated not only obedience and hard work but warfare and iconoclasm, believing that
"whenever God put the sword into the hands of His elect, they
were bound to punish enormities."[53] He trusted to the "efficacy
of true hatred," condemning "all honoring of God not contained
in his holie Word,"[54] especially that worship which relied, for its
insights, upon the sensual beauties of nature. Unlike Calvin, who
merely found the aesthetic experience "insufficient," Knox warned
that "Sathan" tries to ravish our senses "with gazing upon the
visible creatures."[55] Our consciousness of beauty in the objects of
this world, so vital to poets and transcendentalists, represented to
Knox but another evidence of our corruption. The "aesthetic
sense" was no more than a weapon of idolaters, a tool of those
"conjured ennemys of veritie"[56] who smother the voice of God
under painted vestments, statuary, and stained glass. Knox clearly
included the sensual imaginings of the artist in his indictment of
Catholic "harlotrie" and Anglican complacency:

> The Word of God plainlie speikis, that gif a man sall heir
> the curses of Godis Law, and yet, into his heart, shall prom-
> eis to himself felicitie and gude luck, thinking that he sall
> haif peace, albeit he walk after the imaginationis of his awn
> will and heart; to sic a man the Lord will not be mercifull,
> but his wrath sal be kendellit againis him, and he sall dis-
> troy his name from under Heaven.[57]

Like Calvin, Knox disparaged not only self-consciousness but the
temperamental equanimity of men unacquainted with the gravity
of their sins.

Further, Knox's assurances of the divine presence were in no
way symbolic, "mystical," or fantastic, but rather, he believed,
preeminently empirical. Scriptural law and the very *facts* of the
world demanded that he approach life as a conflict of moral forces,
an actual struggle for righteousness in which much that is practically efficacious should be done and much that is speculative and
useless should be abjured. The Puritan's world is not one
of "hieroglyphs" or "appearances" but one of common, obvious
truths: "The factis of men aggrie with the law of God."[58] Divine
justice is acted out in the history of man in simple, intelligible
events. Knox, for example, read the will of God into the defeat
of Scottish Catholics by an army of outnumbered English protes-
tants: "Agane we say, that such as in that sudden dejectioun behold-
is not the hand of God, fighting against pride, for freedom of his
awin litill flock, unjustly persecutted, does willingly and mali-
tiouslie obscure the glorie of God."[59] In such a way does Calvinism
promote a literal, commonsensical view of political history and
daily life.

For the Scots, this spare, practical faith fitted well with the
rigors of their native clime. As one ungentle critic of Puritanism
puts it: "These stiff and austere people were attracted by the stiff
and austere character of the creed, and their character was made
thereby still more stiff and austere by being confirmed in its natural bent."[60] Knox plainly imprinted on Calvinism the dour, rude,
unmusical, even savage qualities of his race. But he was much more

than a man impatient of decoration and fancy, prophesying doom to "craftie flatterers" and "pestilent prelattis": he believed in active resistance to false authority. On the question of conscience versus obedience, he fell out with Calvin, maintaining that it is more righteous to overcome an idolatrous ruler than, by submission to tyranny, to expiate our racial guilt. Knox argued that the "power of spiritual hatred" ought to be vented, in open warfare, against "the accursed kingdome of that Romane Antichrist."[61] It is Knox, rather than Calvin, who is responsible for the image of the Puritan as a zealous "soldier of God," intolerant of every vanity; it is the spirit of Knox that inspired the tumults and fanaticism of the Cromwellian period.[62] Finally, as a man dedicated to censure and to furious activity, it is ironically characteristic of Knox that, at his death, he should confess his own chief failings to be "lacke of fervencye in reproving synne . . . and lacke of diligence in the execution of myne office."[63]

From the preceding picture of Calvin's hostility toward the works of the imagination, Knox's exclusive sympathy with practical reforms in church and state, and the overriding pessimism of both men, it seems reasonable to conclude that Carlyle's intermittent outbursts against literature might have had their origin in the temper of his native Puritanism. For confirmation, let us look first at a cross-section of orthodox opinions of literature written in Scotland and England during the years of Carlyle's childhood. These reflect the continued currency of Puritan principles among protestant critics of the early nineteenth century and give us a clue to the climate of thought in which James Carlyle raised his eldest son.

Some of these latter-day Calvinists raised the old cry that "novels exalt imagination at the expense of judgment," others that they "idealize" life, replacing the hard truths of error and sin with "transport, rapture, bliss and ecstatic joy."[64] One Edinburgh critic, writing in 1805, spoke condescendingly of poetry as "an elegant and charming amusement. . . . But, for influencing the active principles, for guiding our conduct in the ordinary affairs of life, it does not seem so very well suited."[65] One is reminded of Cotton Mather's view of poetry as *"Sauce* rather than *Food,"* as "a little Recreation . . . in the midst of more painful Studies."[66] Puritan critics of the nineteenth century continued to disparage the works of the imagination for their "vicious doctrine of goodness of heart,"[67] their "fantastic and visionary speculations," and their tendency to ignore "duty, justice, prudence and economy . . . in behalf of love, generosity, benevolence, and compassion."[68] The recurrent fear of vanity and self-assertion underlay much of the orthodox Scotsman's opposition; his Calvinist instincts assured him that exposure to fictions rendered the reader "dissatisfied with that more humble station which Providence has assigned him."[69] But of all the necessary virtues the nineteenth-century Puritan saw literature working against, none figured so strongly in his criticism as the simple urge for action, duty, and obedience. Again and again, his Hebraic temper balked at the passivity and impracticality of the artists' world: writing "ought not to be of a romantic or visionary nature. It must be adapted to the actual conditions of human life, and such as . . . is capable of being reduced to practice";[70] the novel consumes "time that might be given to more useful reading or to serious exercise";[71] the benevolence that literature promotes "has been stigmatized rightly, as rather an indolent kind of sympathy, not much to be depended on when any vigorous exertion is required";[72] "those who jog on the plain paths of duty have little need for the heroics of fiction";[73] "Sensation, not action, is the natural state [of literary heroes]. They are governed chiefly by occasional and transient impulses, and incapable of that regular and consistent system of conduct which can alone render a man respectable and useful."[74] It appears, then, that even more than the doctrines of depravity, self-denial, suffering, and silence, the work-ethic of the radical Protestant—that desire for a "regular and consistent system of conduct"—interposes itself between the dogmatic Puritan mind and the spirit of literature.

Yet in order to justify the claim that Calvinist standards dictated the negative pull in Carlyle's ambivalent view of the arts, we must show further that such prejudices were indeed impressed upon him as a child, and that they recurred in his writing at every stage of his development.

The best, and certainly the most authoritative account we have of Carlyle's earliest years is that which he himself has provided in *Reminiscences*. There appears there a sketch of his father (written at the time of James's funeral in 1832) that gives us an adequate picture of the temper of family life in the Ecclefechan environment of Carlyle's youth.[75] Apparently, much of the pessimism and intolerance that animated Knox's pronouncements had found its way into the personality of the Carlyle clan: Thomas's grandfather "did not drink, but his stroke was ever as ready as his word. . . . He was a fiery man, irascible, indomitable";[76] his father had from an early age displayed a predilection for violence and for caustic invective;[77] one old man of the village, in an interview with Espinasse, recalled with distaste the behaviour of the Carlyles: "There was not the like o' them. Pithy, bitter-speaking bodies, and awfu' fighters."[78] In this fanatical, reforming spirit of his father's family, rooted as it was in the Calvinist preoccupation with sin, lies an obvious source for Carlyle's virulence. That "cynical," "gloomy," "anti-philanthropic," "injudicious" mood which for so many years embarrassed Carlyle's literary friends was surely a legacy from the Scotland of Knox. Carlyle had been taught from an early age to respect the efficacy of hatred, righteously directed; for despite the fact that his father was "choleric and we all dreaded his wrath," his indignation nevertheless appeared to be "grounded on the sense of right and in resistance to wrong . . . rending asunder official sophisms."[79] Like most children of Puritan parentage, Carlyle learned to look at life as a kind of endless moral warfare and to accept the zeal and outrage of his father as but one aspect of that battle. For the rest of his life, Carlyle himself often acted as though the reproving of sin and the denunciation of "shams" and "un-verities" were more of a virtue than the delineation and promotion of the beautiful.

At least it would seem he scorned Aristotelian decorum and

Virgilian sonorities in the manner of his writing. This is not the place, while discussing the sources of Carlyle's literary ideology, for a close study of his stylistic models, yet his father's rough-cut Burgher diction was clearly a principal influence. Surely the sudden, arhythmic explosions of contumely, the unexpected clusters of morbid imagery, the spasms of dissonance and vituperation that flame out with such dark fire from the continuum of Carlyle's prose owe as much to the Puritan preference for excited, unlovely speech as to the Rabelaisian eccentricities of Richter.[80]

James Carlyle represented to his son a number of other Calvinist ideals of conduct, especially those that encouraged the habit of material self-denial: "He was thrifty, Spartan . . . abstemious"; "Frugality and assiduity, a certain grave composure, an earnestness . . . were the order of our household."[81] And since Carlyle's father believed primarily in the God of the Old Testament, he naturally attached more significance to the masculine precepts of command and obedience than to the feminine instincts of love and forgiveness. As Carlyle remembers it, his childhood was "wholesome" rather than "joyful," for "an inflexible element of authority surrounded us all."[82] The Hebrew deity, embodied in Carlyle's father, asked but one thing of His earthly children: unquestioning labor in the service of His will. Again and again, work, in the sense of physical action, was offered to Carlyle as the only good: "as a man wholly for action . . . [my father] admired [us] for our 'activity,' our practical valour and skill";[83] "we were particularly taught that work . . . was the only thing we had to do";[84] "food and all else were simply and solely there as the means *for doing work*."[85] As far as James Carlyle was concerned, any other indulgence—of the speaking or writing talents especially—was mere self-consciousness and therefore, by Calvinist lights, vanity. Perhaps because of the Puritan tendency to think in terms of moral contrasts, Carlyle's father condemned unequivocally whatever appeared to distract men from their practical duties. Like many Calvinists before him, he believed that his words should be "wary and few," as became the humble and guilty creature of an outraged

God. According to Carlyle, his father's policy in this regard amounted almost to a gospel of silence; "he had the most entire and open contempt for all idle tattle; what he called clatter"; "he behaved with prudent resolution, not like a vain braggart but like a practically brave man . . . I must admire now his silence. . . . He spoke nothing . . . except only what had practical meaning in it, and in a practical tone. . . . [He was] there not to talk, but to work."[86] And at the same time the young Carlyle was being trained to avoid "flourishes of Rhetoricke," he was also learning to cultivate his common sense. As Puritans, James and Margaret Carlyle had accepted the Bible and the world in literal terms—the facts of sin, punishment, and struggle left them no choice.[87] Their son, in consequence, was taught to suspect those uncommon worlds of fancy or appearance, such as the literary artist or the speculative philosopher devised. His father put it simply: "Man was created to work—not to speculate, or feel, or dream."[88]

In Carlyle's recollections of his childhood, as in the sources of Puritanism itself, we are presented with repeated examples of Calvinist hostility toward the products of the imagination. During the whole of his early life, Carlyle learned nothing of poetry or fiction from his father.[89] As he confessed to Allingham in 1876: "I never heard of Shakespeare there: my father never, I believe, read a word of him in his life."[90] James Carlyle even denied himself and his family any acquaintance with the songs of Burns, although the poet had once been his neighbor. In discussing the differences between these two Scotsmen, Carlyle again touches on that radical Hebraism in his father's nature which alienated him from the world of literature:

> He had never . . . read three pages of Burns' poems. . . .
> The poetry he liked (he did not call it poetry) was
> truth. . . . Burns had an infinitely wider education, my fa-
> ther a far wholesomer. Besides, the one was a man of musical
> utterance; the other wholly a man of action, with speech
> subservient thereto. As a man of speculation—had culture
> ever unfolded him—he must have gone wild and desperate

as Burns, but he was a man of conduct, and work keeps all right.[91]

The whole weight of Calvinist tradition came down against the artist. Scottish Puritans had for centuries found little room in their scheme of things for painting, music, verse, or any of those arts that seemed to them only to please the "carnal appetites." James Carlyle was no exception, and his children grew up under the shadow of his prejudices: "Poetry, fiction in general, he had universally seen treated as not only idle, but false and criminal. This was the spiritual element he lived in."[92] And, we might also observe, it was the spiritual element in which his oldest son lived for fourteen years.

I should qualify, if only slightly, this indictment of Calvinist doctrine as the culprit in Carlyle's schizophrenic view of literature. The prejudices he inherited from his father were in part those of the peasant class in Scotland, regardless of its religion. Carlyle's parents, like most Puritans, were simple people, with little education, living in a hard climate. It was thus natural, as well as spiritually fitting, that James Carlyle should be a man "singularly free from affectation" and wholeheartedly dedicated to the business of stonemasonry. That "there was little place for love and the other tenderer elements of Christianity,"[93] in the Burgher creed was as much a reflection of the lowlanders' primitive environment as a dogmatic loyalty to the precepts of Calvin. So far as literary attitudes were concerned, Puritan preachers only condemned what was already unfamiliar and suspect among the greatest part of their brethren, thereby confirming the unread in their ignorance. Scottish Calvinism offered, in many ways, a set of principles adapted to the instincts of "the plain man, unversed in literature as such and unable to grasp either intricate rhetoric . . . or complicated imagery."[94]

Be that as it may, by the time this apparently natural asceticism had affected the character of Carlyle and his parents, it had long since been overlaid by the justification of religious principle.

Carlyle understood his father's prejudices not as symptoms of ignorance or provincialism but as the necessary corollaries of a traditional faith.

In the years between 1809 and 1832, Carlyle moved gradually but firmly away from this miraculous, dogmatic theology of his parents. We have seen, in the last chapter, the way in which his intellectual and philosophical inquiries led him toward German idealism and a set of values radically different from his father's. More importantly, we have explored the significant connection between his adopted faith of transcendentalism and his advocacy of literature. Now, seeing that his native faith—based on a body of principles quite contrary to those of transcendentalism—encouraged him to vilify the arts, it is my contention that Carlyle's intermittent disparagement of literature represents a reassertion of these Calvinist prejudices. Certainly, since the evidence indicates that Carlyle maintained an ambivalent attitude toward poetry and fiction throughout the whole of his life, it is of crucial importance to trace the course of his instinctive Puritanism after 1809, and to prove that it acted as a counterweight to idealism in all his thought and writing.

There is little question that in the first ten years of his literary career Carlyle, more often than not, defended the artist as the "most perfect of modern spirit-seekers."[95] Yet even in this period of high optimism—as we have seen in chapter one—Carlyle frequently denigrated literature as a wasteful and dangerous pursuit.[96] In letters, notes, and essays written before 1832, he scorned aesthetics as "palabra," Goethe's advice as "twaddle," and literature itself as mere "babble" or the "loud clamour of Nonsense." He offsets his praise of Schiller in the *Life* with his sudden antagonism toward the "impractical," imaginative works of the German poet; his impassioned portrait of Novalis with his nagging distrust of the passivity and effeminacy of the artist; his advice to his brother to cultivate literature as "the most precious of your possessions," with his letter denouncing "all Art" as "mere Reminiscence." Clearly, despite the restorative influence of transcendental faith, and the fundamental allegiance to aesthetic experience that it demanded, Carlyle was not yet free of religious tension nor had he gained a settled view of the value of the imagination.

The Hebraic temper of his native Calvinism, I suggest, worked even here, in the first flush of creative affirmation, against the idealism he had adopted. Carlyle's first project, in 1822, was not, after all, to write a novel or poem in the vein of his German mentors but to reappraise the life and work of Oliver Cromwell. Although the scope of the research eventually forced a postponement of the history, Carlyle's notebook entries for that year indicate his eagerness to study the soldierly character of Puritan reformers. He pored over Clarendon's "excellent descriptions" of religious warfare and felt, much as his father might, that Cromwell was a *"very* curious person" who had been mistreated by Anglican historians.[97] Like the last literary interest of his life—the portraits of Knox—Carlyle's earliest concern as a writer was not with imaginative truth but with the political, religious figures of whom his parents approved. Again, in the early notebooks, he echoes the conventional Scottish attitude toward the imagination when he asks "whether there ought to be . . . *any* class of purely speculative men? Whether all men should not be of active employment and habitude; their speculation . . . incidental thereto."[98] In fact, it appears that although transcendental aesthetics mark the limit of Carlyle's spiritual and intellectual independence during these years, his distrust of beauty and his insistent activism indicate the extent to which his sympathies were still traceable to Calvinist doctrine. It is as the son of a Puritan father that Carlyle can say, in 1823, that idealistic poetry is "enveloped in clouds and darkness, shadowed forth in types and symbols of unknown and fantastic derivation" or that "a playhouse shows but indifferently as an arena for the Moralist," or that literary distinctions are "folly," "blarney," or simply "futile, very futile."[99] Carlyle surely recalls the ingrained Hebraism of his parents and prefigures the intolerant temper of his own later work when, in 1825, he writes in his notes of Sir William Temple: *"He* was no Artist or speculative

Philosopher, but a man of action."[100] Like other Puritans before him, Carlyle faulted the literary man for putting thought ahead of duty, love ahead of strength, talk ahead of silent obedience, the world of his "diseased" fancy ahead of the world of fact, and self-consciousness ahead of self-denial. Although by his own confession the 1820s were among his happiest years, Carlyle's opinions were characterized, then as later, by the chronic unrest of a divided world-view. As Cazamian, in discussing the antipathy between Carlyle's native faith and his adopted transcendentalism, rather theatrically puts it: "The Calvinist's obsession with conduct and the instinctive need for activity in Carlyle lay in wait for this alien individualism."[101] Thus, despite the balm of Kant and Goethe, he did not achieve genuine equanimity in these years; he quarreled with his friends, complained bitterly of his dyspepsia, and was, in short—very much like Knox himself—incapable of living in peace.[102]

Nowhere in the period before 1832 do Carlyle's Puritan prejudices manifest themselves more clearly than in *Characteristics*. It is in this essay that Carlyle first advocates a kind of self-denial that is explicitly austere and Calvinistic, and thus removed in degree and type from Goethe's *Entsagen*. Elsewhere, in "The State of German Literature" and *Sartor,* he appears to accept the less severe German version of renunciation that allows space for imaginative self-consciousness.[103] But that which to the Romantic poet and the Fichtean idealist represents the core of religious experience— namely the "I"s' consciousness of itself—seems to the writer of *Characteristics* to be art's unpardonable sin, her crucial "Error."[104] Certainly transcendentalism does not inspire Carlyle's assertion that through modern literature's self-consciousness, worship of divine truth has been distorted into vanity. No, it is upon an entirely different set of principles, preeminently puritanical ones, that Carlyle condemns the egotism of the arts. Like his father and every dogmatic Protestant since Calvin himself, Carlyle takes issue with the pride of men in their personal creations. The thrust of his argument in *Characteristics* is but a recapitulation of Knox's warning two hundred and seventy years before: "Whosoever boast themselves of the merittis of thair awin workis . . . they boast of thame selfis of that whiche is not, and putt thair trust in damnable idolatrie."[105] Even Carlyle's diction resembles that of the Calvinist reformer, for in the context of such phrases as "mother of Abominations," Knox would surely have been comfortable. We see here, revealed in Carlyle's thought as early as 1831, his father's proscription of literature not only for its idleness but for its self-flattery. In the ensuing years, this call of Carlyle's for "annihilation of the self" resolved itself into an appeal for straightforward asceticism. By degrees, as Cazamian says, "Carlyle twists Goethe's teaching toward the Puritan austerity of his own instincts."[106]

As the analysis of Calvin indicated, the Protestant fear of self-indulgence arises directly out of the doctrine of man's depravity; that is, out of a profound sense of sin. Insincerity, "fleshly longings," and general corruption (contends the Puritan) infect, and will continue to infect, the nature of man; in the name of these evils certain of us constantly challenge the sovereignty of God and are constantly rebuked. This belief in the eternal conflict of virtue and vice is an essential element in the personality of Calvinism, and Carlyle, in many of his early works, acknowledges such an antagonism. He illustrates it most vividly in *Sartor Resartus*. The world picture he paints there is as stern and "everlasting" in its contrasts as any that Knox or Calvin devised: transcendentalism may have determined the general philosophy of the novel, but its frequent moral dichotomies are reminiscent not so much of Kant's speculations as of Puritan sermonizing. Nothing is more familiar to the radical Protestant than the polarities of "elect" and "damned," grace and sin, affectation and truth; by the same token, nothing absorbs Carlyle's interest in *Sartor* so much as "shams" and "verities," "Nos" and "Yeas," "dandies" and "poor-slaves," Byronic demonism and Goethean calm. In *Sartor* as in "Signs of the Times," he feels compelled to break the world into mechanism and dynamism, into the enemies of God and the sons of Light; like

Knox declaiming against the "idolatrous" trappings of the Catholic church, Carlyle is at his best when he is reviling the "self-worship" and "Mammonisms" of the English Christian gentleman. Tutored by his father to admonish his fellow men "whenever occasion shall require," Carlyle was naturally more adept at fault-finding than at panegyric. The world of *Sartor Resartus* is not, after all, simply the untroubled realm of the idealist's dreaming; it is, as well, a universe split into the stern antimonies of the Calvinist creed; imbued, as Holloway says, with "Carlyle's sense of a cosmic fissure between good and bad, real and sham."[107] Teufelsdröckh's name itself suggests the corruption of the flesh and the depravity of our natural state. One critic sees Carlyle's consciousness of evil not only as an adjunct to the Clothes-Philosophy but as the focus of the author's interest:

> The Demon, the Puritan devil, is everywhere in Sartor Resartus. . . . By the circumstances of his education and by the atmosphere of his father's home and the habits of speech in the circle where he had lived, as well as by the authority of the Bible, the Evil Spirit came to take in [Carlyle's] thought the part of an obsessing reality.[108]

Furthermore, Carlyle has begun, even in *Sartor,* to associate imaginative literature with the idleness and vanity of the degenerate Christian, much as the Puritan ministers had linked the theater and poetry to those "nocturnal dissipations" and "boastful imaginings" of the ungodly. Admittedly, it is the "fashionable novel" of literary "half-men" like Bulwer-Lytton that Carlyle here condemns,[109] but his critical position is one that, distorted by the Calvinist instinct for absolute judgments, will later evolve into an intolerance of the serious artist as well. He has, in a sense, reached a kind of balance in *Sartor,* between German aestheticism and the prejudices of his native faith: on the one hand, he appreciates the "rude," active Craftsman toiling after righteousness and "daily bread"; on the other, he exalts the Artist whose labors are internal and whose fruit is the "spiritually indispensable."[110] For the moment at least, Carlyle speaks for the stonemason and the poet, for the Puritan and the idealist without denigrating either: "Two men I honour, and no third."[111]

Throughout the whole of the novel Carlyle's inherent Hebraism rises through the ether of his professed transcendentalism.[112] Paraphrases from the Old Testament, like echoes from the orthodoxy of his childhood, mingle with the more sophisticated rhetoric of Kantian idealism. In a single page of *Sartor,* Holloway points out no fewer than thirty-six biblical references, most of them from Isaiah, Ezekiel, or the Books of Moses.[113] Probably the clearest example, in this early period, of Carlyle's undiminished faith in the Puritan work-ethic of his father occurs at the end of the "Everlasting Yea" section of *Sartor.* Again, almost instinctively, his hero appeals to the authority of Scriptures—this time, to Ecclesiastes:

> I too could now say to myself: Be no longer a Chaos, but a World, or even a Worldkin. Produce! Produce! Were it but the pitifullest infinitesimal fraction of a Product, produce it, in God's name! "Tis the utmost thou hast in thee: out with it then. . . . Whatsoever thy hand findeth to do, do it with thy whole might. Work while it is called Today; for the Night cometh, wherein no man can work.[114]

There is then sufficient evidence in Carlyle's early writings to suggest that he maintained many of the prejudices of Scottish Calvinism despite his efforts to articulate a more "up-to-date" philosophical creed. Certainly in the first ten years of his career, the German influence was the stronger of the two, and in deference to its aesthetic bias, Carlyle generally took a charitable view of literature. But after 1832, his vocational interest shifted rather abruptly from imaginative writing to history and the conflicts in his attitude toward the arts became more pronounced. Without doubt, ambivalence toward poetry and fiction can be traced through the whole of his life, yet Carlyle clearly took issue with literature more openly and more often after the completion of *Sartor Resartus.* If, as it appears, Calvinist instincts are at the root of his negative opinion

of literature, then we must locate that event of the early 1830s
that encouraged the ascendency of his Puritanism.

In January 1832, only a few months after Carlyle had offered
the manuscript of *Sartor to* various London publishers, his father
died. No other event, with the possible exception of Jane's death
thirty-three years later, had such a marked effect upon the character of Carlyle's thought.[115] The direction of his life and his work
had been, since his first years in Edinburgh, away from the teachings of James Carlyle. He had rebelled against the literalism of the
Burgher religion, against a career in the ministry, against the plain,
unspeculative atmosphere of his parents' home. Even in *Sartor,*
when Teufelsdröckh claims to honor the "coarse" Craftsman, it
is honor tempered with the condescension of the philosopher who
has risen above the simple dogmas of his earliest teachers. "We
must," he says, "pity as well as love thee!"[116] As long as Carlyle
looked down at his father's toilings from the "Highest" plane of
"inspired Thinker," there was only an occasional danger that his
inherent Hebraism would conflict with the cutural values of German idealism. But the death of James Carlyle weakened, considerably, his son's sense of having followed a superior calling. In
the weeks after the funeral, as the mood of the sketch in *Reminiscences* makes clear, Carlyle underwent a profound guilt-reaction
over his neglect of the principles by which his father had lived.
The pressure of this guilt forced from him a declaration not only
to tolerate but to promote the world-view of his puritanical parent; he hoped, perhaps, by doing so to earn forgiveness for his
apostasy while justifying the diligence and obscurity of his father's efforts. Again and again, in *Reminiscences,* Carlyle praises
the active virtues of his father at the expense of his own more
sedentary pursuits: "His life was no 'idle Tale' . . . an earnest
toilsome life";[117] "The force that had been lent my father he
honourably expended in manful well-doing. A portion of this
planet bears beneficent traces of his strong hand and strong head.
Nothing he undertook to do but he did it faithfully and like a
true man. . . . No one that comes after him will ever say, 'Here

was the finger of a hollow eye-servant'";[118] "Like a healthy man, he wanted only to get along with his task";[119] "he was among the last of the true men. . . . diligently working on God's earth";[120] "I call a man remarkable who becomes a true workman in this vineyard of the Highest."[121] The implication of these statements is, of course, that tale-telling, in contrast to "real" labor, constitutes the idle, unremarkable, unhealthy, even "false" occupation of mere "eye-servants." But Carlyle did more than recognize, in Puritan terms, the moral discrepancy between his own career and that of his father: he resolved to close the gap between them by the re-direction of his intellectual energies:

> I owe him a noble inspiring example . . . let me do worth-
> ily of him. So shall he live even here in me. . . . I can see
> my dear father's life in some measure as the sunk pillar on
> which mine was to rise and be built . . . I might almost
> say his spirit seems to have entered into me (so clearly do I
> discern and love him); I seem to myself only the continua-
> tion and second volume of my father.[122]

It was obvious to Carlyle, under the influence of this new determination, that there was a specific way in which the spirit of his father might manifest itself in his own writing: "I had the example of a real Man. . . . Let me learn of *him*. Let me write my books as he built his houses."[123] Clearly, James Carlyle had expended the whole force of his genius on concrete externals, on the literal "fact of things." Thus this new commitment behooved his son to follow a similar course in the world of letters—to wrestle, in fact, with the actual, providentially significant problems of political history, rather than to dissipate his powers (as he had been doing) in "vain" eloquence and "idle" story-telling. After 1832, Carlyle consequently made the outer world his primary study. David Masson was the first critic to pinpoint this link between Calvinist determinism and Carlyle's "new," obsessive interest in historical justice (and, by the way, the first to distinguish discretely internal and external biases in his religion):

Carlyle's religion . . . was a compound of two elements, one furnished from within, the other found without. . . . The world without was . . . God working. . . . The superiority of the right and noble over the wrong and ignoble, the conquering power of the right and noble in the long run, and the futility or nothingness of evil, were evident in the actual rule and history of the world, preached in disaster, ruin, retribution. Divine justice stared up at you out of the very fact of things. . . . Hence his preference of History over all other forms of Literature.[124]

Although the reminiscence of 1832 did not come to light until Carlyle's death, it proves conclusively that his declining opinion of aesthetic literature and his increasing interest in history were, in large measure, the result of a Puritan reaction occasioned by the death of his father. That is not to say that the decisions taken in January 1832 resolved Carlyle's religious schizophrenia: theologically, he remained as undogmatic and idealistic as he had been since first reading *Wilhelm Meister:* literarily, he continued to subject his material to a highly wrought, impressionistic style; critically, he still claimed, with intermittent conviction, that the aesthetic writer occupied the first place among the chosen of God. What the crisis of his father's death did do was to join the battle more openly in Carlyle's mind between the spirit of his parents' faith and the spirit of his own adopted creed. From then on, he felt fully justified in promoting, unapologetically, the ascetic, authoritarian, gloomy, pragmatic prejudices of his Puritan ancestry.

Another event of 1832 may have encouraged Carlyle to articulate the Calvinist sentiments that he had thus far muted in his writing. Goethe's death followed close on his father's, but, unlike his father's, it did not rouse in Carlyle any sense of guilt; on the contrary, the passing of the "venerable" poet signified the "innocent" loss of a father-figure to whom Carlyle had openly and unstintingly directed his admiration for eight years. The coincidence of the deaths of the two men must, if anything, have made Carlyle more acutely aware of having transferred his spiritual allegiance from his natural father. At all events, the death of Goethe broke the strongest personal tie Carlyle had with German literature; without that special influence to reinforce his idealism, Carlyle retreated, at frequent intervals, into the simplistic, instinctual world of his childhood.

We should also take account of the profound watershed that 1832 signified in the political and social life of England. Few men of Carlyle's generation or younger failed to respond: the Saint-Simonians proselytized, Mill agitated for democracy, and Dickens reported the great parliamentary debates; Arnold, Ruskin, Morris, and most later Victorians looked back upon the early 1830s as the seedbed of the major political controversies of the century. Undoubtedly the universal excitement surrounding the continental revolutions of 1830, the Reform Bill of 1832, the abolition of slavery in 1833, and the Poor Law Reforms of 1834 conspired with the deaths of James Carlyle and Goethe to launch Carlyle toward less romantic, more matter-of-fact horizons.

However that may be, after 1832 his works confirm his enlarged sympathy with the precepts of Scottish Calvinism. In *The French Revolution,* Carlyle sees that upheaval as one of those inevitable, even providential, clashes between the simple truth of things and the aberrations of our depraved reason; in his 1838 *Lectures,* he asserts that the great ages of literature correspond to eras of "decadent" self-consciousness and impracticality;[125] in *Past and Present,* he offers the disciplined authority of Abbot Samson's regime to his own complacent century as an example of the benefits to be gained by hard work and pious obedience; in *Heroes,* he claims that the "fervencye" of Knox and the often unforgiving rule of Cromwell were as constructive morally and, in many ways, more heroic than the delicacy and perspicuity of poets. Certainly the "Gospel of Work" and the militant aspects of the hero-theory that Carlyle developed in the 1840s appear to be extensions of orthodox Hebraism and the doctrine of election by grace. As he said in a letter to a friend about this time, Calvinism "is at bottom my religion, too."[126] A short while later, in his partisan study of

Cromwell's letters and speeches, Carlyle publicly declared himself an apologist for the Puritan spirit.[127] This exhaustive work was followed, in 1850, by a less careful but even more strident defense of Calvinist values: the terrible impatience and severity of "Model Prisons," "The Nigger Question," and "Jesuitism" among the *Latter-Day Pamphlets* parallel in tone—more closely than anything else Carlyle wrote—the denunciatory "trumpet blasts" of Calvin and Knox. After 1850, probably the least savory aspects of Carlyle's recurrent Hebraism was a disturbing tendency to equate the Puritan action-principle with outright warfare. He had, of course, sufficient authority for such an equation in the battles of the Old Testament, Knox's doctrinal defense of political revolution, and Cromwell's successful application of violent reforms. It is nonetheless unfortunate that in the writings of Carlyle's last years the bogey of militarism intrudes: the "drill-seargeant" and the "City-burner" often overshadow the "spirit-seeker" and the architect of the mind; might, rather than beauty, frequently makes right. Along with Goethe, Kant, and Shakespeare, Carlyle holds up as equivalent heroes Frederick, Dr. Francia, and Governor Eyre.

Throughout the final forty years of Carlyle's career, this antagonism between idealistic values and Puritan prejudices continued to provoke a consistent ambivalence in his attitude toward literature. As we have already seen in the opening chapter, Carlyle frequently juxtaposed paradoxical opinions of the arts in the space of a single essay, a single letter, or even a single conversation. Our concern in the next chapter will be to locate the specific religious bias behind each of these statements, but for now it may be instructive to look briefly at one such cause-and-effect relationship.

During the 1840s, Carlyle was preoccupied with his research into Oliver Cromwell. Like James Carlyle, Cromwell had taught his fellow Puritans that man was created not to love or to dream but to act. Cazamian points out the insistent Hebraism in Cromwell's letters and sermons: "He is dominated by a faith which . . .

tempers men for action. . . . Just as the weakening of their activity was the work of sin, the reflux of divine grace was a torrent
which bore them toward activity."[128] Carlyle, predisposed by his
father's example, entered with shrill enthusiasm into the spirit of
his Calvinist subject. He was chiefly attracted, it appears, by a man
who seemed a "natural Governor," a man determined to apply
"force till right is ready," a man anxious to instruct people in
what was good for them, not in what they wanted. That Cromwell's Calvinism was discrete from the fanatical Presbyterian faith
of the Burghers seems a distinction lost on Carlyle (as earlier he
had blurred the differences between Hume and the *philosophes*
or Goethe's aesthetics and those of Fichte).[129] In his introduction
to the *Letters and Speeches,* he makes a virtue of Cromwell's verbal
"inadequacy" while at the same time disparaging those who value
"musical singing" more highly than "manful" labor: "He that
works and *does* some Poem, not he that merely *says* one, is worthy
of the name of Poet."[130] It is an essential ingredient of the Puritan
creed to denounce all forms of idleness, and Carlyle, galvanized
by the fervor of Cromwell, turned against literature as against an
enemy of righteousness. "Goethe," he said to Espinasse in 1846,
"was the most successful speaker of the century, but I would have
been better pleased if he had *done* something."[131] In 1847, the
second meeting between Emerson and Carlyle was less congenial
than the first, largely for the same reason: Carlyle, under the influence of Cromwell's example, was uncomfortable with "speculative men." In place of the compassionate idealist he had met at
Craigenputtock, Emerson sat down in Chelsea with an inhospita-
ble, thoroughly intemperate Calvinist. One account of their re-
union records that "Carlyle, still full of Cromwell, resented with
needless heat Emerson's refusal to fall down and worship the Puritan hero."[132] And it was certainly no coincidence that at the
same meeting Emerson was saddened by Carlyle's "vehement denunciations of authorship."[133] To accept the spirit of Calvinism
was, for Carlyle, to take a dim view of the value of literature. All
writing that was not specifically practical, that did not contribute

materially to the service of God, was of no consequence; as far as Carlyle was concerned, the poetry and novels of the nineteenth century were part of some gigantic "intellectual prostitution." The arts, he argued, ought to be not a free expression of the individual's concept of beauty but a strictly organized discipline, dedicated—like the reformer pamphlets of the Cromwellian period—to religious utility.[134] Under the Puritan influence, Carlyle's oft-repeated opposition to the Protestant zealots of his own day weakened as well: "[He] might then be heard declaring that among Evangelicals were to be found some of the best people in England."[135] Even the resolve he had made to stay clear of contemporary politics paled in the strong light of Calvinist activism: "Cromwell for a long time coloured his thoughts and waking dreams. . . . I can see him now. . . . Pouring forth in the strongest possible of Scotch accents, an oral Latter-Day Pamphlet, contrasting Cromwell and his Puritans with contemporary English politicians and the multitudes whom they were leading by the nose to the abyss."[136] But more significantly, from the practical, contentious perspective of Puritanism, Carlyle could see little point in the quietism of aesthetic literature. It appeared, in fact, as his father had warned, to be a following "not only idle, but false and criminal," for in its tranquility it bespoke a kind of spiritual pride. At the end of a discussion with Jane and Espinasse on the merits of Cromwell's religion, Carlyle invoked the characteristically Calvinist objection to the artist as vain and self-satisfied: as Espinasse records the incident, "Mrs. Carlyle pointed out to me a portrait of Jean Paul Richter. . . . 'His nose is put out of joint,' Carlyle remarked significantly. German Literature, and a great deal else, was being effaced from him by the Letters and Speeches of Oliver Cromwell, 'the best fellow I have fallen in with,' I once heard him say."[137] We may conclude from this sampling of Carlyle's opinions that, in the 1840s at least, the prejudices of his father's faith dictated his hostility to the arts.

The evidence in this and the preceding chapter demonstrates

that those transcendental and Puritan precepts to which Carlyle owed a dual allegiance, represented, in almost every way, antithetical views of life. In particular, they encouraged opposite and irreconcilable attitudes toward literature. Worst of all, against the current of transcendental optimism, Carlyle as Puritan was bound to set the Calvinist obsession with guilt and evil. In doing so, he ran against his own espousal of "natural supernaturalism" and found himself condemning the very vision of aesthetic unity that he had taken such pains to articulate. With the transcendental Artist's appeal to the ultimate through the sensuous "his Puritan character was acutely uncomfortable. . . . His loathing for shams, for cant . . . stifled in him the taste and joy of the beautiful."[138]

1. Espinasse, *Literary Recollections*, pp. 197–98, 209.

2. Masson, *Carlyle Personally and in His Writings*, p. 209.

3. A. Swinburne, *Letters*, II, 121.

4. Ibid., II, 33, 102.

5. Allingham, *A Diary*, p. 119.

6. A. Haultain, *Goldwin Smith, His Life and Opinions*, p. 44. This verdict undoubtedly owed much to the vicious controversy over Governor Eyre in the 1860's, during which Carlyle and Smith had become prominent antagonists.

7. Henry James, *Notes of a Son and Brother*, p. 185.

8. *Autobiography*, I, 386.

9. Maitland, *Life and Letters of Leslie Stephen*, p. 231.

10. Allingham, *A Diary*, p. 206.

11. Espinasse, *Literary Recollections*, p. 228.

12. *A Diary*, pp. 209, 254.

13. Ibid., p. 166.

14. *Literary Recollections*, p. 212.

15. Ibid., p. 180.

16. *Carlyle Personally and in His Writings*, p. 33.

17. Espinasse, *Literary Recollections*, p. 159.

18. Ibid., p. 265. Amy Cruse discusses at some length the mixed reaction of Carlyle's contemporaries to his later works, especially *Latter-Day Pamphlets* (*The Victorians and Their Books*, pp. 134–50).

19. "Carlyle's 'Past and Present,'" in *Miscellaneous Pieces*, p. 177.

20. Espinasse, *Literary Recollections*, p. 265.

21. Masson, *Carlyle Personally and in His Writings*, p. 37.

22. *Carlyle*, pp. 6, 3.

23. *First Forty Years*, II, 256. See also ibid., I, 200, on the "offense" German aestheticism gave to Carlyle's Calvinistic sensibilities.

24. "Thomas Carlyle," *Studies in Early Victorian Literature*, p. 57.

25. H. Walker, "The German Influence: Thomas Carlyle," p. 31.

26. *A Diary*, p. 254.

27. *Carlyle Personally and in His Writings*, p. 33.

28. Allingham, *A Diary*, p. 289.

29. *Carlyle*, p. 279.

30. *Institutes of the Christian Religion (A Compend)*, ed. H. T. Kerr, p. 43.

31. Ibid., p. 49.

32. Ibid., p. 48.

33. Ibid., p. 101.

34. Ibid., p. 41.

35. Ibid., p. 32.

36. Ibid., p. 18.

37. Ibid., pp. 11–12.

38. Ibid., pp. 13–14.

39. Ibid., p. 6.

40. Ibid., pp. 96–97.

41. Ibid., pp. 104–5.

42. *Culture and Anarchy*, ed. D. Wilson, p. 129.

43. Kerr, *Institutes of the Christian Religion*, pp. 180–81.

44. Wilson, *Culture and Anarchy*, p. 135.

45. *The Works of John Knox*, ed., D. Laing, V, 30. This six-volume edition was a favorite of Carlyle in his last years; he kept it within arm's reach of his writing desk in the attic study, where it can be seen today.

46. Ibid., III, 23.

47. The Calvinist attitude toward election should not be confused with eighteenth-century Methodism, in which the doctrine of salvation by faith was often invoked as an excuse for misconduct.

48. See especially *Heroes*, pp. 144–53, and "The Portraits of John Knox," *Essays*, V, 313–67.

49. *Works of John Knox*, II, 103–4.

50. Ibid., III, 196.

51. Ibid., III, 34.

52. *Essays*, V, 319. Carlyle remarks further that "no man saw any sign of mirth in him" (p. 343).

53. Quoted in Edwin Muir, *John Knox: Portrait of a Calvinist*, p. 143.

54. *Works of John Knox*, II, 189.

55. Ibid., pp. 252–53.

56. Ibid., I, 100.

57. Ibid., III, 169.

58. Ibid., II, 449.

59. Ibid., I, 88–89.

60. Andrew MacPhail, *Essays in Puritanism*, p. 16. For more detailed criticism of the effect Calvinism had upon the culture of Scotland, see two articles by D. H. Fleming in the *Scottish Historical Review*: "The Influence of Knox," and "The Influence of the Reformation on Social and Cultural Life in Scotland." On the same subject, Edwin Muir remarks significantly: "What did Calvinist Scotland produce? . . . In philosophy, profane poetry, the drama, music, painting, architecture, nothing. Whatever was done in literature . . . came from the opponents of Calvinism or from men out of sympathy with it. . . . It frowned on all prose and poetry which was not sacred. For its imaginative literature it was confined more and more to the Old Testament" (*Portrait of a Calvinist*, pp. 307–8). Carlyle himself points out the barrenness of Scottish culture before Burns and, comparing it to that of Geneva, blames their mutual backwardness on too much "theological ink" (*Essays*, I, 288).

61. *Works of John Knox*, I, 100.

62. Not so much in Cromwell himself, who distrusted rampant religious enthusiasm, as in those dissident sects of the era that claimed in their monopoly of "true religion" a right to monopolize political authority: namely, Presbyterians, Fifth Monarchy Men, Diggers, Levellers, doctrinaire Republicans, and so on.

63. *Works of John Knox*, III, 271.

64. Quoted in W. F. Gallaway, "The Conservative Attitude toward Fiction, 1770–1830," pp. 1044, 1047. R. J. Cruickshank, in his study of early Victorian England, believes that in the Sunday sermon, the Puritan permitted himself his only surrogate for the drama and "narrative power" of literature: "Among strict Evangelical and Nonconformist families who regarded the playhouse as being under Satan's management and the novel as a corrupter of the young, the pulpit was in some part a moral substitute for both" (quoted in Nicholas Bentley, *The Victorian Scene, 1837–1901*, p. 192).

65. Hugh Murray, *The Morality of Fiction*, p. 37.

66. Cotton Mather, *Manuductio ad Ministerium*, pp. 38, 42.

67. Henry Fielding was one of the first novelists to be accused of propounding such an unclassical morality, especially in the creation of heroes like Tom Jones.

68. Gallaway, "The Conservative Attitude toward Fiction," pp. 1050, 1045, 1051.

69. Murray, *The Morality of Fiction*, p. 5.

70. Ibid., p. 26.

71. Gallaway, "The Conservative Attitude toward Fiction," p. 1048.

72. Murray, *The Morality of Fiction*, p. 134.

73. Gallaway, "The Conservative Attitude toward Fiction," pp. 1053–54.

74. Murray, *The Morality of Fiction*, p. 140.

75. Cazamian, who is more aware than most critics of the Puritanism in Carlyle's character, says plainly: "The touching tribute to his father in the

Reminiscences is among the essential texts for the understanding of Carlyle" (*Carlyle*, p. 5).

76. Reminiscences, I, 31.

77. Ibid., p. 39.

78. Espinasse, *Literary Recollections*, p. 262.

79. *Reminiscences*, I, 13.

80. G. B. Tennyson reviews the peculiarities and chief sources of Carlyle's style succinctly in his introduction to *A Carlyle Reader*, pp. xxxi–xxxviii.

81. *Reminiscences*, I, 26, 55.

82. Ibid., p. 55.

83. Ibid., pp. 23, 25.

84. Ibid., p. 55.

85. Ibid., p. 26.

86. Ibid., pp. 12, 62.

87. See Harrold, *Carlyle and German Thought*, p. 29.

88. *Reminiscences*, I, 10.

89. This fact invites a comparison with Mill's early circumstances (see *Autobiography*, chap. 5), and supports the commonly held opinion that Puritanism is but religious Utilitarianism (or vice versa).

90. Allingham, *A Diary*, p. 247.

91. *Reminiscences*, I, 17, 19.

92. Ibid., p. 19.

93. Harrold, *Carlyle and German Thought*, p. 27.

94. K. Murdock, "Puritan Literary Attitude," in *Literature and Theology in Colonial New England*, p. 43.

95. *Note Books*, p. 140.

96. Harrold sees a number of contradictory strains in Carlyle's opinions at this time: "In dealing with this early reflective period . . . it is necessary constantly to bear in mind the very sturdy unmystical aspects of Carlyle's genius. For his work reveals a curious blend of stoicism, Hebraism, Calvinism, and transcendentalism" ("The Mystical Element in Carlyle, 1827–34," p. 434).

97. *Note Books*, pp. 5, 17. A preliminary view that, it later developed, was perfectly just.

98. Ibid., p. 263.

99. Ibid., pp. 42, 41, 46, 47.

100. Ibid., p. 84.

101. Cazamian, *Carlyle*, p. 92.

102. Harrold points to Carlyle's unrest as a sign of his dissatisfaction with transcendental values: "The absence of harmony and joy from his life and writings argues a dissonance in such mysticism as he did profess. . . . He . . . never ceased to show, in the tumult of his prose . . . how little joy and peace . . . he ever attained" ("The Mystical Element in Carlyle," p. 463).

103. Carlyle also restates the Goethean ideal in his first essay on Richter: "The great law of culture is: Let each become all that he was created capable

of being . . . casting off all foreign, especially all noxious adhesions" (*Essays,* I, 19).

104. *Essays,* III, 23.

105. *Works of John Knox,* II, 108.

106. Cazamian, *Carlyle,* p. 91. Elsewhere, he speaks of the perversion of *Entsagen* per se: Carlyle "colors with Christian asceticism Goethe's favorite precept of renunciation: instead of a sacrifice, he interprets it as a mutilation, an amputation from the spirit of a number of its faculties" (p. 44).

107. John Holloway, *The Victorian Sage,* p. 57. This is, of course, an archetypal distinction hardly exclusive to Puritanism.

108. Cazamian, *Carlyle,* p. 108.

109. See *SR,* pp. 220–22. In her study *The Dandy: From Brummell to Beerbohm,* Ellen Moers suggests that the vehicle of the Clothes-Philosophy may have been adopted as a result of Carlyle's introduction to Bulwer-Lytton's novels (see chapter 8, "England in 1830 and the Anti-Dandiacals"). See also Carlyle's journal entry for December 1831, in which he speaks of Bulwer-Lytton as "the mystagogue of the dandiacal body" (Froude, *First Forty Years,* II, 253). Sterne, Swift, even Shakespeare, nevertheless are more likely antecedents.

110. *SR,* p. 81. G. Levine, in " 'Sartor Resartus' and the Balance of Fiction," has remarked on this state of equilibrium: "*Sartor* exhibits a tension between a commitment to speculative philosophy and a commitment to unself-conscious work" (p. 136). It displays "his dual impulses (toward self-consciousness . . . self-assertion, for example, as well as work, humility, and self-denial)" (p. 147).

111. *SR,* p. 81.

112. Or conversely, as Harrold perorates: "His mysticism shines like a golden gleam through the darker texture of his Calvinism" ("The Mystical Element in Carlyle," p. 475).

113. Holloway, *The Victorian Sage,* pp. 24–25.

114. *SR,* p. 157, and Ecclesiastes 9:11.

115. It is a curious feature of Carlyle's temperament, and perhaps a further proof of his Puritan morbidity, that he was apparently most deeply stirred by the emotions of guilt and remorse.

116. *SR,* p. 181.

117. *Reminiscences,* I, 17.

118. Ibid., pp. 5–6.

119. Ibid., p. 10.

120. Ibid., p. 9.

121. Ibid., p. 7.

122. Ibid., pp. 6, 65.

123. Ibid., p. 15.

124. Masson, *Carlyle Personally and in His Writings,* pp. 88–90.

125. See also his paean to Knox in an article on Scott in 1838 (*Essays,* IV, 42–44) and "Baillie the Covenanter," a review printed in 1841 (*Essays,* IV, 226–60).

126. 30 May 1844, in *New Letters of Thomas Carlyle*, ed. A. Carlyle, I, 314 (hereafter cited as *New Letters*).

127. Though perhaps at the time it was a necessary overcompensation for the partisan studies it superseded.

128. *Carlyle*, pp. 228–29.

129. For a definitive treatment of Carlyle's distortions of the Cromwell of history, see C. H. Firth's introduction to the three-volume edition of the *Letters and Speeches* (London, 1904), ed. S. C. Lomas.

130. *Cromwell*, I, 78. It is a sure mark of the extent of Carlyle's ambivalence that, despite his Puritan mood, he holds on to the *word* "Poet" as a synonym for the worthiest kind of man.

131. Espinasse, *Literary Recollections*, p. 92.

132. Ibid., p. 156.

133. Ibid., p. 159.

134. Ibid., pp. 87–88.

135. Ibid., p. 75. Albert Potter, who died at 94, just after World War II, also told of how Carlyle listened at the porch of a Methodist church near his Chelsea home and was heard to comment, "They talk sense, these Methodists" (anecdote reported to me by Harold Brooks, 21 July 1969).

136. Ibid., p. 82.

137. Ibid., p. 69.

138. Cazamian, *Carlyle*, p. 253.

Chapter Five

Carlyle on Literature: Transcendental Faith versus Puritan Temper

> The poet's eye in a fine frenzy roll-
> ing,
> Doth glance from heav'n to earth,
> from earth to heav'n;
> And as imagination bodies forth
> The forms of things unknown, the
> poet's pen
> Turns them to shapes, and gives to
> airy nothing
> A local habitation and a name.
>
> —Shakespeare

Before we immerse ourselves in literary particulars, let us briefly reexamine the determining characteristics of both creeds.

The Scottish dissenter faults the artist and his work for their express self-consciousness; the poem or play or novel reflects a private vision; it is vain because it springs, not from God, but from the corrupted fancy of the individual. Furthermore, the Puritan condemns imaginative literature as sham: it does not accord with the stern realities of God's lower world; it frequently neglects the fact of evil in order to paint pretty, idealized "fictions." Lastly, the Calvinist is contemptuous of art because it encourages contemplation and general passivity where action and practical morality are required. It is thus wasteful, unmanly, and frivolous. That the poet is active in delineating and arranging selectively the materials he perceives does not satisfy the Protestant dissenter: in disavowing an externally imposed system of conduct, the aesthetic writer appears to him to be "doing" nothing at all.

157

The transcendentalist, on the other hand, looks to literature as to the organ of a new religion: it is among the best repositories for spiritual truths in the modern age. The artist's value consists, for him, first of all, in the ability to transcend the apparent self-sufficiency of logic, to escape the contradictions of the senses (what the Kantian calls the Understanding). In an age of popular empiricism, literature alone recognizes the infinite significance of the imagination. Second, the arts perform, for the transcendentalist, a vital function in reconciling the phenomenal with the noumenal world. Fancy, as Kant says in the *Critique of Aesthetic Judgment,* bridges the gap between the actual and the real, the seen and the unseen; in the apprehension of beauty, in the music of poetry, man's Understanding and man's Reason—his nature and his soul—are harmonized. Finally, for the transcendentalist, the "Poet" or "Literary Man" assumes the stature of a messiah: he is spoken of as "hero" or "high-priest" for it is he who *sees* into things themselves, reads their symbolic significance to the rest of us, and reveals the moral basis of the universe. Gifted with divine vision, he alone uncovers "mystical" meanings and amplifies, as it were, the "soul-music" within the time element.

In his advocacy of literature, Carlyle's attitude corresponds closely to that of the transcendental idealist. He, too, considers the essential purpose of art to be a religious one and presumes its whole significance to rest upon the articulation of spiritual values. Often Carlyle points up this principle of high seriousness by saying what art is not: "It should be recollected that Literature positively has other aims than this of amusement from hour to hour; nay, perhaps that this, glorious as it may be, is not its highest or true aim."[1] Again, he appeals to a religious standard in excluding certain writers from the domain of "true Literature": "We cheerfully acquitted Mr. Taylor of Religion; but must expect less gratitude when we farther deny him any feeling for true Poetry, as indeed the feelings for Religion and for Poetry of this sort are one and the same."[2] Even Jeffrey, although "a newspaper critic on the great scale," has no true sense of "Literature" or "Poetry" because he lacks the aptitudes of a "priest."[3] On the positive side, Carlyle accepts Schiller as a genuine poet because "there is something priest-like in that Life of his,"[4] and Carlyle recognizes that German literature, "alone of all existing Literatures," retains some claim to "that ancient inspired gift, which alone is Poetry."[5] More specifically, he believes that "a consistent philosophy of life . . . is the soul and ultimate essence of all Poetry."[6] In a letter to Goethe (previously quoted), he suggests that German artists in particular have adopted the unique spiritual doctrine or philosophical ground plan that will allow art its true scope.[7] Elsewhere, he refers explicitly to Kant's idealistic philosophy as the basis upon which the modern poet may safely build his images of reality:

> Such men as Goethe and Schiller cannot exist without effect in any literature or in any century: but if one circumstance more than any other has contributed to forward their endeavors, it has been this philosophical system; to which, in wisely believing its results . . . all that was lofty and pure in the genius of poetry, or the reason of man, so readily allied itself.[8]

Reinforced by the principles of a new faith, art assumes for Carlyle the potency of a gospel. He writes to Goethe in the fervour of his commitment: "Literature is now nearly all in all to us; not our speech only, but our Worship and Lawgiving; our best Priest must henceforth be our Poet."[9] Thus he shares with the transcendentalist that intense reverence for literature as the implement of a new religion; it aims, of course, to delight and instruct, but its highest purpose, as Carlyle and the German idealists understand it, is spiritual revelation.

Kant and Fichte and their advocates among the Romantic poets of Germany emphasize further that literature should be a liberating vocation. The creative imagination, rightly employed, allows man to reach beyond the relative values of his senses and his intellect; it permits him to transcend the Understanding and escape the enervating contradictions of present circumstances and time. Art alone opens the window to ultimacy—neither "pure reason" nor dogmatic religion, which are trapped by their own literalism, can do so much. Carlyle, in his devotion to literature, shares the Kantian's faith in its special properties. It cannot, he agrees, be judged as one judges of external things, by its "utility": it is impervious to "logic-chopping," "cause-and-effect," "pleasure-pain principles," and so on, for it springs from the "I," from the absolutes of Reason: "To inquire after [Art's] *utility,* would be like inquiring after the utility of a God, or, what to the Germans would sound stranger than it does to us, the *utility* of Virtue and Religion!"[10] In his contempt for the standards of "utility," "pleasure," and "effects," Carlyle means to indict the mechanical philosophies of Bentham and Hume; at the same time, he indicates his sympathy with the more liberal-minded "Germans." In other passages, from the preface to *Wilhelm Meister* and the sketch of Edward Irving, he labels as "rude" or "philistine" men who attempt to apply quantitative measures to the innate beauties of art.[11] Moreover, Carlyle frequently invokes the yardstick of transcendental vision in evaluating the contribution of a particular writer. On one occasion, he denies Hoffman "the name of an artist" because he "failed to discover that 'agreeable sensations' are not the highest good": "It was not things, but 'the shows of things,' that he saw; and the world and its business, in which he had to live and move, often hovered before him like a perplexed and spectral vision."[12] Unlike the idealistic poets who were his contemporaries, Hoffman could not rise above "appearances"; he could not see through the phenomena of nature into the quieter realms of spiritual reality. In contrast, what Carlyle called "genuine" literature occupies a place higher than, and discrete from, material involvements:

> Poetry is not dead; it will never die. Its dwelling and birth-place is in the soul of man, and it is eternal as the being of

man. In any point of Space, in any section of Time, let there
be a living Man; and there is an Infinitude above him and
beneath him . . . and tones of Sphere-music, and tidings
from loftier worlds, will flit round him . . . and visit him
with holy influences, even in the thickest press of triviali-
ties, or the din of busiest life.[13]

Thus, to the poet, "all objects are as windows through which [he]
looks into Infinitude itself."[14] If we fail to respond to his insights,
preferring "the coarse passions and perceptions of the world," he
becomes "a Martyr"—the spokesman for "universal, everlasting
Beauty" in an age of "modish Elegance," "Regularity," and
"Method."[15] If, however, we suspend the mechanical processes of
thought, the poet then lifts us free of prosaic mists and, like some
Prospero, "transports us into a holier and higher world than our
own; everything around us breathes of force and solemn
beauty. . . . The enchantments of the poet are strong enough to
silence our scepticism."[16] In *Reminiscences,* Carlyle recalls that
his own escape into a "holier and higher" realm came about
through the mediation of a poet:

> [In the early days] I found that I had conquered all my
> scepticisms, agonizing doubtings, fearful wrestlings with the
> foul and vile and soul-murdering Mud-gods of my epoch
> . . . and was emerging free in spirit into the eternal blue of
> ether, where, blessed be heaven! I have for the spiritual part
> ever since lived, looking down upon the welterings of my
> poor fellow-creatures, in such multitudes and millions still
> stuck fast in that fatal element. . . . In a fine and veritable
> sense, I, poor, obscure, without outlook, almost without
> worldly hope, had become independent of the world. . . .
> I then felt, and still feel, endlessly indebted to Goethe in
> this business.[17]

Poetry represents—for Carlyle as much as for the transcendentalist—a key to the independence of the soul, a release from the
"Not I." As Fichte puts it, "in the contemplation of beauty, the

limitations of the material and the sensuous are broken through and the spirit returns to itself."[18]

Again and again, Carlyle sets literary values above the "limitations of the material" and argues for art as a higher calling than purely practical concerns. In his essay on Burns, he speaks of the man of war, the "conqueror," as a species with which "the world could well dispense": his victories are those of the "hard intellect" only. In *Past and Present,* the poet's is the one "sacred voice" heard amidst "the dreary boundless element of hearsaying and cant, of twaddle and poltroonery, in which the bewildered Earth . . . has *lost its way.*"[19] In *Sartor,* the artist's words, rising from the immutable regions of the soul, will "outlast all marble and metal . . . . in this so solid-seeming world."[20] In the *Life of Sterling,* Carlyle claims for the "Poet or Singer" a "depth of tune" missing in the mere "Speaker."[21] Clearly, he accepts the idealist's notion of the poet as one who transcends the senses and touches a profundity of meaning unknown to the "earth-creeping" mind. Carlyle recalls both Fichte and Kant when he praises the artist at the expense of the politician: "Understand well . . . that to no man is his political constitution 'a life, but only a house wherein his life is led'; and hast thou a nobler task than such house-pargeting and smoke-doctoring, and pulling down of ancient rotten rat-inhabited walls, leave such to the proper craftsman; honour the higher Artist."[22] The politician, in effect, reconstructs appearances, phenomena, the "Not I," whereas the literary artist applies his genius to "things themselves," to the essential, transcendent "I."

The peculiar gift of the creative imagination to lift our spirits free of time-bound paradoxes and "welterings" lends literature, in Carlyle's mind, a higher value than that even of formal religion. Christianity, he believes, unlike art, attempts to explain itself in terms of a causal reality and thus wastes its power in endless arguments with "the mind of the flesh." The literalism of miracles and divine justice diminishes the church's central vision for Carlyle. He sees with grief that to the dogmatic Christian as well as to the Newtonian scientist, miracles consist simply in the violation of natural law. Both might be excited to wonder by the fact of a man reaching out his arm to touch the sun, but neither, like the poet, would wonder that a man reaches out his arm at all.[23] Only the artist has escaped the tyranny of the space-time element and can speak for the spirit with an unmuddled voice. And literature, in Carlyle's estimate, is religion's "greenest branch,"[24] her new "Church": "The true Pope of Christendom is not that feeble old man in Rome. . . . It has been said, and may be repeated, that Literature is fast becoming all in all to us. . . . The true Autocrat and Pope is that man . . . who finds his Hierarchy of gifted Authors . . . whose Decretals [are] written not on parchment, but on the living souls of men."[25] Carlyle conjectures that "Art is higher than Religion" because it avoids the soul-destroying contradictions that arise from an accommodation with the Understanding. Evil, for example, as a reality to the orthodox Christian, must be met with "hostility," but as an appearance to the transcendental artist, it may be comprehended with "peacefulness."[26]

That unique tranquility of insight—enforced by the artist's superiority to the mechanical world—is a crucial element in German idealism. Carlyle continually reveals his attachment to this Kantian principle of freedom in his defense of literature. Poetry, he says, demands "a certain Infinitude, and spiritual Freedom; that elevation above the Fate and Clay of this Earth in which alone, and by virtue of which . . . soul-music is possible."[27] Nowhere does Carlyle argue for literature's potentialities from a more explicitly transcendental perspective than in his *Unfinished History of German Literature:*

> Literature . . . does not plead to us by logical demonstration and computation, yet awakens mysterious and far more potent impulses than these: the deep tones of Imagination, the gay melodies of Fancy. . . . We err much when we suppose that Understanding, the part of our nature which can be moved by syllogisms, is stronger than Imagination: which last, we may rather say, is as the boundless Invisible to the small Visible, as the infinite Universe to the little horizon

we command with our eye. It is but a small portion of any
life that is determined by the perception of things seen: the
dullest worldling worships not his golden or clay idols, of
guineas or acres, but a divinity which lies hidden in
these. . . . Our very senses, whether for pleasure or pain,
are little more than implements of Imagination. . . . Is not
all vision based on Mystery, all Matter Spirit? . . . Fearful,
majestic, unfathomable, in these hearts of ours, is the Witness and Interpretess of that Unknown! . . . Our whole
life has been shaped and moulded by [the poet]; our
thought, our will still hangs on his words: his domain is all
the Infinite in man.[28]

The concept of a supersensible reality, glimpsed through the
superior aesthetic consciousness of the poet, reinforces Carlyle's
favorable views of literature at every stage in his career: "Literature . . . is the eye of the world; enlightening all, and instead of
the shows of things unfolding to us things themselves."[29] In this,
Carlyle's vocabulary as well as his convictions reveals an enormous
debt to transcendental philosophy, especially to the categories and
conclusions of Kant's first and second Critiques.

But art, for Fichte as well as for Kant, has a wider purpose than
that of facilitating man's escape into a world of pure forms. As
Kant contends in his *Critique of Aesthetic Judgment* and Fichte in
The Nature of a Scholar, imaginative genius serves to reconcile the
natural and the spiritual realm; to link, through the faculty of
aesthetic awareness, the moral absolutes and the objects of sense.
The world of the Understanding, what Fichte calls the "Not I," has
an intrinsic symbolic value; it lies, like the "Garment of God,"
atop the unseen, giving it a shape to the eye. Through the heightened perceptions of the poet, argues Kant, the invisible kingdom
of Reason is articulated for us in tangible forms. In the fine arts,
moral ideas are rendered visible, love becomes "the preparation
for virtue," for duty, and wisdom achieves a unique compatibility
with knowledge. There is then no antagonism between the actual

and the ideal, no schism between body and spirit. Nature, in Goethe's words, is an "open secret," the reflex of faith; its "thousand changes / But one changeless God proclaim." In Fichte's more academic manner, the world of objects is "the posited experiential context in which the I conceives of itself."[30] Art, in effect, compels us to acknowledge the interrelation of our two natures. For Kant, this simultaneous revelation of truth and annihilation of conflict "alone confers happiness, [for] under its influence every being forgets that he is limited."[31]

Carlyle, too, embraces the concept of material ideality in his apologies for literature. He writes in his notebook in 1831, "The only Sovereigns in these days are the Literary Men," for in their minds alone do "all forms, and figures of men and things . . . become ideal."[32] Elsewhere he reflects that "the poet's imagination *bodies forth* the forms of things unseen, his pen turns them to shape."[33] Unquestionably, Carlyle attached special significance to the poet as a harmonizer of disparate human faculties. Wordsworth warrants, for him, the name of poet because he reconciles the external and internal, the commonplace and universal:

> To our minds, in these soft, melodious imaginations of his, there is embodied the Wisdom which is proper to this time; the beautiful, the religious Wisdom, which may still, in these hard, unbelieving, utilitarian days, reveal to us glimpses of the Unseen but not unreal World, so that the Actual and the Ideal may again meet together, and clear Knowledge be again wedded to Religion, in the life and business of men.[34]

The passage displays a number of affinities with Kantian thought: Carlyle appreciates a "Wisdom" that takes account of "these hard . . . utilitarian days," Kant wrote, in the first *Kritik* at least, to refute Hume; Carlyle's poet "glimpses . . . the Unseen"—Kant's "glances" at the "supersensible"; in Carlyle's conception of the artist the "Actual and the Ideal" meet, "Knowledge" and "Religion" are wedded—in Kant's the gap between "the phenomenal and the noumenal" is bridged, *Verstand* and *Vernunft* unite. In "Characteristics," Carlyle insists that this "revelation of the God-like" is literature's true purpose; that through art, "Religion has again become possible and inevitable for the scientific mind."[35] The poet incorporates "Nature" into "Art" in such a way that the Understanding, those "sister Faculties" of the Imagination, "will not contradict" the validity of his perceptions.[36] Carlyle again paraphrases Kant's aesthetics when he writes in 1828, "Poetry . . . aims not at 'furnishing a languid mind with fantastic shows and indolent emotions,' but at incorporating the everlasting Reason of man in forms visible to his Sense, and suitable to it."[37] He believes, as the transcendentalists do, that literature must accommodate its intuitive world to the mechanical realm of the intellect, and appeal to the sublime through the rational: "Whatever [literature does] not in some sort address itself to all men and to the whole man, to his affections as well as to his intellect, were no longer Literature."[38] Poetry, properly understood, consists of "Spirit mingled . . . in trustful sisterhood with the forms of Sense."[39] He declares in his journal in July, 1832, that the task of the literary artist amounts to nothing less than the articulation of the *"unaussprechlichen."*[40] His art is thus, as Fichte would have it, "a revelation of the Infinite in the Finite,"[41] an "imaging forth in shadowy emblems the universal tendencies and destinies of man."[42] Carlyle can speak of the yoking of sense and spirit without contradiction because German idealism has convinced him that they are but different aspects of a single reality. The body, nature, science, time, and space are mere appearances, the "garment of the Unseen."[43] Because, as he asserts in his journal, "the Natural *is* the Supernatural,"[44] and the earth is *"the reflex of the living spirit of man,"*[45] the harmonies of art are possible.

For Kant, of course, the world of Reason is the world of the moral law. The artist's function is ultimately moral: his insights constitute sensible truth. Carlyle argues, too, for the poet's fictions as "purest truth." Novels, he cautions, "ought to be moral," and poetry should ever be "melodious human verity."[46] In that last expression Carlyle catches the essential point of Kant's aesthetics: through the "melodious" taste for beauty, our outward humanity and our inward "verity" are joined. His sympathy for the Artist's aesthetic awareness—what he calls the "eye for the Beautiful"—rises directly from his concern for moral revelation. The poet's "celestial brightness" can be justified only if his "morality, too, is of the highest and purest."[47] Carlyle contends that "the best bit for me in Kant" is the philosopher's simultaneous reverence for "the Starry Heavens and the Sense of Right and Wrong in the Human Soul."[48] And like Fichte, who sees in our sensitivity to beauty "the preparation for virtue," Carlyle believes the "love of Poetry" to be "the necessary parent of good conduct."[49] Clearly, Carlyle has no patience with "capricious sports" of the "Fancy" for their own sake: to him that poetry only is noble which leads us to contemplate and obey the dictates of the Categorical Imperative. The best impulses in literature help man toward Reason itself.[50]

Yet despite his passion for unseen truths, even the idealist intends that literature should make its immediate study the natural world. The poet "excites," with his more acute consciousness, the elements of actuality into symbols of the ideal; he perceives significance where, to the prosaic eye, there is none. Carlyle, too, looks on nature as a storehouse of divine symbols, opaque until interpreted by the artist. In the *History of German Literature,* he speaks of the "loveliness and mystic significance of Nature . . . revealed [in] Poetry,"[51] and in *Sartor,* of the "Godlike" "rendered visible" in the "prison of the Actual."[52] Later, in *Heroes,* he acknowledges the transcendental origins of this concept:

> Literature, so far as it is Literature, is an "Apocalypse of Nature," a revealing of the "open secret." It may well enough be named, in Fichte's style, "a continuous revelation" of the Godlike in the Terrestrial and Common. The Godlike does ever, in very truth, endure there; is brought

out, now in this dialect, now in that, with various degrees
of clearness: all true Singers and Speakers are, consciously
or unconsciously, doing so.[53]

Of Goethe's poetry he says, "it is . . . no looking back into an
antique Fairyland," but a successful reconstitution of the "real
world itself" so that ordinary things appear "holier to our eyes."
Carlyle accepts with Goethe the Fichtean view of nature as a
"solemn temple" furnished with myriad "emblems" of the spirit.[54]
Equipped with these deepened affections, the true poet studies
every element of the sensible world, "from the solemn phases of
the starry heaven to the simple floweret of the meadow," for "his
eye and his heart are open for nature's charms and her mystic
meanings."[55] In *Heroes,* Carlyle himself singles out one of the
more poignant hieroglyphs of the veiled truth behind appearances:
" 'The lillies of the field—springing up there in the humble
furrow-field; a beautiful *eye* looking out on you, from the great
inner Sea of Beauty! How could the rude Earth make these, if her
essence, rugged as she looks and is, were not inwardly Beauty?"[56]
He understands, too, that these objects are not in themselves sufficient to excite the sleeping soul of the world. "Art," he admits in
his introduction to *Wilhelm Meister,* must do with "Nature,"
what nature did "of old." Thus the very works of the literary man
become divine symbols as well. When Carlyle encourages Browning, in a letter of 1856, to pursue poetry for its "symbolic help,"
he speaks in the language of transcendental aesthetics; and when
he writes further that "melody" adds "finish" or "perfection" to
the ordinary products of the mind, he echoes Kant's conviction
that an acute sense of beauty harmonizes the lower and the higher
spheres.[57]

There is a fourth major characteristic of the transcendental attitude toward literature to which Carlyle's views conform. The
idealists of the German school, convinced of the close relationship
between beauty and truth, tend often to deify the artist. Kant puts
the poet in the "first rank" of men; Fichte makes a hero-priest of

the "Literary man"; to Schiller the artist is "like the son of Agamemnon" descending into the world "to purify it"; to Goethe the "World-Poet" is he who "brings the gods down to us."[58] For each, the literary man is uniquely gifted and an object of intense admiration. The nature of that gift that sets him above ordinary men is variously defined by Kant and Fichte, but in either case it amounts to the same thing: the artist *sees,* in the profoundest sense of the word. Inspired by "Imagination," "Reason," or a "Divine Idea of the World," the aesthetic writer looks beneath the shows of things and deciphers the moral basis of the universe. When he speaks sympathetically of the arts, Carlyle himself owns to such a messianic vision of the literary man. He, too, bases his reverence upon the conviction that the true poet manifests a depth of insight impossible for the rest of mankind. The "music" or "melody" of great art results from "Sphere-Harmonies" heard in deepest thought, from the richness of a mind able to grasp the larger unity of things. In *Heroes,* Carlyle argues for the primary, everlasting need to see:

> Poetry, therefore, we will call *musical Thought.* The Poet is he who thinks in that manner. At bottom it turns still on power of intellect; it is a man's sincerity and depth of vision that makes him a Poet. See deep enough, and you see musically; the heart of Nature *being* everywhere music, if you can only reach it.[59]

Clearly it is contemplation to which Carlyle refers when he speaks of "vision"—that is, internalized sight. In the foregoing passage he takes a stand immeasurably distant from the Calvinist's preference for "doing to thinking." There are, as well, distinct overtones of Platonic arrogance in such phrases as "power of intellect." Contemplative men constitute for him not only a cultural curiosity but a cultural elite. In his last essay on Goethe, Carlyle reiterates the central importance of "seeing"—that is, clarity and depth of thought—to the poet:

> As the first gift of all, may be discerned here utmost Clear-

ness, all-piercing faculty of Vision; whereto, as we ever find it, all other gifts are superadded; nay, properly they are but other forms of the same gift. A nobler power of insight than this of Goethe you in vain look for, since Shakespeare passed away. . . . Shakespeare too does not look *at* a thing, but into it, through it . . . the thing melts, as it were, into light under his eye, and anew *creates* itself before him. That is to say, he is a Thinker in the highest of all senses: he is a Poet. . . . What are the *Hamlets* and *Tempests,* the *Fausts* and *Mignons,* but glimpses accorded us into this translucent, wonder-encircled world; revelations of the mystery of all mysteries, Man's Life as it actually is?[60]

The essence, then, of poetry is transcendent vision; the artist looks *through* the actual into "mysteries" and timeless truths. Carlyle insists upon this perspicuity in all his favorable comments on literature:

> The poet's eyes are opened: he sees the changes of many-coloured existence, and sees the loveliness and deep purport which lies hidden under the very meanest of them; hidden to the vulgar sight, but clear to the poet's; because the "open secret" is no longer a secret to him, and he knows that the Universe is *full* of goodness; that whatsoever has being has beauty.[61]

The artist, blessed with vision, stands apart from the mass of men —those dull "worldlings" equipped with "vulgar sight." Carlyle, in this passage, takes an unequivocally idealistic view, believing, as Schiller and Novalis had come to believe, that "whatsoever has being has beauty." His mood is more than optative; it is assured. There are no reservations for him—as there would be for the Calvinist—occasioned by the appearance of evil or the frailty of man. The true artist exposes the realities of the supersensible and the very existence of such men makes possible for Carlyle "a life of joy and peace." Poetry, as he understands it, is the organ of transcendental faith: "[The poet] is a *vates,* a seer; a gift of vision has been given him. . . . For him the Ideal world is not remote from the Actual, but under it and within it: nay, he is a poet, precisely because he can discern it there."[62] The literary man must not, of course, approach the sensible world with trepidation; he must not fear, as the Puritan does, to engage himself with "the Creature." Carlyle's archetypal artist "not only loves Nature, but he revels in her; plunges into her infinite bosom, and fills his whole heart to intoxication with her charms."[63] Only then can he read her "mystic meanings." The poet's involvement, Carlyle carefully emphasizes, is not with the material for its own sake—that would be, in transcendental terms, as unworthy as asceticism. A "Divine Idea of the World" should stand always "in clear ethereal light before his mind"; he should apprehend "the Invisible, even under the mean forms of these days" and strive "to represent it in the Visible, and publish tidings of it to his fellowmen."[64] Thus, as a "recogniser and delineator of the Beautiful,"[65] the literary man can not fail to further the spiritual progress of the world.

Specifically, the artist's outstanding quality for Carlyle is a power of intellect—or extraordinary fusion of sensibilities that enables him to outstrip the merely rational thinker. The poet alone transcends the prison house of "logic-utterance." Carlyle feels that such a distinction between modes of thought has been made possible in his century through the idealistic philosophy of Kant and Fichte, and he welcomes the freedom from categories that their categories have permitted:

> It begins now to be everywhere surmised that the real Force, which in this world all things must obey, is Insight, Spiritual Vision and Determination. The thought is parent of the Deed, nay, is living soul of it, and last and continual, as well as first mover of it; is the foundation and beginning and essence, therefore, of man's whole existence here below. . . . The true Sovereign of the world, who moulds the world like soft wax, according to his pleasure, is he who lovingly sees into the world; the "inspired Thinker," whom in these days we name Poet.[66]

The concept of the essence of existence as sublime thought derives clearly from Carlyle's transcendental sources and parallels his commentary in *Lectures* on Kant's view of the material world as pure spirit.[67] In such a philosophical context, the "World-Poet," admitted "Sovereign" in the realm of transcendental vision, is, for Carlyle, "the eye and revealer of all things."[68] Elsewhere he speaks of the poet with the same unqualified reverence: he is "of all heavenly figures the beautifulest we know of that can visit this lower earth."[69] In *Past and Present,* Carlyle equates "genius" with poetry and names the poet, much as Schiller had, a "sacred voice," a purifying force "usefuller," "nobler," and "heavenlier" than any other.[70] He consistently deals in superlatives, even in his notebooks, when treating of the poetic intellect.[71] But Carlyle seldom reserves his praise for the poet solely—that is, for the hero-figure as Kant, Schiller, and Goethe defined him. He widens the circle, with Fichte's approval, to include the prose artist, the *Gelehrte* or "Literary Man":

> Men of Letters are a perpetual Priesthood, from age to age, teaching all men that a God is still present in their life; that all "Appearance" whatsoever we see in the world, is but a vesture for the "Divine Idea of the World," for "That which lies at the bottom of Appearance." In the true Literary Man there is thus ever, acknowledged or not by the world, a sacredness: he is the Light of the world; the world's Priest; guiding it, like a sacred Pillar of Fire, in its dark pilgrimage through the waste of Time.[72]

Such moods of "fine frenzy" notwithstanding, Carlyle seldom suspends his critical or discriminatory powers. He frequently denigrates one artist or national literature in comparison with another, but these comparative judgments depend, without exception, upon the criteria of transcendental aesthetics. The value of literature, according to disciples of German idealism, rests on its ability to articulate spiritual truths in a manner adapted to the complexities of modern thought. For Carlyle, the works of Goethe

and Schiller appear to herald such a religious awakening and to
incorporate an intense consciousness of the dilemmas that confront
the post-Renaissance man. When Carlyle writes, in an unpublished
letter to Forster, of his disillusionment with European literature,
it is disillusionment occasioned by the desertion of contemporary
writers from the standards and ideals of these transcendental
artists: "I have had nothing to do with foreign literature for a
number of years past. . . . German Literature in these new days
seems all to have run to threads and thrums. The French Literature of G. Sand and Co., which many people told me was a new-
birth, I found to be a detestable putrefaction,—new life of nothing
but maggots and blue bottles."[73] His estimate of individual artists
depends on transcendental principles as well. In *German Romance*
and the early essays, he denies to Musaeus, Hoffman, and Kotzebue
the name of "Poet" on the grounds of their absorption in the
"shows of things." By the same token, he excludes Voltaire from
the literary elite: "His view of the world is a cool, gently scornful,
altogether prosaic one: his sublimest Apocalypse of Nature lies
in the microscope and telescope: the Earth is a place for producing
corn; the Starry Heavens are admirable as a nautical timekeeper."[74]
In consequence, Carlyle finds Voltaire's ideas fitting "in a mere
Man of the World," but "very defective, sometimes altogether out
of place, in a Poet and Philosopher."[75] Here, clearly, Carlyle manifests the Kantian's distaste for quantitative measurements in nature; he reveals, too, the commonplace transcendental assumption
of an affinity between the artist and the metaphysician. Later in
the same essay, he quotes directly from the *Critique of Aesthetic
Judgment* in order to point up the distance between Voltaire's
"creations" and those of the genuine poet:

> A Tragedy, a Poem, with him is not to be "a manifestation
> of man's Reason in forms suitable to his sense"; but rather
> a highly complex egg-dance. . . . The deeper portion of
> our soul sits silent, unmoved under all this; recognizing no
> universal, everlasting Beauty, but only a modish Elegance,

less the work of a poetical creation than a process of the toilette.[76]

Carlyle condemns Voltaire, in effect, for living purely in the domain of the Understanding, for appealing to the intellect without appealing to the affections. There is apparently no room in his world-view for the sublimities of Reason; to Carlyle, he is utterly lacking in depth of insight:

> Poetic Method . . . must be the fruit of deep feeling as well as of clear vision—of genius as well as talent; and is much more likely to be found in the compositions of a . . . Shakespeare than of a Voltaire. The Method discernible in Voltaire, and this on all subjects whatever, is a purely business Method. The order that arises from it is not Beauty, but, at best, Regularity.[77]

In contrast to his estimate of Voltaire, Carlyle finds a superior faculty in the character and works of Dr. Johnson. Unlike his French contemporary, "it does not appear [to Carlyle] that at any time Johnson was what we call irreligious"; he possessed, not a skeptical nature, but that "first grand requisite, an assured heart."[78] In common with the transcendental artist, he valued his "choicest gift,—an open eye and heart," and perceived, with the light of Reason, the ultimate unity or "coherent Whole" that the "fragments" of the actual world "tend to form."[79] Moreover, Carlyle believes that Johnson accepted, as Kant did in his second *Kritik,* the innate existence and infinite value of the moral law in the individual: "Knowledge of the *transcendental,* immeasurable character of Duty we call the basis of all Gospels, the essence of all Religion: he who with his whole soul knows not this, as yet knows nothing, as yet is properly nothing. . . . Happily for him, Johnson was one of these that knew . . . it stood forever present to his eyes."[80]

Carlyle is uniformly hard on those imaginative writers who do not understand or seek to promote the moral instincts in man.

Walter Scott, for example, draws Carlyle's censure because he had "no message whatever to deliver to the world: wished not the world to elevate itself, to mend itself . . . except simply to pay him for the books he kept writing."[81] He seems from his novels, Carlyle allows, "one of the *healthiest* of men,"[82] but his health is of an external, shallow sort: "His life was worldly, his ambitions were worldly. There is nothing spiritual in him; all is economical, material, of the earth earthy."[83] Scott never accepts, as the German idealists do, that the subject, not the object, of experience is the artist's essential concern: "Your Shakespeare fashions his characters from the heart outwards; your Scott fashions them from the skin inwards, never getting to the heart of them!"[84] He has, in fact, no acute consciousness of "the great Mystery of Existence," is not, "as the Transcendentalists speak, possessed with an *idea*."[85] In the end, Carlyle refuses Scott admission to the "Priesthood" of true literary men for the same reason he denies it to Voltaire and Hoffmann: the novelist lacks any profound awareness of a noumenal reality. "He for the most part transcended but a little way the region of the commonplace."[86] "Literature," as Carlyle concludes, "is the Thought of thinking Souls,"[87] and Scott, healthy, active, and practical as he was, appears to his critic deficient both in soulfulness and deep thought.

Diderot, too, he contends in an 1833 article, "was little better than an Encyclopedic Artisan," a man who by his mere "copying of Nature" spoke only the "half-truth" of Art.[88] Unanimated by a "Divine Idea of the World," he was able only "to distort and dislocate . . . all things he laboured on"; at best, his works argue the insights of "no Seer, but only possibilities of a Seer, transient irradiations of a Seer, looking through the organs of a Philosophe."[89] Carlyle disparages Diderot's mechanistic, fragmentary *Weltanschauung*, especially in comparison with the intuitive, microcosmic awareness of the transcendental poet: "Your true Encyclopedical is the Homer, the Shakespeare; every genuine Poet is a living embodied, real Encyclopedia,—in more or fewer volumes . . . the whole world lies imaged as a whole within him."[90] In this,

Carlyle echoes Fichte's definition of the "I" and deplores, by implication, the incompleteness of Diderot's phenomenological atheism.[91] Later in the essay, he condemns openly his subject's analytical approach to truth:

> Beyond the meagre "rush-light of closet-logic," Diderot recognized no guidance. . . . He dwelt all his days in the "thin rind of the Conscious"; the deep fathomless domain of the Unconscious, whereon the other rests and has its meaning, was not, under any shape, surmised by him. Thus must the Sanctuary of Man's Soul stand perennially shut against this man; where his hand ceased to grope, the World ended.[92]

From this and other passages we may safely conclude that Carlyle's good opinion of literature depends, almost entirely, upon the degree to which that literature conforms to the principles of transcendental philosophy. No artist or work of the imagination that is out of keeping with the high seriousness of the German aesthetic appears to command Carlyle's favor: he is as incapable as Kant or Schiller or Novalis of condoning literature that does not, in some sense, encourage a spiritual "new-birth."

Yet there is, as we have long since discovered, an entirely different perspective from which Carlyle often looks at imaginative writing and its value. When he assumes such an attitude, his execrations are unmitigated: the artist and his art, however well-intentioned, are simple futile. Carlyle, at such times, does not trouble to differentiate between the *philosophe* and the "World-Poet," the newspaper article and the lyric poem—each and all contribute nothing to the spiritual well-being of man. Like the orthodox Calvinist, Carlyle bases his contempt, for the most part, upon one of three grounds: literature is either vain, that is, it betrays the sin of unrepentant self-consciousness; or it is false to the "facts of things"; or it displays and spreads idleness among its adherents. This is not to say that Carlyle's negative comments necessarily reveal, as the conventional Presbyterian's would, an exact reliance upon the dogmas of Calvin: Carlyle's desertion from Christian *theology* is entire and genuine; his loyalty is to the temper, not the letter, of his father's religion.

Often in his attacks on the "verbal arts," he manifests more than one of these Puritan antagonisms. Passages from the 1832 review of Boswell's *Life*, written within months of Carlyle's father's death, echo James's warning, recorded in *Reminiscences*, against both the vanity and idleness of "talk":

> He who . . . has clapped no bridle on his tongue, but lets it run racket, ejecting chatter and futility, is among the most indisputable malefactors omitted, or inserted, in the Criminal Calendar. To him that will well consider it, idle speaking is precisely the beginning of all Hollowness, Halfness, *Infidelity*. . . . Was the tongue suspended there . . . only that it might utter vain sounds, jargon, soul-confusing, and so *divide* man, as by enchanted Walls of Darkness, from union with man? . . . Consider the significance of Silence: it is boundless . . . unspeakably profitable to thee! Consider that chaotic hubbub, wherein thy own soul runs to waste, to confused suicidal dislocation and stupor: out of Silence comes thy strength.[93]

In this instance, Carlyle condemns the "speaking-talent" both as an instrument of "Infidelity" and idleness and as a device to wrap man in "soul-confusing" devilment: the human spirit, easily misled or "enchanted" by sophistical arguments, is best employed in the "profitable" realm of "Silence."[94] Much later, in a letter to his brother in 1870, Carlyle again argues that speculative literature is of an unprofitable nature—neither fitting one for action nor taking account of the potential for error and misconduct in a fallen world: it is "in general much too ideal and unpractical and impracticable—totally *neglecting* the frightful amount of Friction and perverse Impediment, perverse but insuperable, which attends every one of us in this world!"[95] Curiously, it is of Emerson's transcendental essays that Carlyle here specifically speaks, thus marking out sharply the differences between his inherited and his adopted beliefs. Yet the danger of literature, for the Puritan, is not so much in its naïveté as in its sinister, self-congratulatory appearance. In *Cromwell*, Carlyle reveals precisely that note of distrust: the literary man, he contends, aims at "eloquence" rather than truth, at "adroitness" and the "superfluity" of "eloquent speaking" rather than the "Heroic insights" of conviction. Oliver Cromwell, on the other hand, scorned the use of "boastful" decoration in his letters: he represents, in fact, Carlyle's Calvinist ideal; that is, the humble man of action who "does" his poems. Carlyle had earlier attacked the arts on these twin points of inaction and self-esteem in his *Lectures on the History of Literature*. There he compares the Romans' "genius" for practicality to the "dreaming," "unhealthy" intellect of the Greeks and concludes that those epochs are most decadent in which the artist occupies a central position in national culture. The flowering of art signals a movement toward self-absorption, passivity, and complacency; in Carlyle's sometime Calvinist universe of tireless battle and obligatory asceticism, the taste for literature presages damnation. Rather than the "Sovereign" or saviour of his age, the "World-Poet" dwindles for Carlyle as Puritan into a talisman of the devil. The aesthetic writer's contribution to society is then of infinitely smaller value than the transcendentalist presumes it to be; for Carlyle in these *Lectures,* it amounts to an ultimately corrupt extension of man's energies.

But Carlyle, while maintaining his opposition to literature on the grounds of a need for self-denial, does not always fault it as an occupation for "idle fools." Frequently, the impetus for his attack is a Calvinist allegiance to "the facts of things"—that literal representation of the world for which the poet and novelist feel little responsibility. Knox had argued that man must recognize, in the reality of conflict, God's judgments and his own imperfect state: to idealize the actual is to ignore the omnipresence of evil. Carlyle inherited from his Puritan father an enormous respect for these concrete truths and a consequent impatience with the imagined kingdoms of the artist. In his less tolerant moments, Carlyle describes literature as a more sophisticated species of *"lying."*[96] He finds, for example, in his 1875 essay on Knox, that Puritanism was of greater value than all the artistic achievements of the Renaissance, because it, in contradistinction to poetry and drama, refused "to believe what is not a Fact in God's Universe"; it alone avoided that "mingled mass of self-delusions and mendacities" to which the heterodox individual is subject.[97] The arts, on the other hand, condone both self-consciousness and fantasy, caring nothing, as Carlyle wrote in 1851, for "nature and her verities." He variously describes the artist's words as "windy gospels," "a nebulous kind of element," even "the temporary dilettante cloudland of our poor Century."[98] But in the *Life of Sterling,* as openly as in *Cromwell,* Carlyle indicts the aesthete for deeper crimes than these apparently innocent "untruths." Imaginative literature reveals, to a man of Carlyle's Puritan instincts, a strain of "hypocrisy" from which "earnest men . . . are admonished" to keep their distance. Surely, he warns, such hypocrisy is a function of the literary man's unchecked self-consciousness; the result, more or less, of his "love of the love of greatness." In his journal in 1848 Carlyle, with unguarded acerbity, writes of "the kind of hunger for pleasure of every kind, and want of all other force. . . . There is perhaps no clearer evidence of our universal *immorality* and cowardly untruth than even in such sympathies."[99] The "immorality" that Carlyle reads into the character of Keats results, it seems, both from the poet's self-indulgence ("the hunger for pleasure") and from his complacent "falsehoods."

For the most part, however, Carlyle grounds his derogation of literature not so much on the Puritans' distaste for vanity and fabrication as on their respect for hard work and accuracy of judgment. Frequently, it is true, Carlyle confuses such accuracy or "sincerity" with the degree to which an author allows historical phenomena to dominate his world-picture. Thus he moderates his praise of Shakespeare by claiming, "It is not the Fiction that I admire, but the Fact; to say truth, what I most of all admire are the traces he shows of a talent that could have turned the *History of England* into a kind of . . . *Bible*."[100] In this, Carlyle echoes the Calvinist concept of history as a set of moral object-lessons—a treatment of events best exemplified in the Old Testament. Again, when he asserts that "the Bible itself . . . is the *truest* of all Books," Carlyle seconds Calvin's opinion in the *Institutes* that the "received word" is the strongest source of light for man. Earlier, in *Past and Present,* Carlyle confirms his complimentary belief in historical providence, in what he calls the "Bible of Universal History": "This is . . . God's-book, [in] which every born man, till once the soul and eyesight are extinguished in him, can and must, with his own eyes, see God's Finger writing."[101] All other lights appear, upon closer examination, to be "walls of Darkness"; particularly that "fantastical air-Palace" known as literature. Carlyle believes it to be an unfit habitation for the "serious souls" of his generation:

> "Fiction,"—my friend, you will be surprised to discover at last what alarming cousinship *it* has to *Lying:* don't go into "Fiction," . . . nor concern yourself with "Fine Literature," or Coarse ditto, or the unspeakable glories and rewards of pleasing your generation. . . . In general, leave "Literature," the thing called "Literature" at present, to run through its rapid fermentations . . . and to fluff itself off into Nothing, in its own way,—like a poor bottle of soda-water with the cork sprung;—it won't be long. . . . In fifty years, I should guess, all really serious souls will have quitted that mad province, left it to the roaring populaces; and for any *Noble*-man or useful person it will be a credit rather to declare, "I have not written anything";—and we of "Literature" by trade, we shall sink again, I perceive, to the rank of street-fiddling. . . . Of "Literature" keep well to windward, my serious friend![102]

Just as the conventional Puritan might, Carlyle despises art primarily for its dissipation of vital energies—its flippancy toward, as well as its distortion of, the stern realities of the moment. In a world of conflict, he believes, its passivity is the measure of its wantonness. Not surprisingly, he periodically loses patience with those who "waste themselves in that inane region of Art, Poetry, and the like."[103] In an essay of 1867, he declares his Hebraic position in much the same language he had adopted in a letter to his brother thirty-four years earlier:[104] "Poetry? It is not pleasant singing that we want, but wise and earnest speaking:—'Art,' etc. are very fine and ornamental, but only to persons sitting at their ease: to persons still wrestling with deadly chaos, and still fighting for dubious existence, they are a mockery rather."[105] Again, in the *History of Frederick*, Carlyle dismisses the charms of literature as idle fantasies, unfit for the ear of Prussia's most valiant, "truth-loving" prince.[106] From such statements one clear association emerges: work and truth are often linked in Carlyle's mind. Furthermore, remembering *Reminiscences,* we may be sure that this equation derives from the precepts and example of his Puritan father. "The Doable," as he says in *Past and Present,* "reaches down to the World's centre"; "it is her Practical Material Work alone that England has to show for herself!"[107] The converse is equally true for Carlyle; that is, the identification of speech or writing with whatever is false and shallow: "The Speakable . . . lies atop, as a superficial film"; "the spoken Word of England has not been true . . . [has been] trivial; of short endurance; not valuable. . . . A Cant; a helpless involuntary Cant, nay too often a cunning voluntary one . . . the Voice not of Nature and Fact, but of something other than these."[108] By contrast, there is nothing "cunning," "light," or "adroit" in hard work; for Carlyle in his Calvinist temper, physical suffering and obedience seem the best measure, not only of sincerity, but of manliness. "A man that can succeed in working is to me always a man. . . . The Practical Labour of England is *not* a chimerical Triviality; it is a Fact . . . which no man and no demon will contradict."[109] Carlyle was influenced in this, as in the sketch of his father, by an inherent regard for "manful well-doing"; his childhood sympathy for the "strong hand" of the "true workman" was apparently ineradicable. Literature, he often said, unlike "Practical Labour," merely increased "contemporary confusion," for it detached itself from the exigencies of the moment and blurred the moral realities—"ofttimes making wrong right," as the Calvinist would say: "O ye Playwrights, and literary quacks of every feather, weep . . . over yourselves! Know . . . that the wind-bag, are ye mad enough to mount it, will burst, or be shot through with arrows, and your bones too shall act as scarecrows."[110] The faults of the artist, as Carlyle depicts them in his essay on Novalis, are twofold: "a want of rapid energy; something which we might term *passiveness*"; and an inability to distinguish between the fantastic and the real: "He *sits*, we might say, among the rich, fine, thousandfold combinations, which his mind almost of itself presents him; but, perhaps, he shows too little activity in the process."[111] The aesthetic thinker, according to Calvin and Knox, allows himself to be seduced by the "phantasms of his own brain" from a proper loyalty to the "factis of men." These facts, declared to us in the countless shocks of daily life, demand not "idle sitting," but "laborious activity." The idealist's tranquil temper, seen through Puritan eyes, proceeds not from some "depth of insight" that pierces the actual, but from straightforward moral indolence: the artist simply refuses to discriminate between the false and the true or to work manfully for the salvation of the world. Knox, as Carlyle described him in 1875, stands in the strictest and most praiseworthy opposition to the pallid "unrealities" of art: "Truly it was not with what we call 'Literature,' and its harmonies and symmetries, addressed to man's Imagination, that Knox, was ever for an hour concerned; but with practical truths alone, addressed to man's inmost Belief, with immutable Facts, accepted by him . . . as the daily voices of the Eternal."[112] As testaments to Carlyle's Puritan distrust of literature and his reverence for hard work and literal truth, there are no better illustrations than his frequent letters to literary aspirants. To one hopeful, unpublished author in June 1862, he writes that "Literature" is not a "truly noble human career," but rather "a loud clamor of Nonsense," neither useful nor "authentic"; better, he suggests, for earnest, vigorous men to ignore such "palaver" and follow "a *silent* course of activity."[113] In another such letter, dated twenty years earlier, Carlyle invokes nearly every argument the Calvinist was likely to use in condemning the literary life:

> My dear young friend, you must learn the indispensable significance of hard, stern, long-continued *labour.* Grudge not labour, grudge not pain, disappointment, sorrow or distress of any kind—all is for your good, if you can endeavor and endure. . . . You must learn the meaning of *silence.* . . . Pray that you may be *forced* to hold your tongue. . . . I would advise that you resolutely postponed, into the unexplored uncertainty of the Future, all concern with literature. . . . As a trade, I . . . describe it as the frightfullest, fatallest, and too generally despicablest of all trades now followed under the sun. . . . A steady course of professional industry has ever been held the usefullest support for *mind* as well as body; I heartily agree with that. . . . My decided advice is, that you stand resolutely by medicine, determined to find an honest livelihood . . . and do a man's task in that way. Then is there a solid *backbone* in one's existence.[114]

From this it would seem that the standard by which all things ought to be judged is the Puritan one of moral usefulness—a position that contrasts sharply with Carlyle's loud and frequent defenses of the "sacred" non-utility of literature. And surely, in his insistence on "a steady course of professional industry," Carlyle exhibits the fundamental Calvinist longing for "a regular and consistent system of conduct." There is, in fact, only one Puritan objection to the arts that Carlyle fails to raise in the preceding passage—that of the dangers of licentiousness and vanity—and he implies even this in advocating an enforced silence.

Frequently Carlyle's antipathetic comments on literature reveal all the major Puritan prejudices at once: he ranks Cromwell above the aesthetic writer, for example, because there is no taint of self-flattery in his words—nothing "glib" or "eloquent"; further, the English reformer never distorts "the naked truth of things" but studies always to tell "God's Facts" rather than some "euphemistic story"; lastly, he does not sit idly amidst the "rich harmonies" of his imagination, but "grapples like a giant, face to face" with the evils of the actual world.[115] In the last of the *Latter-Day Pamphlets,* Carlyle amplifies these misgivings about the worth of literature. First of all, he takes exception to the literary man's private, and therefore depraved, concept of divinity: "All arts . . . are tainted to the heart with foul poison; carry not in them the inspiration of God, but (frightful to think of!) that of the Devil calling and thinking himself God; and are smitten with a curse for ever-more."[116] This is an obvious echo of Knox's warning that "all wirschipping, honoring, or service inventit by the braine of man in the religioun of God . . . is Idolatrie." Carlyle then unwinds a sustained diatribe against the premeditated falsehoods of imaginative writing—falsehoods that waylay and confuse the unselfcon-scious workman:

> The Fine Arts . . . are sure to be the parent of much empty talk, laborious hypocrisy, dilettantism, futility; involving huge trouble and expense and babble, which end in no result, if not in worse than none. The practical man, in his moments of sincerity, feels them to be pretentious nothingness; a confused superfluity and nuisance, purchased with cost—what he in brief language denominates a *bore.* It is truly so.[117]

He recalls, a few pages later, his equation of fiction with "lying" and implies, in the process, that truth exists only in its narrowest acceptation, that is, as literal fact:

> Truth, fact, is the life of all things; falsity, "fiction" or whatever it may call itself, is certain to be death. . . . [The arts] are to understand that they are sent hither not to fib and dance, but to speak and work; and, on the whole, that God

Almighty's *Facts,* such as are given us, are the one pabulum which will yield them any nourishment in this world.[118]

Carlyle goes as far as the dogmatic Calvinist in designating the fountainhead or authority for those "facts" which are "given us": "The Hebrew Bible, is it not, before all things, *true,* as no other Book ever was or will be?"[119] All other written "sources," particularly of the imaginative, artful sort, amount to "pretentious nothingness" or "confused superfluity." It seemed to Carlyle, as he finished his pragmatic "latter-day" tracts, that the company of poets and novelists had been engaged, for "centuries long," in the merest "wool-gathering"—"wandering literally like creatures fallen mad!"[120]

Yet despite his towering intolerance of "Poetries,"[121] Carlyle condescends in the same pamphlet to admit the singularity of Shakespeare's genius: "In Shakespeare, more than in another, lay that high *vates* talent of interpreting confused human Actualities."[122] For the moment, Carlyle dampens his Calvinist fury and dwells instead on those "divine melodious Ideals" of the transcendentalist and the poet. But almost immediately the dominant tone of contemptuousness returns, and he despairs, as Cromwell himself might have, that Shakespeare wasted his talent for discerning truth in the idle, morally purposeless realm of literature: "Alas, it was not in the Temple of Nations, with all intelligences ministering to him and co-operating with him, that his workshop was laid; it was in the Bankside Playhouse that Shakespeare was set to work, and the sovereign populace had ware for their sixpence from him there!"[123] Profound indeed is the perversity of a religious temper that compels Carlyle to wish Shakespeare had been a politician.[124] In one final onslaught on the legion of "wits, story-tellers" and "Ballad-singers," Carlyle displays the fullest measure of Puritan iconoclasm:

Fiction, I think, or idle falsity of any kind, was never tolerable, except in a world which did itself abound in practical lies and solemn shams; and which had gradually impressed

on its inhabitants the inane form of character tolerant of
that kind of ware. A serious soul, can it wish, even in hours
of relaxation, that you should fiddle empty nonsense to it?
A serious soul would desire to be entertained, either with
absolute silence, or with what was truth, and had fruit in
it, and was made by the Maker of us all. With the idle soul
I fancy it far otherwise; but only with the idle.[125]

He agrees here with his father's dicta as well as Knox's: all three
tolerate nothing written except the Bible; all associate the decoration of language with the "shams" and "idolatries" of a decadent,
Catholic spirit; and all exhibit an ingrained Hebraism that bridles
at the relative passivity of the artist. It is, moreover, curiously in-
dicative of the Puritan nature of Carlyle's bias that such a sustained
attack on the arts should occur in the context of a polemic against
Jesuitism.

For the most part, however, Carlyle does not concentrate so
much Calvinist anger in a single passage. It is seldom that he rails,
in one breath, against the "idle falsity" of the "Devil . . . thinking
himself God"; more frequently, his negative opinions of literature
fall into one of three discrete categories. The first of these includes
his objections to art as a violation of the principle of self-denial.
Highly wrought language appears to him then as a species of corruption, undermining the need in man for submission and mute
obedience. In "Characteristics" and Lectures on the History of
Literature, Carlyle declares that self-consciousness is a sickness, a
symptom of depravity. He has, for example, a strong temperamental aversion to the confessional novel, as a letter to Forster in 1849
demonstrates: "Froude's Book [Nemesis of Faith] is not . . . worth
its paper and ink. What on earth is the use of a wretched mortal's
vomiting up all his interior crudities, dubitations, and spiritual,
agonizing bellyaches into the view of the public, and howling
tragically, 'See!' "[126] A strange remark from Carlyle, especially when
one considers his early fondness for Rousseau and his own efforts
along similar lines in Wotton Reinfred, Sartor, and Reminiscences.

Yet even in *Sartor* itself, he cannot resist a judgment against the obfuscating egotism of speech:

> Silence is the element in which great things fashion them-
> selves together. . . . Not William the Silent only, but all
> the considerable men I have known . . . forbore to babble
> of what they were creating and profecting. Nay, in thy own
> mean perplexities, do thou thyself but *hold thy tongue for
> one day:* on the morrow, how much clearer are thy pur-
> poses and duties.[127]

The silence Carlyle here advocates is not the quietism of the mystic or the transcendentalist, but that shamed, obedient silence of which the devout Presbyterian—especially James Carlyle—was so jealous. Given man's fallen state, the mute individual is the only one who can expect to please God. And when Carlyle writes to Sterling that "on the whole *Silence* seems to me the Highest Divin- ity on this Earth at present. Blessed is *Silence:* the giver of all Truth, of all good,"[128] he voices the same ascetic principle by which his father and most of the Puritan commonality studied always to live. Carlyle objected, as his contemporaries were often reminded, to the vanity of "phrase-making" in particular. There seemed to him something highly dishonest about the artist's efforts to refine his utterance; it amounted, he believed, to an assertion of the pos- sibility of human perfection. Not only was such quibbling self- congratulatory but, because its aim was illusory, it usurped time that might be spent upon practicable matters: "Learn to do it *honestly . . . perfectly* thou wilt never do it. . . . Time flies; while thou balancest a sentence, thou art nearer the *final* Pe- riod."[129] Here, as in his advice to Sterling, Carlyle looks at the poetic talent not as a divine gift, but as the merely gratuitous inter- ference of self with sense.

A larger number of Carlyle's depreciations of literature manifest another Puritan bias; that is, a tendency to reproach the artist simply for mouthing "shams." It should be remembered that the

Protestant apologist insists, as much as the empirical philosopher, upon the logical aspects of his system: he has an enormous, almost exclusive, respect for common sense. The roots of the Scottish dissenter's faith lie, after all, in the cogent, legalistic arguments of Calvin's *Institutes*. Believing as he does that "the factis of men aggrie with the laws of God," the devout Puritan naturally feels uneasy in the presence of "dreams and phantasms"—whether those of decadent artists or superstitious Catholics. Carlyle, like his father, often exhibits a low tolerance for fantasy. In the *Life of Schiller*, he ranks "the love of knowing things as they are" above the talent for "painting things as they should be." He sets in opposition—as the transcendentalist seldom would—the "love of truth" and the "dreamy scenes of the Imagination" and treats the former as a more "earnest," "calmer province."[130] Again, in a letter to von Ense in 1842, Carlyle speaks pejoratively of art as "speculation" and claims there is "almost nothing of the so-called Poetry that I can bear to read at all."[131] Earlier, in 1828, he projects something of the Puritan literalist's impatience with idealism when he writes to his brother that Goethe's ideas are "to redolent of *twaddle*."[132] Certainly, Carlyle's scorn for the "hazy infinitudes" of Coleridge, in the eighth chapter of *Sterling* and an 1824 letter to John (previously cited), arises in part from his loyalty to the Calvinist instinct for fact. Another passage, from a letter to Sterling in 1842, announces unequivocally Carlyle's commitment to concrete realities:

> Of Dramatic Art, tho' I have eagerly listened to a Goethe speaking of it, and to several hundreds of other persons mumbling and trying to speak of it, I find that I, practically speaking, know yet almost as good as nothing. Indeed of *Art* generally (*Kunst* so-called) I can know almost nothing: my first and last secret of *Kunst*, is to get a thorough *intelligence* of the *fact* to be painted, represented, or in whatever way set forth.[133]

Elsewhere, he speaks of the historian's craft as alone "authentic":

the act of "writing down many a thing that he with his own heart and eyes has *known*."[134] Wordsworth's sonnets, on the other hand, strike him as "bewildered, benighted, ghost-ridden,"[135] and aesthetic theories and poetry in general amount to a "jingle" of *"palabra"* and "Nonsense."[136] That commonsensical impulse directs Carlyle, in his lecture on the "Hero as Poet," to qualify Goethe's declaration that "the beautiful is higher than the Good; the Beautiful contains in it the Good." As any down-to-earth Scottish Calvinist, aware of the fallibility of our tastes might do, Carlyle immediately appends a warning: "the *true* Beautiful; which however, I have said somewhere, 'differs from the *false* as Heaven does from Vauxhall!' "[137] Of course, Carlyle thereby clouds his meaning, but in doing so he displays openly the tension within him between transcendental principles and Calvinist prejudices. His intermittent exasperation with "untruths" often led him to make absurd generalizations about literature. In two articles on Boswell's *Life of Johnson,* for example, he claims genuine literary merit for only one work of art—the *Iliad*—and that solely on the basis of its verisimilitude:

> Fiction . . . has ever an, in some degree, unsatisfactory character . . . the Epic Poems of old time, so long as they continued epic, and had any complete impressiveness, were Histories, and understood to be a narrative [sic] of *facts*. In so far as Homer employed his gods as mere ornamental fringes, and had not himself . . . a belief that they were real agents in those antique doings; so far did he fail to be *genuine;* so far was he a partially hollow and false singer. . . . None but the earliest Epic Poems can claim this distinction of entire credibility, of Reality; after an *Iliad* . . . the rest seem by this rule of mine, to be altogether excluded from the list. Accordingly, what are all the rest, from Virgil's *Aeneid* downwards, in comparison? Frosty, artificial, heterogeneous things; more of gumflowers than of roses; at the best, of the two mixed incoherently together.[138]

Although Carlyle has not lost entire faith in the Imagination, as the Puritan inevitably does, he has gone so far as to make individual fancy the merest gloss upon actuality. Such a shift in priorities, from subjective to objective criteria, would amount, for the Kantian idealist or the Romantic artist, to an abnegation of belief. Later, in the first of these essays, Carlyle does moderate his dissatisfaction with the arts, but he quickly returns to the need for factual truth:

> Here and there, a *Tom Jones,* a *Meister,* a *Crusoe,*[139] will yield no little solacement to the minds of men; though still immeasurably less than a *Reality* would, were the significance thereof as impressively unfolded. . . . Quitting these airy regions, let anyone bethink him how impressive the smallest *historical fact* may become, as contrasted with the grandest *fictitious event.*[140]

In the same review, Carlyle treats the high purposes of the transcendental artist in a manner that approaches outright condescension. "They are," he admits, "right in their precept, they mean rightly."[141] What they fail to understand (unconverted as they are to Carlyle's regard for "facts") is "that History, after all, is the true Poetry . . . that even in the right interpretation of Reality and History does genuine Poetry consist."[142] Such a declaration of values recalls Carlyle's admiration for the "done Poem," his resolve to write as his father had built his houses, even his odd desire to "raise" Shakespeare to the stature of a politician. Only thus, by rededicating himself and his literary world to the truths of actual existence, did Carlyle believe he might be justified or forgiven by a Calvinist God.

The third Puritan influence revealed in Carlyle's antagonism toward literature—that of radical Hebraism—is the most insistent. Often, the dichotomy between art and action is clearly drawn and Carlyle's evaluation is explicit: "Homer will one day be swallowed up in time. . . . But actions will not be destroyed."[143] At other times the work-ethic is implied by Carlyle's reliance upon "usefulness" or "practicability" as the measure of the worth of a man's invention. Judged by such a standard, imaginative literature naturally suffers in Carlyle's opinion: "There is a number, a frightfully increasing number, of books that are decidedly, to the readers of them, not useful."[144] Literature, he warns, does not teach us "what is necessary to be known . . . [that is] faithful obedience, modesty, humility, and correct moral conduct."[145] These last are precisely the virtues that every Scots Presbyterian, schooled in the stern disciplines of Old Testament logic, learned from an early age to revere. Out of a guarded silence, Carlyle contends, the individual acquires both humility and those principles of common sense that the orator and the artist consistently abuse.[146] In his Edinburgh address, Carlyle longs for a "more practical and concrete way of working," doubts of "the salutary effect of vocal education altogether," and finally admonishes his audience to "keep out of literature . . . as a general rule."[147] At other times, particularly in conversation, he upbraids poets and critics for their passivity and "uselessness": Novalis seems "womanish" in his idleness; Goethe would have been better employed "if he had *done* something";[148] Tennyson appears "distinctly rather wearisome; nothing coming from him that [does] not smack of utter indolence, what one might almost call torpid sleepiness and stupor";[149] Coleridge's writing is "vague and purposeless"; Lamb "had no practical sense in him"; Shelley was simply "a poor shrieking creature who had said or sung nothing worth a serious man being at the trouble of remembering"; and Wordsworth was "essentially a cold, hard, silent practical man, who, if he had not fallen into poetry, would have done effectual work of some sort in the world."[150] Again, in his published histories, he argues that human wisdom ought not to be judged through this "idle element of speaking," ought not to depend upon "a thing of *vocables*"; rather, let us strive "to develop a man into *doing* something."[151] At such times, Carlyle believes with Calvin that labor, not thought, is our prime duty in a fallen world. He does, of course, occasionally imply, in letters to his brother and a few scattered essays, that after we have rid ourselves of error and sin there will be opportunities to "sing and paint," to dwell in art's imagined ideal.[152] Literary men, it seems, have value even to Carlyle as Puritan, but it is a value much diminished by their "want of force." They may prove, perhaps, more than "a noisy crew"; they may yet entertain an enlightened humanity; but "at present" it behooves the earnest soul "to be shy [of them] rather than otherwise." After all, "To speak, to write, Nature did not peremptorily order thee; but to work she did."[153] "The Speakable," the "written Poem," are indeed of some ornamental consequence to Carlyle, but the "Doable," the "done work," are of infinitely greater moment: they alone tell us "whatsoever of strength the man had in him."[154] Carlyle writes contemptuously in his early notebooks of "female geniuses," men who invariably have "a taste for Poetry," and whose minds "admire and receive, but can hardly create."[155] Again he exhibits the Calvinist's blind spot—an inability to conceive of creation in any but the physical sense. In a letter to Jane in 1845 and one to Browning a few years later, Carlyle complains that literature consists of "little other than a Newspaper," for it is at best a reporting of deeds, a reminiscence of action.[156] To another correspondent, he declares his open envy of the "true workman" and his personal disappointment with the fruits of a literary career:

> It is a real blessing for a man that lives by tilling of the soil! Were it ugly as sin, every stroke of good labour you bestow on it, will make the place beautifuller;—what "beauty" is there in Fairyland itself compared with the aspect of order produced out of disorder by one's own faithful toil? That is the real beauty that will make a man feel some reconcilement to his ugly lot, however ugly it look.[157]

Gavan Duffy recalls a conversation with Carlyle in which he indulged, with complete candor, that same Hebraic vision of imaginative writing: "Modern literature was all purposeless and distracted, and led he knew not where. Its professors were on the wrong path just now, and he believed the world would soon discover that some practical work done was worth innumerable

'Oliver Twists' and 'Harry Lorrequers,' and any amount of other
ingenious dancing on the black rope."[158] As early as 1831, Carlyle
questioned the value of art in a world where there were yet enormous practical improvements to be made: in his journal, he considers, sympathetically, the active alternatives to his present way
of life:

> Meanwhile, what [is] the true duty of man? Were it to stand
> utterly aloof from politics . . . or is not perhaps the very
> want of this time an infinite want of Governors, of knowl-
> edge how to govern itself? Canst thou in any measure
> spread abroad reverence over the hearts of men? . . . Is it
> to be done by art? or are men's minds as yet shut to art,
> and open only at best to oratory?[159]

Here, even before the deaths of Goethe or his own father, Carlyle
suspects the effectiveness of art; later these misgivings led him to
endorse the dogmatism of the Hebrew prophets and the brutality
of "drill-sargeants." But his early sentiments, moderate as they appear, nonetheless parallel those of the orthodox Puritan, for both
strip literature of contemporary relevance and tend to dismiss it
as "a little Recreation" in the midst of serious, unfantastical concerns.[160] Carlyle's unhappiness with literature deepened as he aged
and had obviously reached a critical stage when he divulged, in an
1835 letter to his mother, his plans to abandon writing for politics:

> I have grave doubts about . . . books in general, for all is
> in the uttermost confusion in that line of business here. . . .
> There are some two or even three outlooks opening on me
> unconnected with books. One of these regards the business
> of national education which Parliament is now busy upon,
> in which I mean to try all my strength to get something to
> do, for my conscience greatly approves of the work as use-
> ful.[161]

Although his momentary determination came to nothing, Carlyle
continued for many years "to try all [his] strength to get something

to *do.*" When the last realistic opportunities for that had passed, he persisted in advising everyone young enough to choose, to re-dedicate himself to a practical livelihood. This Scots Calvinist bias in favor of an active, externally directed life figures prominently in a letter from Carlyle to a literary aspirant in 1847:

> [You are] not by any means to quit the solid paths of prac-tical business for these inane froth oceans which, however gas-lighted they may be, are essentially what I have called them somewhere, base as Fleet Ditch, the mother of dead dogs. Surely it is better for a man to *work* out his God-given faculty than merely to speak it out, even in the most Augustan times.[162]

In his reference to the need for toil even in "Augustan" eras, Carlyle seems to deny to literature a legitimate function in any epoch, however stable or just. There is no question that Carlyle's discouragement with his own idleness was, at times, profound. He writes despairingly to Forster in 1870: "My life [is a] dwelling mainly . . . in the vague, in the cloudy and (to practical purposes) mournful and inane. I read 3 or 4 hours daily; goodish Books . . . though of what *use* it is . . . I could not in the least explain to myself or another."[163] Yet work, for Carlyle and for the Calvinist, is not simply desirable on the grounds of utility. It has another purpose, for it alone "reduces us to submission" and acquaints us with the necessary miseries of our corrupt condition. In the post-lapsarian world, imaginative creation, unlike "true" labor, does not entail sufficient suffering to offset the natural depravity of men. Carlyle implies as much in a journal entry for February 1848:

> Neither does Art, etc., in the smallest hold out with me. In fact, that concern has all gone down with me, like ice too thin on a muddy pond. I do not believe in 'Art'—nay, I do believe it to be one of the deadliest *cants.* . . . In brief, nothing is—but by *labour,* which we call sorrow, misery, etc. Thou must gird up thy loins again and work another stroke or two before thou die.[164]

Work, then, constitutes, for Carlyle and the orthodox Puritan, an expiation of guilt. Doggedness, in both cases, is often overlaid with morbidity; and like the Calvinist, Carlyle takes an almost masochistic pleasure in the wretchedness of his tasks. Although denied the exquisite sufferings of the laboring poor, he attempts, in later life, to compensate for his "sinful" good fortune by applying himself to scholarly projects that are basically joyless. He admits, for example, that he has no real enthusiasm for writing *Frederick,* yet one suspects from numerous letters that he hoped, by continually fronting a loathsome subject, to earn some measure of forgiveness from the spirit of his father. The effort to complete the eight-volume history,[165] he tells Forster in 1861, "has fairly broken my heart" and excels all other activities "in disgusting bother . . . and discouragement"; nonetheless, he will "compel" himself to finish it, following the "true example" of his father's perseverance in all things.[166] In such a context, literary practice has no intrinsic significance for Carlyle; it serves only as a hair shirt.

At about the same time Carlyle was finishing *Frederick,* he spoke to Froude of his disillusionment with the arts. As Froude recalls the monologue, Carlyle based his antipathy upon Hebraic principles, upon his own unfulfilled longing to work as his father had worked. The passage is remarkably close, in language and in temper, to the sketch he had written of James Carlyle thirty years earlier. The sentiments are straightforwardly Calvinistic and include a nagging suspicion of the honesty and humility of artists:

> A "man of letters" . . . was generally someone who had gone into it because he was unfit for better work, because he was too vain or too self-willed to travel along the beaten highways, and his writing, unless he was one of a million, began and ended in nothing. Life was action, not talk. The speech, the book, the review or newspaper article was so much force expended—force lost to practical usefulness. . . . He once said to me that England had produced her greatest men before she began to have a literature at all. A man . . . was made better by being trained in habits of industry, by being

enabled to *do* good useful work and earn an honest living
by it. . . . "If there be one thing," he said, "for which I
have no special talent, it is literature. If I had been taught
to *do* the simplest useful thing, I should have been a better
and a happier man."[167]

1. *Essays*, II, 2. In an article on Scott nine years later, Carlyle repeats, almost verbatim, his objections to "amusing" literature. See *Essays*, IV, 76. Carlyle detested writers who appealed only to the sensations—what he called the "stomach"; he writes in such a vein to Forster on 11 April 1853; "That was a capital article on *Smith*, the new "Poet" they [the *Times*] have discovered! . . . In his present course he seems to be but proclaiming, in an eloquent manner, that his stomach is bottomless . . . I, for my own solitary share, am inexpressibly wearied of all that" (from an unpublished letter in the Forster Collection, Victoria and Albert Museum, III, no. 175).

2. *Essays*, II, 360.

3. Journal extract in Froude, *First Forty Years*, II, 130–31. Despite the many years Jeffrey had spent reviewing poetry, he did give occasional evidence of what Carlyle called his "prose spirit." See especially his review of *Wilhelm Meister* in 1825, in which he labels Goethe's ideas "unclassical," "heretical," and lost in "the region of mysticism." The book, he says, amounts to a jumble "of misty metaphysics, and superstitious visions . . . [with which] it would be a baseness to be acquainted" (*Contributions to the Edinburgh Review*, pp. 120–42).

4. *Essays*, II, 175.

5. *Unfinished History of German Literature*, p. 11.

6. *Essays*, I, 389–90.

7. *Goethe Letters*, pp. 32–33, 190–91. On his view of poetry as "another form of Religion," see also *Essays*, I, 314.

8. *Essays*, I, 78.

9. *Goethe Letters*, p. 256.

10. *Essays*, I, 56.

11. *Reminiscences*, I, 232, and *WM*, I, 22.

12. *GR*, II, 18–19.

13. *Essays*, I, 85–86.

14. *SR*, p. 57. See also *Essays*, IV, 476.

15. *Essays*, I, 449, 452, 459.

16. *LS*, p. 78.

17. *Reminiscences*, I, 287–88.

18. *Science of Knowledge*, p. 286.

19. *PP*, p. 86.

20. *SR*, pp. 138, 158.

21. P. 195.
22. *Essays*, II, 442.
23. *SR*, p. 209.
24. *Essays*, III, 23.
25. Ibid., II, 369–70.
26. *Note Books*, p. 204.
27. *Unfinished History of German Literature*, p. 87.
28. P. 3.
29. *Essays*, II, 133.
30. *Science of Knowledge*, p. 129. See also above, p. 111 n. 117.
31. *Critique of Judgment*, ed. J. H. Bernard, p. 117.
32. *Note Books*, pp. 184, 187.
33. *Essays*, I, 244. Compare *Midsummer Night's Dream*, V.i.12–17.
34. *Essays*, I, 208.
35. Ibid., III, 41.
36. *WM*, I, 29.
37. *Essays*, I, 255.
38. *Unfinished History of German Literature*, p. 12.
39. *GR*, I, 266.
40. Froude, *First Forty Years*, II, 294.
41. Ibid., p. 213.
42. *GR*, I, 266.
43. *Essays*, II, 29.
44. Froude, *First Forty Years*, II, 359.
45. Ibid., p. 294.
46. *GR*, I, 266; and *Sterling*, p. 156.
47. Allingham, *A Diary*, p. 263.
48. Ibid., p. 264. See also Meredith's sonnet "On a starred night Prince Lucifer arose."
49. *Essays*, II, 185.
50. Ibid., p. 283.
51. *Unfinished History of German Literature*, p. 87.
52. *SR*, p. 178.
53. *Heroes*, p. 163.
54. *Essays*, I, 65.
55. *GR*, II, 125.
56. *Heroes*, p. 81.
57. *MSB Letters*, pp. 297–98.
58. The particular reverence of the transcendentalist for the literary man carries over into the American school. See especially Emerson's essays "Nature" and "The Poet."
59. Pp. 83–84.

60. *Essays*, II, 437.

61. Ibid., I, 225. Carlyle says much the same thing in his 1832 article, "Death of Goethe." See *Essays*, I, 377.

62. *Essays*, I, 272.

63. Ibid., II, 142.

64. Ibid., p. 159.

65. *Sterling*, p. 266.

66. *Essays*, II, 377.

67. *Lectures*, p. 205.

68. *Essays*, II, 375.

69. Ibid., p. 407.

70. *PP*, p. 86.

71. *Note Books*, p. 140.

72. *Heroes*, p. 157.

73. Undated letter, Forster Collection, XIV, no. 251. My approximate date of 1841, based upon internal evidence, is conjectural.

74. *Essays*, I, 427.

75. Ibid., p. 425.

76. Ibid., pp. 454, 452.

77. Ibid., pp. 448–49.

78. Ibid., III, 111.

79. Ibid., p. 112.

80. Ibid., pp. 110–11.

81. Ibid., IV, 54.

82. Ibid., p. 38.

83. Ibid., p. 35.

84. Ibid., p. 75.

85. Ibid., pp. 36, 37.

86. Ibid., pp. 35–36.

87. Ibid., p. 83.

88. Ibid., III, 242, 244.

89. Ibid., pp. 234–35, 228.

90. Ibid., pp. 227–28.

91. For Carlyle's evaluation of Diderot's philosophy, see ibid., pp. 232–34.

92. Ibid., p. 234.

93. Ibid., pp. 84–85.

94. For orthodox views on this aspect of literary influence, see Murdock, *Literature and Theology in Colonial New England*, pp. 31–65.

95. *New Letters*, II, 266.

96. *Essays*, III, 49.

97. Ibid., V, 359–60.

98. *Sterling*, pp. 174–75.

99. Froude, *Life in London*, I, 484.

100. *Essays*, V, 26.

101. P. 165.

102. *Essays*, V, 25–26.

103. Ibid., p. 24.

104. For a comparison of these passages, see letter, quoted above, p. 29.

105. *Essays*, V, p. 24.

106. *HFG*, I, 431–32; quoted above, p. 7.

107. Pp. 159, 168.

108. Ibid.

109. Ibid., pp. 159, 169.

110. *Essays*, I, 360.

111. Ibid., II, 52.

112. Ibid., V, 351–52.

113. *Note Books*, facsimile letter appended to final page.

114. *Counsels to a Literary Aspirant*, ed. J. H. Stirling, pp. 11–15.

115. *Heroes*, p. 209.

116. P. 319.

117. Ibid., pp. 320–21.

118. Ibid., p. 322.

119. Ibid., p. 323.

120. Ibid., p. 326.

121. Mrs. Tillotson has aptly described this sort of terminology as the "dismissive plural," in a lecture delivered at the University of London, winter, 1968. Some other examples: "Puseyisms"; "Scoundrel Protection Societies" (prisons); "Talking-Apparatuses" (the Houses of Parliament).

122. *LDP*, p. 326.

123. Ibid., p. 327.

124. Compare this to Carlyle's earlier scorn for politics, quoted above, p. 162.

125. *LDP*, p. 327.

126. *New Letters*, II, 59. Alexander Carlyle dates the letter "Spring 1848," but I find the conjectural date in the manuscripts—March 21, 1849—more probable. See Forster Collection, III, no. 164.

127. *SR*, p. 174.

128. *New Letters*, I, 27.

129. *Note Books*, p. 265.

130. *LS*, p. 84.

131. Quoted in Sanders, "Carlyle, Poetry, and the Music of Humanity," p. 54n.

132. *Goethe Letters*, p. 81.

133. *New Letters*, I, 254.

134. Ibid., p. 283.

135. Ibid., p. 250.

136. *Note Books*, pp. 41, 42, 151.

137. *Heroes*, pp. 81–82.

138. *Essays*, III, 49–51.

139. It is particularly appropriate that Carlyle should appreciate the works of Defoe, since both men not only place a high value on prosaic realism in literature but share, as well, a lifelong enthusiasm for the Presbyterian cause.

140. *Essays*, III, 52, 54.

141. Ibid., p. 78.

142. Ibid., p. 79.

143. *Lectures*, p. 72.

144. *Essays*, IV, 465.

145. Ibid., p. 470.

146. Ibid.

147. Ibid., pp. 472, 471, 481.

148. According to a conversation he held with John Tyndall, Carlyle wished for Goethe the same political destiny he had elsewhere hoped for Shakespeare: "Goethe's life as a writer he considered a tragic one. Such a man ought to have room to *act* in the world. I retorted that writing was really action. He replied it was a poor species of action. . . . Such a soul ought to have governed Germany; he ought to have been King of Germany." Recalled by Tyndall in a letter to Hirst, May 1855; see Eve and Creasey, *The Life and Works of John Tyndall*, pp. 74–75.

149. To John Carlyle, 15 November 1873, *New Letters*, II, 301.

150. Duffy, *Conversations with Carlyle*, pp. 59, 86, 63, 55.

151. *HFG*, I, 434.

152. There is a curious parallel between these sentiments of Carlyle and those of Tennyson in "The Palace of Art," especially lines 245–56 and 293–96.

153. *LDP*, p. 212.

154. *PP*, pp. 158–59.

155. *Note Books*, pp. 188–89.

156. *Letters to His Wife*, p. 210, and *MSB Letters*, p. 192.

157. *New Letters*, I, 309.

158. Duffy, *Conversations with Carlyle*, pp. 212–13.

159. In Froude, *First Forty Years*, II, 210–11.

160. Again, in his journal for 1831, he wonders about the efficacy of art "in this late era" (ibid., p. 214).

161. Froude, *Life in London*, I, 49.

162. Ibid., p. 441.

163. Unpublished letter, Forster Collection, XXIV, no. 162.

164. Froude, *Life in London*, I, 453.

165. Six volumes as originally published, 1858–65.

166. Unpublished letter, Forster Collection, XXIV, no. 119.

167. Froude, *Life in London*, II, 264–65.

Chapter Six

The Faltering Victorian Vision

> Life without industry is guilt, and
> industry without art is brutality.—
> John Ruskin

Unquestionably, the transcendental-Puritan tension revealed in Carlyle's literary attitudes often resolves itself into a conflict between contemplation and action, vision and conduct. Bearing in mind such considerations, one may be tempted to uncomplicate the terminology by reducing the elements of the antagonism to the lowest common denominators; that is, to a struggle in Carlyle between Hellenic and Hebraic impulses. There are certainly compelling arguments for doing so, especially if we agree to define Hellenism and Hebraism as Arnold does in *Culture and Anarchy*. Understood thus, German idealism and Hellenism share a respect for intelligence, "spontaneity of consciousness," sensitivity "to things in their essence and beauty," and spiritual calm; by the same token, Puritanism and Hebraism mutually promote common sense, "strictness of conscience," obedience, awareness of evil, and spiritual unrest. Arnold himself makes the connection between the instincts of the Hebrew tribes and those of the Reformation sects: "All which Protestantism was to itself clearly conscious of, all which it succeeded in clearly setting forth in words, had the character of Hebraism rather than Hellenism."[1] More specifically, Arnold links the British Puritan to the Old Testament Jew through their identical preference for "doing to thinking." The action principle "knits in some special sort the genius and history of us English, and our American descendents across the Atlantic, to the genius and history of the Hebrew people. Puritanism . . . was originally a reaction of Hebraism against Hellenism."[2] Certainly it is upon this exact point of "cultivated inaction" that Carlyle most frequently attacks those spiritual descendents of Hellenism—the modern aesthetic writers. He even attempts, at one point, to place the contemporary polarities in Arnold's classical perspective: "Socrates," Carlyle observes, "is terribly at ease in Zion."[3] There are, as well, infrequent occasions when Carlyle not only suffers from the tension between these primitive instincts but recognizes their hostility. In a letter to Forster in 1845, he writes that the contemplation of nature is "all very 'beautiful,' but amounting to the most perfect state of *Donothingism* the mind of man could well conceive! That is the drawback of it: alas, you cannot do hard work and be quite beautiful; labour, says the apostle, is not joyous, it is grievous!"[4] A few years earlier, in an account to Sterling of his visit to Ely Cathedral, Carlyle acknowledges the same conflict, and claims, unconvincingly, to have resolved it within himself:

> Tonight, as the heaving bellows blew, and the yellow sunshine streamed in thro' those high windows, and my footfalls and the poor country lad's were the only sounds from below, I looked aloft, and my eyes filled with very tears to look at all this, and remember beside it (wedded to it now and reconciled with it for me) Oliver Cromwell's "Cease your fooling, and come out, Sir!" In these two antagonisms lie what volumes of meaning![5]

"Volumes of meaning" indeed, especially if the antagonism should be invoked as an answer to the contrariety in Carlyle's literary attitude. Yet Hebraism is ultimately a more limiting, not a wider, concept than Puritan temper when applied to Carlyle.

His dissatisfaction with the arts depends as much upon a respect for humility and factual truth as it does upon the impulse for action. Without the terminology derived in these pages, the critic would be compelled to trace Carlyle's negative views, as Harrold did thirty-five years ago, to "a curious blend of stoicism, Hebraism, Calvinism."[6] "Puritan temper" has the distinct advantage of encompassing all three of these strains. "Transcendental faith," on the other hand, serves better than Hellenism to characterize Carlyle's sympathy for literature: first of all, because, through the aesthetics of Kant and Fichte, that philosophy recommended to Carlyle a particular reverence for the artist, and second, because it suggests moral and metaphysical doctrines without which Carlyle believed all cultural movements nugatory. Moreover, to label the poles of Carlyle's thought "Hellenic" and "Hebraic" is, in fact, to reduce the conflict to a strict Kierkegaardian struggle between the aesthetic and ethical faculties in man. The question for Carlyle is not "either-or," but a choice between the affirmation of an equilibrium (transcendental faith), on the one hand, and a thorough-going rejection of beauty in favor of "grievous" duty on the other. At no point in Carlyle's life or writing does he embrace the amorality of a "pure" aesthetic.

Other, minor, adjustments in the terms of the equation prove equally unsatisfactory. For example, if one changes "transcendental faith" to Kantian idealism or simply to transcendentalism proper, Carlyle then immediately becomes responsible for a philosophical exactitude that he never maintained in his thinking. By the same token, if one substitutes the pejorative term "mysticism" for "transcendental faith," one loses both critical impartiality and historical specificity in the process. Except those upon which we have already determined, no connotative or denotative phrases will be found to indicate, so precisely, the special nature of the case. "Transcendental faith" and "Puritan temper" suggest at once the deeply religious aspects of Carlyle's struggle and the decided tension in him between German and Scottish authorities.

Finally, I should like to point up the importance of these discoveries within the pattern of nineteenth-century aesthetics. In recent years, it has become common critical practice to trace the decadence or fragmentation of romanticism among the later Victorians—most notably in studies by J. H. Buckley, Graham Hough, John Holloway, D. G. James, and David DeLaura.[7] I do not wish to wash out Carlyle's unique literary ambivalence in the murky light of "Romantic vs. Victorian," for we have sharply underlined those elements of his experience which were singular, yet it would be equally unjust to isolate his aesthetic dilemma from the dynamics of his age.

Though born nearly a generation before most of the writers whom he knew and influenced, Carlyle was no more impervious than they to the political and religious contretemps of mid-century England. "Signs of the Times," "Chartism," *Past and Present, On Heroes and Hero-Worship,* "Shooting Niagara—and After?", all evidence the man of letters' eagerness to reach beyond his writing desk and join battle with the Philistines and scientific Liberals. The impulse of his era was, initially at least, toward optimistic prescription and social activism. That earnest, sanguine engagement of Tennyson in *Locksley Hall* and "The Palace of Art," of Dickens in *Household Words,* the early novels and *Hard Times,* of Ruskin in *Unto this Last,* "Nature of the Gothic," and "Traffic," of Morris in *News from Nowhere* and his lectures on medieval craftsmanship, and of Newman and Arnold as well,[8] parallels Carlyle's compulsion to close the gap between the artist and his times.

In most cases, what we witness is a brave attempt at applied romanticism: Ruskin and Morris mediate between the naturalism of Pre-Raphaelite painting or Gothic architecture and the mindless vulgarity of middle- and working-class tastes; Arnold and Newman promote Goethe's aesthetic of a "harmonious balance of the faculties" under the banner of liberal education for the sons of "Utilitaria"; and Carlyle, long before the others have begun to preach, is busy "Germanizing the public," transplanting the bloodless, academic categories of Kant into the popular mind in phrases like "mechanics and dynamics," "organic filaments," and "natural supernaturalism." In fact, it is Carlyle, as we have seen in chapter three, whose early example pointed the direction for, and infused the thinking of, so many Victorian men of letters. Ruskin, for example, though he had no firsthand acquaintance with German idealism, knew enough Carlyle to paraphrase Fichte in defining great art as "the revelation of immaterial values hidden behind the veil of material beauty."[9] And, like Carlyle, he carried his *Weltanschauung* beyond the realm of aesthetics in his middle years.

Predictably, it is also Carlyle who first retreats from the general assault on the anaesthetic man or, more properly, exhibits those self-contradictory tensions which we associate with the decline of romanticism. Until now, he has been viewed chiefly as some inviolate, early Victorian monolith, the polar opposite to Newman in religion or to Mill in economics. Or perhaps too many critics have taken their cue from Arnold who, in later life, wrote off the Sage of Chelsea as an overindulged Hebraic "desperado." Yet Carlyle, too, had often wished to make the Goethean ideal prevail and had cajoled the "Mud-gods of this present Epoch" as hopefully as Arnold lectured the "Barbarians." True, the manner of his retreat took its own peculiar, injudicious form: there is nothing in his rude militarism or strident Calvinist harangues so pleasing as the lyric escapism of Morris's verse, nothing so forgivable as *Locksley Hall Sixty Years After,* nothing so poignant as Ruskin's decline after the Whistler trial, nothing so eloquent in its despair as *Empedocles on Etna,* "Stanzas from the Grand Chartreuse," or "Dover Beach," nothing so sombre and moving as the last novels of Dickens, nothing so exquisite as the attenuated utterances of the *fin-de-siècle.* Whenever Carlyle believes himself embattled by ignorant, uneducable "armies of the night," he reverts not to dreaming medievalism or Hellenic isolation but to the fierce misanthropy of his father's clan. Such apprehensions of man's depravity seem to accord, after all, with the intimations of his childhood and thus excite righteous anger rather than fine melancholy in his prose. For Carlyle, born in eighteenth-century Scotland, the Kantian Aesthetic could never be more than an acquired property of the mind: under threat from an unregenerate populace, it is entirely unnatural for him to cling, as later generations of Victorian writers did, to "the supreme theme of Art and Song." Nonetheless, Carlyle's divided consciousness, his inability to resolve the tension between art and the exigencies of the contemporary world, presage the schizophrenic temper of mid-Victorian romanticism. And much as he would resist the devolution, Carlyle's fluctuating literary vision may, in fact, represent the first signal of disintegration in the unified moral aesthetic of Wordsworth and Goethe—a disintegration that is arrested only by the proud parochialism of the nineties.

Last of all, one may be tempted to consider the effect of Carlyle's religious contrariety on his nonliterary pronouncements—especially his attitude toward history, politics, and culture. A number of critics have looked into these areas, but always at the Calvinist side of Carlyle's temperament and with a tendency to dismiss as irrelevant, or unintelligible, the "mystical elements" in his personality.[10] Even in a more balanced approach, one would have to proceed with caution. As we have already seen, there are points at which Puritanism and transcendentalism become confused in Carlyle's mind: Goethe's *Entsagen* mergers with Calvin's doctrine of asceticism; James Carlyle's "gospel of silence" appears to be complemented by the quietism of the pantheist. If we should expand our discussion to include Carlyle's historical ideas, we would face further ambiguities, such as the hero-theory—the exact derivation of which remains unclear. It is probable that Carlyle took the germ of his doctrine from Fichte or Hegel and narrowed it over the years to fit the Calvinist concept of divinely elected political rulers.[11] This, and other features of Carlyle's world-view—the phoenix theory,[12] the individual's "cosmic knowingness,"[13] the growing sense of historical determinism—would demand close attention and a willingness on the critic's part to incorporate variables and thus to dilute his largely valid argument. To work with

Carlyle, after all, is to study a man of immense eccentricity and to accustom oneself to a prose style that bristles with crotchets. Our hypotheses may illuminate facets of his writing, but he never quite surrenders his humanity to the efforts of the "logic-chopper."

1. P. 140.

2. Ibid., p. 142.

3. Quoted in ibid., p. 135.

4. This excerpt, from an unpublished letter in the Forster Collection, III, no. 142, has been printed in Wilson's biography of Carlyle, III, 307.

5. Letter of September 1842, in *New Letters*, I, 269.

6. See above, p. 000 n. 00.

7. *The Triumph of Time, The Last Romantics, The Victorian Sage, Matthew Arnold and the Decline of English Romanticism*, and *Hebrew and Hellene in Victorian England*, respectively.

8. At the opposite pole, among the scientists and political economists, the urge to reach beyond the traditional sphere of a single discipline was equally strong. Thus Darwin incorporates Spencerian sociology in later editions of *The Origin of Species* or descants on the "moral sense" in *The Descent of Man*; thus Mill invokes Goethe's dictum "the Beautiful is greater than the Good" in *On Education* or attempts to humanize *Utilitarianism* with a paean to the "exalted feelings" of Socrates, Plato, and Demosthenes.

9. On Ruskin's amateurism as philosopher and sociologist, see Frederick Harrison's report in *John Ruskin*, pp. 97, 103.

10. Notably, Holloway in *The Victorian Sage*, Harrold in a brief article "The Nature of Carlyle's Calvinism," and S. Gwilliam in a longer, more recent study "Thomas Carlyle, Reluctant Calvinist." Froude, Frederick Harrison, Matthew Arnold, and even Harrold in *Carlyle and German Thought* make the same mistake of deemphasizing transcendentalism either because Carlyle's brand is too "popular" a form for their purist sentiments or because they would prefer to avoid the "hazy infinitudes" of Kantism. Even Basil Willey, who condemns conventional Christian analyses of Carlyle's religion, can offer only indefinite labels in their place, such as "escaped Puritan" or "religious Romantic" (see *Nineteenth Century Studies*, especially pp. 105–25).

11. See B. H. Lehman, *Carlyle's Theory of the Hero*, especially pp. 104–29.

12. For an appraisal of Carlyle's "flirtation" with the Saint-Simonians in the early 1830s, see Neff, *Carlyle and Mill*, pp. 210–15; and for his correspondence with the society, see *New Quarterly* (London, 1909), II, 277–88.

13. See R. Sharrock, "Carlyle and the Sense of History," p. 91. This essay includes an interesting discussion of changes in Carlyle's historical method between the writing of *The French Revolution* and *Cromwell*.

Emerson and Carlyle

Emerson does, clearly, owe many of his ideas and some of his language to *Sartor,* although in most cases, especially in "Nature," it is impossible to say whether the debt is to German philosophy itself or to Carlyle's interpretations. Carlyle, for example, speaks of nature as "the reflex of our own inward force"; and Emerson declares it to be "a metaphor of the human mind," but then so do Kant and Fichte. Again, Carlyle and Emerson employ the terms "Me" and "Not Me" in their conceptualizing, but seem more indebted to Fichte's "Ich" and "Nicht Ich" than to each other. In one sense, Emerson's exposition of transcendental metaphysics marks a clear advance on Carlyle's: he rearranges and relabels the categories of the German and English systems, so as to make their idealism into a graphically intelligible picture of the universe. His approach is less poetic than Carlyle's—there are no ghosts or fiery war-horses hasting from one Inane into the next—but he makes a stronger appeal to the intellect of his reader. Nature is not simply a "Shadow-system gathered round our Me," or a "revealed Force," but "all that is separate from us . . . both nature and art, all other men and my own body."[1] Further, he introduces the term "Over-

soul" as a substitute for Kant's "supersensible," Goethe's "All,"
Fichte's "Divine Idea of the World," and Carlyle's "Immensities
and Infinitudes." Thus its relation to the soul of man, the seat of
"Justice, Truth, Love, Freedom" in the individual,[2] is established
linguistically as that of macrocosm to microcosm. And nature functions not as an "open secret" or "garment of God" but as a "trans-
parent eyeball"[3] linking the human to the divine mind; it is a
kind of two-way glass or mirror, the "present expositor" or "projection of God"[4] as well as a set of physical correspondences to the
spiritual consciousness of every man: "The world is emblematic.
. . . The laws of moral nature answer to those of matter as face
to face in a glass. 'The visible world and the relation of its parts,
is the dial plate of the invisible.' "[5] The fragments of the actual
have no meaning in themselves; their value is entirely symbolic,
and they acquire beauty only as they are integrated, by the soul,
into a coherent idealism: "A single object is only so far beautiful
as it suggests this universal grace."[6] It is possible from Emerson's
definitions, as it is not from Teufelsdröckh's insights, to summon a
mental image of the transcendental cosmos. In the center sits the
soul, or Me, looking out upon the variety of nature, the elements
of which, unified, reflect man's own divinity and reveal, in part,
the sublimities of the enclosing Oversoul. Of course, the Oversoul
has alike created the hieroglyphs of Nature (in order to externalize
the Divine Essence), so that the world of objects reverberates both
outward toward God and inward toward the innate Reason of the
individual. As Whitman, drawing on Emerson's ideas, later puts it,
"these tend in-ward to me, and I tend outward to them/ . . . .
the unseen is proved by the seen,/Till that becomes unseen and
receives proof in its turn."[7]

Emerson's aesthetics adhere even more closely than his metaphysics to the spirit of Carlyle's asseverations in *Sartor*. For Teufelsdröckh, the true work of art is a divine symbol, "the Godlike
rendered visible," a synthesis of nature's variety. For Emerson, it
is "nature passed through the alembic of man. . . . The production of a work of art throws a light upon the mystery of humanity.

A work of art is an abstract or epitome of the world.''[8] Both men affirm that beauty is sensible truth; that it alone is the key to the reconcilement of appearances and reality. Emerson allows, first of all, that "Beauty is the mark God sets upon virtue. . . . The world thus exists to the soul to satisfy the desire of beauty. . . . No reason can be asked or given why the soul seeks beauty. Beauty is one expression for the universe."[9] But, like Carlyle, he does not trust to the merely passive perception of beauty. He believes, rather, that a gift of vision or poetic intellect must be present to "excite" meaning from natural objects: "Beauty in nature is not ultimate. It is the herald of inward and eternal beauty, and is not alone a solid or satisfactory good."[10] Specifically, it is the mind of the artist that Emerson reverences: "There is a property in the horizon which no man has but he whose eye can integrate all the parts, that is, the poet. . . . The lover of nature is he whose inward and outward senses are still truly adjusted to each other."[11] Carlyle attaches to art the significance of a "Church-Homiletic"; he avers that poets "first made Gods for men," and Emerson agrees that literature contains the seeds of "new thought," the inspiration that helps man "to break the chains" of his empirical consciousness: "The world seems always waiting for its poet. . . . Every one has some interest in the advent of the poet. . . . All that we call sacred history attest that the birth of a poet is the principle event in chronology."[12] The poem or novel or play, rightly conceived, has for Emerson as much as for Carlyle, a sacred quality, affirmative and revelatory: "The creation of beauty is Art. . . . In art does Nature work through the will of a man filled with the beauty of her first works."[13]

As they aged, Emerson and Carlyle drew farther apart on many of these issues: the former maintaining, without compromise or serious contradiction, the idealism of his early days,[14] the latter retreating frequently, as Emerson himself deplored, into a "deification of the Practical." Their correspondence,[15] which continued until Emerson's death, when not about publishing costs and royalties, deteriorated into a contest of incompatible temperaments.

Allingham describes the antagonism that many of the letters reveal: "C thot E too much in the air, and E thot C too much on the ground. You hear E calling 'Come up!' and C calling 'Come down!' C's genius wants the poetic flavour of the feminine. . . . E holds up a mild steady lamp, like the full moon: C brandishes a huge torch."[16] There is some justice in Carlyle's criticism of Emerson, for the American's essays often read like a group of brilliant but bloodless aphorisms; there is a decided want of concrete images, and one wishes for more breadth or liveliness or application of principles. His attempts at poetry seldom rise beyond the realm of pallid abstraction, and Mrs. Carlyle dismissed much of Emerson's later writing as "affected, stilted, mystical."[17] Carlyle himself never went as far as his wife, although he admitted to her that "certain sides" of the man's nature were "overlaid with mad rubbish."[18] Emerson seemed to Carlyle on their second encounter in 1847 to be "a pure-minded elevated man: *elevated,* but without breadth, as a willow is, as a reed is; no fruit at all to be gathered from him."[19] Jane was again more outspoken on this occasion: she confessed to Lady Ashburton that the "theoretic geniality" of "this Yankee-Seraph . . . leaves me cold."[20] Emerson, for his part, cooled toward the Carlyles considerably and in late years expressed his disaffection in occasional reviews and lapses of correspondence.[21] He nonetheless understood his own limitations and realized that in his passion for ideological purity he had lost the warmth and eloquence that the transcendental aesthetic demanded. Both Carlyle and Emerson fell short of their intended goal of sustained poetry, for neither was able to adjust perfectly "his inward and outward senses."[22] It was left to others, particularly to Thoreau and Whitman, to achieve that balance of sensibilities which their predecessors admired but seldom struck.

1. *Works of Ralph Waldo Emerson,* II, 372.
2. Ibid., p. 385.
3. Ibid., p. 374.

4. Ibid., p. 409.

5. Ibid., p. 388.

6. Ibid., p. 383.

7. From "Song of Myself" in *Leaves of Grass*.

8. *Works*, II, 382–83.

9. Ibid., p. 380.

10. Ibid., p. 383.

11. Ibid., pp. 373–74.

12. Ibid., I, 202–3.

13. Ibid., II, 383.

14. Although in late essays, like "Experience," he seems a bit weary of the effort and admonishes himself, "Up again: old heart! . . . There is victory yet for all justice" (ibid., I, 246).

15. Originally published by C. E. Norton in two volumes in 1883, but recently reedited in one volume with an excellent introduction by J. Slater.

16. *A Diary*, p. 220.

17. Letter to Sterling, 1840, quoted in L. and E. Hanson, *Necessary Evil: The Life of Jane Welsh Carlyle*, p. 259. Arnold also argues that Emerson was unable to write "great poetry" (see *Discourses in America*, pp. 150–59).

18. L. and E. Hanson, *Necessary Evil*, p. 357.

19. Ibid., p. 358.

20. Ibid., p. 357.

21. Despite his reputation as a "universal cynic," it is Carlyle who seemed most willing to forget intellectual differences for the sake of friendship. With Emerson as with Mill, Carlyle was always first to write the conciliatory letter.

22. Although R. Hertz, in an article "Victory and Consciousness of Battle: Emerson and Carlyle," asserts that Emerson's achievement of ideological stasis amounted to a kind of triumph. For a more detailed study of their philosophical relationship, see W. Vance, *Carlyle and the American Transcendentalists*.

A SELECTED
BIBLIOGRAPHY

Works by Carlyle

Correspondence between Goethe and Carlyle. Edited by C. E. Norton. London, 1887.

Correspondence of Thomas Carlyle and Ralph Waldo Emerson. Edited by J. Slater. New York, 1964.

Counsels to a Literary Aspirant. Edited by J. H. Stirling. Edinburgh, 1886.

Early Letters of Thomas Carlyle, 1814–1826. Edited by C. E. Norton. 2 vols. London, 1886.

Last Words of Thomas Carlyle. Edited by R. Preuss. London, 1892.

Lectures on the History of Literature. Edited by J. R. Greene. London, 1892.

Letters and Speeches of Oliver Cromwell. Edited by S. C. Lomas. 3 vols. London, 1904.

Letters of Thomas Carlyle, 1826–1836. Edited by C. E. Norton. 2 vols. London, 1888.

Letters of Thomas Carlyle to John Stuart Mill, John Sterling and Robert Browning. Edited by A. Carlyle. London, 1923.

Letters to His Wife. Edited by T. Bliss. London, 1953.

Letters to John Forster. Mss. Forster Collection, volumes III and XXIV. Victoria and Albert Museum, London.

Love Letters. 2 vols. London, 1909.

New Letters of Thomas Carlyle. Edited by A. Carlyle. 2 vols. London, 1904.

New Letters of Thomas Carlyle to Eckermann. Edited by W. Speck. New Haven, Conn., 1926.

Reminiscences. Edited by J. A. Froude. 2 vols. London, 1881.

Two Notebooks of Thomas Carlyle, from 23rd March, 1822 to 16th May, 1832. Edited by C. E. Norton. New York, 1898.

Unfinished History of German Literature. Edited by Hill Shine. Lexington, Ky., 1951.

Works of Thomas Carlyle. Centenary Edition. Edited by H. D. Traill. 30 vols. London, 1896–99.

Secondary Sources

Abbott, T. K. *Kant's Theory of Ethics.* London, 1898.

Abrahms, M. *The Mirror and the Lamp.* New York, 1953.

Adrian, A. "Dean Stanley's Report of Conversations with Carlyle," *Victorian Studies* 1 (1957): 72–74.

Allingham, W. *A Diary.* London, 1907.

Arnold, M. *Culture and Anarchy.* Edited by D. Wilson. Cambridge, 1965.

———. *Discourses in America.* London, 1912.

Baker, J. E. "Our New Hellenic Renaissance." In *The Reinterpretation of Victorian Literature.* Princeton, N.J., 1950. Pp. 207–36.

Baumgarten, M. "Carlyle and 'Spiritual Optics.'" *Victorian Studies* 11 (1968): 503–22.

Beckson, K., ed. *Aesthetes and Decadents.* New York, 1966.

Bentley, N. *The Victorian Scene, 1837–1901.* London, 1968.

Buckley, J. H., ed. *The Pre-Raphaelites.* New York, 1968.

———. *The Triumph of Time.* Cambridge, Mass. 1967.

Calder, G. *The Writing of Past and Present.* New Haven, Conn., 1949.

Calvin, J. *The Institutes of the Christian Religion* (A Compend). Edited by H. T. Kerr. London, 1964.

Cazamian, L. *Carlyle.* Translated by E. K. Brown. New York, 1932.

Coleridge, S. T. *Aids to Reflection.* Edited by D. Coleridge. 8th ed. London. 1859.

———. *Biographia Literaria.* Edited by J. Shawcross. 2 vols. Oxford, 1907.

———. *The Friend.* London, 1844.

Cruse, A. *The Victorians and Their Books.* London, 1935.

Cudworth, R. *A Sermon Preached before the Honourable House of Commons.* Cambridge, 1647.

Darwin, C. *Selected Writings.* Edited by P. Appleman. New York, 1970.

DeLaura, D. "Arnold and Carlyle." *PMLA* 74 (1963): 104–16.

———. *Hebrew and Hellene in Victorian England.* Austin, Tex., 1969.

Dicey, A. V. *Lectures on the Relation between Law and Opinion in England during the Nineteenth Century.* London, 1905.

Dickens, C. *Hard Times.* Edited by George Ford. New York, 1966.

Downame, J. *Christian Warfare.* London, 1609.

Duffy, C. G. *Conversations with Carlyle.* London, 1892.

Eliot, G. *Essays of George Eliot.* Edited by T. Pinney. London, 1963.

———. *Letters.* Edited by G. S. Haight. 7 vols. London, 1955.

Emerson, R. W. *English Traits.* Boston, 1896.

———. *Miscellaneous Pieces.* London, 1913.

———. *Works of Ralph Waldo Emerson.* 4 vols. London, 1913.

Espinasse, F. *Literary Recollections.* London, 1893.

Eve and Creasey. *Life and Work of John Tyndall.* London, 1945.

Fichte, J. G. *Popular Works of J. G. Fichte.* 2 vols. London, 1844.

———. *Science of Knowledge: A Critical Exposition,* by C. C. Everett. Chicago, 1892.

Fleming, D. H. "The Influence of Knox." *Scottish Historical Review* 2 (1905): 131–35.

———. "The Influence of the Reformation on Social and Cultural Life in Scotland." *Scottish Historical Review* 15 (1917): 1-30.

Froude, J. A. *My Relations with Carlyle.* London, 1903.

———. *The Nemesis of Faith.* London, 1849.

———. *Thomas Carlyle: A History of the First Forty Years of His Life: 1795–1835.* 2 vols. London, 1882.

———. *Thomas Carlyle: A History of His Life in London, 1834–1881.* 2 vols. London, 1884.

Fruman, N. *Coleridge, the Damaged Archangel.* New York, 1971.

Galloway, W. F. "The Conservative Attitude toward Fiction, 1770–1830." *PMLA* 55 (1940): 1041–59.

Garnett, R. *Life of Thomas Carlyle.* London, 1887.

Gascoyne, D. *Thomas Carlyle.* Supplement to *British Book News,* No. 23. London, 1952.

Gibbon, E. *The Decline and Fall of the Roman Empire.* 6 vols. London, 1846.

Glover, T. *Poets and Puritans.* London, 1915.

Green, J. R. *Letters of J. R. Green.* Edited by Leslie Shephen. London, 1901.

Gwilliam, S. "Thomas Carlyle, Reluctant Calvinist." *Dissertation Abstracts* 36:4628 (Columbia University).

Halliday, J. *Mr. Carlyle My Patient: A Psychomatic Biography.* London, 1949.

Hanson, L. and E. *Necessary Evil: The Life of Jane Welsh Carlyle.* London, 1952.

Harrison, F. *John Ruskin.* New York, 1902.

———. *Memories and Thoughts.* London, 1906.

———. "Thomas Carlyle." *Studies in Early Victorian Literature.* London, 1895. Pp. 40–63.

Harrold, C. *Carlyle and German Thought, 1819–34.* New Haven, Conn., 1934.

———. "The Mystical Element in Carlyle: 1827–34." *Modern Philology* 29 (1932): 459–75.

———. "The Nature of Carlyle's Calvinism." *Studies in Philology* 33 (1936): 475–86

Haultain, A. *Goldwin Smith, His Life and Opinions.* London, 1913.

Hertz, R. "Victory and Consciousness of Battle: Emerson and Carlyle." *Personalist* 45 (1964): 60–71.

Holloway, J. *The Victorian Sage.* New York, 1965.

Hooker, R. *The Works of Richard Hooker.* 3 vols. Oxford, 1807.

Horne, R. H. *A New Spirit of the Age.* 2 vols. London, 1844.

Hough, G. *The Last Romantics.* London, 1949.

Howe, M., ed. *The Pollock-Holmes Letters.* 2 vols. Cambridge, 1942.

Hume, D. *Theory of Knowledge.* Edited by D. C. Yalden-Thomson. Edinburgh, 1951.

Hutton, R. H. *Brief Literary Criticisms.* London, 1906.

———. *Criticisms on Contemporary Thought and Thinkers.* 2 vols. London, 1894.

James, D. G. *Matthew Arnold and the Decline of English Romanticism.* Oxford, 1961.

Jeffrey, F. "Wilhelm Meister's Apprenticeship: A Novel from the German of Goethe (1825)." *Contributions to the Edinburgh Review.* London, 1853. Pp. 120–42.

Jewsbury, G. *Zoe: A History of Two Lives.* London, 1845.

Johnson, W. S. *Thomas Carlyle: A Study of His Literary Apprenticeship, 1814–1831.* New Haven, Conn., 1911.

Kant, I. *Critique of Aesthetic Judgment.* Translated by J. C. Meredith. Oxford, 1911.

————. *Critique of Practical Reason.* Translated by T. K. Abbott. London, 1898.

————. *Critique of Pure Reason.* Translated by N. K. Smith. London, 1934.

————. *Critique of Judgment.* Translated by J. H. Bernard. London, 1892; 2d ed., London, 1914.

————. *Religion within the Limits of Reason Alone.* Translated by T. M. Greene and H. H. Hudson. New York, 1960.

————. *Theory of Ethics.* Translated by T. K. Abbott. London, 1898.

Kingsley, C. *Alton Locke: Tailor and Poet.* London, 1850.

Knox, I. *The Aesthetic Theories of Kant, Hegel and Schopenhauer.* London, 1958.

Knox, J. *The Works of John Knox.* Edited by D. Laing. 6 vols. Edinburgh, 1846–64.

LaValley A. *Carlyle and the Idea of the Modern.* New Haven, Conn., 1968.

Lehman, B. H. *Carlyle's Theory of the Hero.* Durham, N.C., 1928.

Leopold, W. *Die religiöse Wurzel von Carlyles literarisher Wirksamkeit.* Halle, 1922.

Levine, G. " 'Sartor Resartus' and the Balance of Fiction." *Victorian Studies* 8 (December 1964): 131–60.

Lewis, C. S. *Surprised by Joy.* London, 1959.

Lindberg, J. "Decadence of Style: Symbolic Structure in Carlyle's Later Prose." *Studies in Scottish Literature* 1 (1964): 183–95.

MacGregor, G. *The Thundering Scot.* London, 1958.

MacPhail, A. "Jonathan Edwards." In *Essays in Puritanism.* London, 1905. Pp. 1–51.

Maitland, F. W. *The Life and Letters of Leslie Stephen.* London, 1906.

Martineau, H. *Autobiography.* 3 vols. London, 1877.

Martineau, J. *Essays, Philosophical and Theological.* 2 vols. New York, 1879.

Masson, D. *Carlyle Personally and in His Writings.* London, 1885.

Mather, C. *Manuductio ad Ministerium.* Boston, 1726.

Mill, J. S. *A Selection of His Works.* Edited by J. M. Robson. New York, 1966.

————. *Autobiography.* London, 1873.

Miller, P., and T. H. Johnson. *The Puritans.* New York, 1938.

Moers, E. *The Dandy: From Brummel to Beerbohm.* London, 1960.

Moore, C. "Persistence of Carlyle's Everlasting Yea." *Modern Philology* 54 (1957): 187–96.

————. "Sartor Resartus and the Problem of Carlyle's Conversion," *PMLA* 70 (1955): 662–81.

Morley, J. V. *Recollections.* 2 vols. London, 1917.

Muir, E. *John Knox: Portrait of a Calvinist.* London, 1929.

Muirhead, J. H. *Platonic Tradition in Anglo-Saxon Philosophy.* London, 1931.

Müller, F. M. "Goethe and Carlyle." *English Goethe Society Publications,* No. 1. London, 1886. Pp. 3–24.

Müller, G. *The Life and Letters of Friedrich Max Müller.* 2 vols. London, 1902.

Murdock, K. "Puritan Literary Attitude" and "A Little Recreation of Poetry." In *Literature and Theology in Colonial New England.* New York, 1949. Pp. 31–65, 137–72.

Murray, H. *The Morality of Fiction.* Edinburgh, 1805.

Neff, E. *Carlyle and Mill.* New York, 1926.

Nelson, J. *The Sublime Puritan: Milton and the Victorians.* Madison, Wis., 1963.

Nettleship, R. L. *Memoir of T. H. Green.* London, 1906.

Parr, P. C. Introduction to *On Heroes, Hero-Worship, and the Heroic in History,* by Thomas Carlyle. Oxford, 1910. Pp. v-xxxii.

Paul, H. *The Life of Froude.* London, 1905.

Pears, D. F., ed., "Hume on Religion." In *David Hume: A Symposium.* London, 1963.

Roe, F. W. *Carlyle as Critic of Literature.* New York, 1910.

————. "Thomas Carlyle, 1795–1881." In *Victorian Prose.* Madison, Wis., 1947. Pp. 3–5.

Roellinger, F. "Early Development of Carlyle's Style." *PMLA* 72 (1957): 936–51.

Ruskin, J. *Unto This Last* and "Traffic." New York, 1967.

Ryan, A. "The Attitude toward the Reader in Carlyle's Sartor Resartus." *Victorian Newsletter,* No. 23 (Spring, 1963). Pp. 15–16.

Saintsbury, G. *The History of Criticism.* 3 vols. London, 1917. Especially III, 495–99, 527–39.

Sanders, C. R. "Carlyle, Poetry, and the Music of Humanity." *Western Humanities Review* 16 (1962): 53–66.

————. "The Byron Closed in *Sartor Resartus.*" *Studies in Romanticism* 3 (1964): 77–108.

————. "Carlyle's Letters." *Bulletin of the John Rylands Library* 38 (1955): 199–224.

Schilling, B. N. "Carlyle." In *Human Dignity and the Great Victorians.* New York, 1946. Pp. 74–95.

Sharrock, R. "Carlyle and the Sense of History." *Essays and Studies* 19 (1966): 74–91.

Shine, H. "Carlyle and the German Philosophy Problem during the Year 1826–27." *PMLA* 50 (1935): 807–27.

Slater, J. "Goethe, Carlyle, and the Open Secret." *Anglia* 76 (1958): 422–26.

Smeed, J. "Thomas Carlyle and Jean Paul Richter." *Comparative Literature* 16 (1964): 226–53.

Spencer, H. *Autobiography.* 2 vols. London, 1904.

Storrs, M. *The Relation of Carlyle to Kant and Fichte.* Bryn Mawr, Pa., 1929.

Strawson, P. F. *The Bounds of Sense.* London, 1966.

Sutton, M. K. " 'Inverse Sublimity' in Victorian Humor." *Victorian Studies* 10 (December 1966): 177–92.

Swinburne, A. *Letters.* 2 vols. London, 1918.

Symons, J. *Thomas Carlyle.* London, 1952.

Taine, H. A. *The History of English Literature.* Translated by H. van Laun. Edinburgh, 1871.

Tennyson, G. B., ed. *A Carlyle Reader.* New York, 1969.

———. "Carlyle's Poetry to 1840: A Checklist and Discussion, A New Attribution, and Six Unpublished Poems." *Victorian Poetry* 1 (1963): 161–81.

———. *Sartor Called Resartus.* Princeton, N.J., 1966.

Tillotson, K. "Matthew Arnold and Carlyle." *Proceedings of the British Academy* 42 (1956): 133–53.

———. *Novels of the Eighteen Forties.* London, 1959.

Trevelyan, G. M. *Carlyle: An Anthology.* London, 1953. Pp. 1–11.

Tulloch, J. "Thomas Carlyle as a Religious Teacher." In *Movements of Religious Thought in Britain.* London, 1885. Pp. 169–208.

Unamuno, Miguel de. *The Tragic Sense of Life.* London, 1921.

Vance, W. *Carlyle and the American Transcendentalists.* Chicago, 1944.

Walker, H. "The German Influence: Thomas Carlyle." In *The Literature of the Victorian Era.* Cambridge, 1921. Pp. 23–79.

Walker, T. *A Vindication of the Discipline and Constitutions of the Church of Scotland.* Edinburgh, 1774.

Watkins, C. "Browning's 'Red Cotton Night-Cap Country' and Carlyle." *Victorian Studies* 7 (1964): 359–74.

Wellek, R. *Immanuel Kant in England, 1793–1838.* Princeton, N.J., 1931.

———. *The Later Eighteenth Century* and *The Romantic Age.* History of Modern Criticism, 1750–1950, vols. 1 and 2. London, 1955.

West, P. "Carlyle's Creative Disregard." *Melbourne Critical Review*, no. 5 (1962), pp. 16–26.

Whitman, W. "Death of Carlyle." In *Essays from the Critic*. Boston, 1882. Pp. 31–27.

Willey, B. *Nineteenth Century Studies*. London, 1949.

———. "S. T. Coleridge." In *The English Moralists*. London, 1964.

Williams, R. *Culture and Society, 1780–1950*. London, 1958.

Willison, J., and others. *A Fair and Impartial Testimony . . . against the Backslidings, Corruptions, Divisions, and Prevailing Evils, Both of Former and of Present Times*. Glasgow, 1765.

Wilson, D. A. *Carlyle till Marriage*. London, 1923.

———. *Carlyle to the French Revolution*. London, 1924.

———. *Carlyle on Cromwell and Others*. London, 1926.

———. *Carlyle at His Zenith*. London, 1928.

———. *Carlyle to Threescore-and-Ten*. London, 1932.

Wilson, S. "The Theology of Thomas Carlyle." In *The Theology of Modern Literature*. London, 1899. Pp. 131–78.

INDEX